FROM TRASH TO TREASURES

Inspired by God

Eva Dimel

This book was printed in the United States of America.

To order additional copies of this book contact:

Eva Dimel
Phone -614-875-9263
EDimel9775@sbcglobal.net

Published by
FWB Publications
Columbus, Ohio

FWB

Table of Contents

He raiseth up the poor out of the dust, and lifteth up the beggar from the dunghill, to set them among princes, and to make them inherit the throne of glory: for the pillars of the earth are the Lord's, and he hath set the world upon them (I Samuel 2:8, KJV).

Dedication

I would like to dedicate this book to my sister Marjorie, without her by my side growing up I don't know how I would have made it. She always put her sister's first in her life and everyone else. She is one of the reasons this story was written. The love I have for her could never be measured. She is and always will be my hero.

God Bless You Marjorie
Love You- Eva Dimel

INTRODUCTION

Virtually every book, irrespective of its genre, somewhere near the beginning, makes certain claims about its content. The reader, of course, has the right to expect the book to live up to its claims. But let it also be said that not every reader will come away with the same opinion after reading the same book. And with only these three sentences, whoever is reading this introduction has already begun to formulate in his or her mind, perhaps not an opinion, but a certain anticipation as to what this book – this novel, is all about. Then let us save some time and effort by jumping into the pond with both feet.

But first – it will be advantageous to tell the reader the negative aspect of this book – what it is **_not_** about. It is not about the triumph of the human spirit over adversity. It includes that, of course, but it goes far beyond it. It is not about the resiliency and adaptability of humans to their present environment and all the different aspects of that environment, although it includes these also, but transcends all of them.

Positively, this book is about the love and grace of the one and only true and living God, who alone is able to take hold of the reins of human lives that are being driven toward Hell at breakneck speed, and turn those lives into something more beautiful than human language is capable of describing. This book will take you to the utmost depths of human shame and depravity. And depending upon your own personal relationship to God, it will raise you to the utmost heights of joy. These are pretty big claims for a book, are they not? Now, let us see if these claims can be substantiated.

Arvil Jones, editor.

ACKNOWLEDGEMENT

I would like to thank my very special friend and author Arvil Jones for all of his time and work he put into this book with me. He not only took everything I wrote and sent him and brought it to life, he also edited it, while encouraging me on this journey – a journey which hasn't always been easy for me. I know in my heart God brought us together to write this book with God's guidance leading the way. I appreciate Avril's patience, kindness and prayers for this book, while reassuring me this book needed to be written. I thank God for him and everything he has done to help me bring this book to life. I could not have done it without him.

Eva Dimel

Dr. Arvil Jones, Th.M., Ph.D.
Books: *Heavenly Places* (co-authored with Ernestine Collins).
The Townsend Legacy – Heavenly Places II (co-authored with Ernestine Collins).
Giving The Devil His Due
Poems of Inspiration
Order from the author, or online.
cjones156@cinci.rr.com
(513) 907-7751
1304 Bonacker Ave.,
Hamilton, OH 45011

FORWARD

There is an old expression that goes, "The truth will out!" God's glory is often revealed in mysterious ways. This is a story that had been a long time coming, but a story that must be told, that needs to be heard. Many doors have had to open for this truth to be let out: Doors of courage and strength, Doors of shame and guilt, and Doors of concern for the welfare of others. It has been told!

To quote the author, Eva Dimel, from her story, "Shelly had no idea how far her influence had already gone, and no idea how far it was yet to go. Shelly's heart desire was to reach out to others who were hurting, many of whose lives were quite similar to her own. She realized there are thousands, if not millions of young girls around the world who may have suffered many, if not all, of the same things she had been through, but were too afraid, and too ashamed for their stories to be publicized."

Shelly is here to speak and to be heard for all of them!

This is a story that runs the full gamut of life from the loving warm, tender embraces through the innocent eyes of a three year old to the horrific experiences and traumatic memories that haunt an individual throughout their life.

This is a story of reality through the real eyes of a woman who has achieved the realization that she has something of value to share, an awareness that must be brought to the surface for the protection and the effectiveness of every child and parent out there. Only when the true story is told will this valuable learning experience achieve its goal. The truth will out!

Darryl S. Doane, Rose D. Sloat
The Learning Service, Ltd.
Former Publisher, Founders:
Life's Journey - Professional & Personal Wholeness **Magazine**

TESTIMONIES

I affectionately refer to Eva Dimel as the "Unknown Woman." You would never know from meeting her, the trials and tribulations she went through to become the woman she is today. I've always known her as a spiritual person who is full of love and devotion to God and family. Most of what you'll read in this book has been locked away in her soul for many years - and for good reason. Get ready for a journey of a woman who refused to let the devil win. A woman who refused to let her story be untold or "unknown." This is a journey of a woman who found God and let him guide her to peace - and to the light of today.

Dan E. Zuko, Radio Personality

It has been several years since the first time I read a poem by Eva Dimel on Facebook. Since reading that first one, I haven't stopped reading her poems since. Every poem she has written has been a source of comfort, healing, and encouragement to me. But more than anything else, Eva's poems always point the reader to someone far greater than the author, and the reader. You will soon discover that her book does the same. The book itself is destined to become a treasure to all who read it.

Carolyn Jordan-Jones

Eva Dimel's poetry, Eva's Inspirations, has been a regular feature in our Christian Newspaper, The Good News Just Keeps Coming since October 2012 and is a favorite of our readers everywhere.   God has given Eva a special gift of praise to him and a true insight of His love for us through her poetry.

It is only through God's love that she has been able to heal from her dysfunctional family and childhood abuse.   Her forgiveness and love for others is nothing short of a miracle from God and I am so blessed to have met her and call her my friend and sister in Christ.

Diana Boring, Editor
The Good News Just Keeps Coming

Eva Dimel's book, entitled "From Trash to Treasures", is an overall heartfelt story based on her true life experiences.   The story's plot is straightforward, leaving little to the imagination as to the life into which she was born, and her finding the life that set her free.   Her story is quite rich and moving.   It will touch you, the reader, in a very personal way.   It's wonderful to see a woman heal, and be made strong through the grace and mercy of God.   I feel blessed to know Eva Dimel as an author, radio host, and woman of faith.

Susan Kay Box Brunner,
Author, Motivational Speaker, & Radio Personality

I am so glad that Eva came into my life at the time she did. My son is one of the many living testimonies to what God has done through Eva's poetry. When he lost his grandma, my son was devastated. His life was headed in the wrong direction, until Eva wrote a very beautiful and touching poem for him, as if it was from his Grandma in Heaven. That poem changed my son's life, and for the better. He and I have since come to know Eva as a dear and faithful friend. All of her poems come from the heart, and have touched countless other hearts. I am proud to call Eva my friend. I love her dearly.

Dannette Krugel, Owner
Dannette's Floral Boutique,
Grove City, OH

It has to have the quality of anticipating the next word for me to want to continue reading a book, and this one has that quality. Eva's words have a way of putting you in her story; walking with her through her pain until you find yourself walking out of your own.

It's like you're reading a movie script and getting to watch GOD take a wounded "Humpty-Dumpty" heart, heal it, and fit all the pieces back together again, like it was never broken. I have had the unforgettable privilege of seeing this transformation in Author, Eva Dimel, first hand, and have experienced emotional healing in my own life as a result of witnessing Eva's story. I believe you will also.

Dawn Gwin
Author, Texas

From Trash To Treasures

One of the many horrific, traumatic memories, and the very first she could remember, that haunted Shelly's dreams for many years happened at home, when she was only three years old. And just as most statistics show, it involved another family member – someone she knew, loved and trusted. From that moment, little Shelly's life would be forever enshrouded by that memory – a life of shame, fear and dread.

One moment she was sitting on the couch, feeling perfectly safe next to her Mom who she loved and trusted. The next moment there was a knock at the door. It was her Dad's cousin Fred - a big man who had come over to visit several times before. But this visit would be different from every other visit he had made to their home. With not much more than a hello, he walked straight toward Shelly, picking her up and lifting her onto his shoulders as he walked upstairs to the bathroom. Innocent and unsuspecting, Shelly hung on tightly to his head, afraid she would fall off his shoulders while he peed. Before zipping his pants, he swung her downward, making sure she saw his manhood, smiling and winking as if to gain her approval. She had no idea what was going on, and no idea what was about to happen to her.

Carrying her out into the narrow hallway, his pants still unzipped, and his manhood fully aroused, he laid Shelly down and proceeded to pull her panties down. At this point, she knew something was not right with this. Consumed with his own insatiable lust, Fred held his hand over her mouth as she started to scream. Her Mom, Sheila, heard the first scream, but never responded. She sat motionless on the sofa, knowing her little girl was about to be raped.

Shelly kept kicking and fighting with every ounce of her strength, but to no avail. Fred continued to try to force himself on her. He had never experienced so much fierce resistance from a child so small and fragile. She fought him as hard as a three year old could fight, screaming and kicking her little legs until he finally gave up. He picked her up as if nothing had happened, put her on his shoulders, zipped his pants, and carried her down the steps, placing her gently beside her Mom, walking out the door without even saying goodbye.

Shelly sat there trembling, wondering what had just happened, with tears streaming down her little face. In her own innocent, stammering language, she tried to tell her Mom in her own words what the big man had just done to her. Mom simply looked into her eyes, sternly warning her to never tell her Daddy what happened. She then turned away from her little girl – no soothing words, no holding her in her arms, and no motherly examining of her daughter's quivering body. Little Shelly Smith, a three-year-old girl, sat there trembling, feeling as if she had done something terribly wrong.

Shelly's life only became worse from there. Six months beyond her third birthday, she ran away from home for the first time. There would be several more attempts before she reached the age of ten, and even more attempts thereafter. Her first ride in a police car was the result of her running away from home. The policeman picked her up at the little corner store not far from her home.

She screamed, cried, and kicked at the glove box all the way home, thinking the cop was surely taking her to jail.

Shelly's sister, Marcy, had been visiting some friends. It was mid-summer, and very hot. On her way back home, she took a shortcut through an alley which led to the Smith family's back yard. Nearing the end of the alley, looking toward the house, she thought she saw something, or someone, tied to the big oak tree in the back yard. Running forward, she quickly recognized it was her little sister, Shelly, who was tied to the tree with ropes. Her face was ashen, she was weak, and severely dehydrated, sweltering in the hot sun. Marcy's first thought was to get her sister some cool water. Marcy ran inside to the kitchen, hurriedly filling a bowl with water. But before she made it to the back door, her Mom, Sheila, angrily knocked the bowl of water out of her hands. Marcy couldn't believe what she was seeing and hearing. Her Mom forbade her from taking Shelly any water, telling her that tying Shelly to the tree was her way of punishing Shelly for running away from home.   Marcy's heart sank in despair. In that moment she didn't know which was worse – her hatred of her Mom, or the fact that she could do nothing for her little sister out there in the hot sun, tied to a tree.

Finally, just before Shelly fainted, just before her Dad came home from work, Sheila allowed Marcy to go out and untie Shelly from the tree. Again Marcy filled the bowl with water, hurrying to her sister, pouring some of the water on her face to revive her, then holding the bowl to Shelly's lips. Shelly was too weak to talk or walk. Marcy lifted Shelly's right arm around her left shoulder, half carrying and half dragging her sister into her bedroom, where she kept dampening Shelly's face with a wet washcloth, slowly giving her water to drink. When she was relatively certain that Shelly was going to survive, she held her in her arms, crying and comforting her sister as best she knew how.

Shelly was the second of three sisters, between Marcy and Beth. Some of Shelly's happier moments were whenever she was with her two sisters. Even though Marcy was only eighteen months older than Shelly, to Shelly she always seemed much older, mature, and more like a mother than a sister. Marcy was always the one who, as best she knew how, helped take care of Shelly and her sister Beth.

Shelly's family lived next door to Brother Parker and his wife, Mrs. Parker. Brother Parker was a preacher, and Pastor of a little church where he and Mrs. Parker would take Shelly and her sisters on Sunday morning. Shelly loved attending the little church, especially at Christmas time, when each child would receive a little box of candy after the Christmas program was over. Shelly's Mom and Dad never attended church, but seemed to have no objection to their children going. But there was always one part of the worship service that seemed a little more special to Shelly than any other part – the time of prayer. There was a certain gentle warmth that touched her heart each time she heard the Pastor and the people praying. In that brief period of time, she felt safe, and somehow distanced from the awful atmosphere that pervaded her home so often. During those moments of prayer, she held onto the hope that one day God could love her, even after the bad thing she had done with her Daddy's cousin Fred - a secret she would never tell.

As it had happened so many times before, the day came when the Smith family had to move again. Shelly and Beth never quite understood why they had to move so often, and Marcy, the oldest sister, although she knew the reason, was afraid to tell her younger sisters, for fear of being whipped by her Mom or Dad, or both. The reason the family had to move so often was the result of Hank Smith's addiction to gambling, drinking, and paying for sex with prostitutes. The money he earned at his job, he spent on his habits. And, as has so often been said – "*a gambler loses much more than he wins.*" Hank Smith spent much of his adult life "*changing addresses.*"

When he wasn't working, he was either at the racetrack, or at the house (and in the bed) of another woman, many of whom were prostitutes, or the wives and girlfriends of friends he knew.

And as if the moving itself wasn't hard enough on the children, the fighting that ensued between Mom and Dad only added to the drama and the trauma. The only times the children ever saw their Mom and Dad hug each other were the few times Hank would pick the winning horse, and bring   a few roses home to his wife Sheila. The sheer joy of a single moment, seeing Mom and Dad embraced in a momentary hug, momentarily displaced the hours and days of loud shouting and screaming they so often endured. These were the only moments of happiness her young heart could treasure up. Those moments were few, and far between. Hank Smith didn't spend a lot of time at home with his family. And among the many things which some parents fail to notice is the fact that their children do notice. And Shelley and her sisters noticed a lot. They noticed that Mom seemed just a bit happier and more relaxed, and even a bit more motherly whenever Hank was absent. In fact, she seemed not to miss him at all.

A few more of Shelly's happier moments came when she and

her sisters got to visit their maternal grandpa and grandma, Ed and Eloise Johnson, who lived one street over from Shelly and her family. Grandma Johnson always had something good to eat, and they would stay all night, sleeping in Grandma's big feather bed with her. But even here, the girls couldn't help but notice a few things that seemed *"out-of-character"*.   Grandpa slept across the hall, and Grandma had lots of locks on her bedroom door, and a baseball bat beside the door. The reasons for the locks and baseball bat would later become all too clear to the girls, but especially to Shelly. But in Grandma's bed, with her two sisters snuggled close, Shelly felt safe, and that feeling of safety brought with it a sense of family, something she seldom felt in her own home.

Although most children didn't begin school until age five, Shelly was allowed to start earlier, because she was about to turn five in two months. But going to school only added to the trauma, the fear, and sinking sense of inferiority in her young life. Among the many things that brought her shame, anxiety, and that awful feeling of inferiority was the fact that she seldom had the nickel to pay for her milk. Each time the teacher came around to collect the milk money from the children, Shelly wanted to hide. Her heart sank as she watched the other children happily drop their nickel into the teacher's hand, knowing that she would have to do without her carton of milk, and endure the stares and jeers of the other children.

But one of the many reasons she loved her sister Marcy so much was because of the many times Marcy would give her the nickel she needed for milk. At the time, it really didn't matter to her how Marcy had come by that nickel, and she never asked. It wouldn't be until their adolescent years that Marcy would finally tell Shelly how she managed to have two nickels every day at school.   Sometimes when they were walking to school

Marcy would secretly toss a nickel on the ground, then take Shelly's head in her hand, pushing her head downward so she could see the nickel on the ground. As she saw the big smile on Shelly's face, Marcy would laugh, exclaiming – *"Why looky there Shelly at what you found, you found a bootie nickel."*

After finding a *"bootie nickel"* several times in several weeks, Shelly's curiosity was   just a bit aroused, wondering why it was that the only times she found a bootie nickel was when Marcy was with her. But the sheer happiness of knowing that today she wouldn't have to endure the shame of not having a nickel for milk overshadowed her youthful curiosity, and so she never asked Marcy how she had gotten the nickels. To her young mind, that nickel was worth more than a dime, not only because it was bigger than a dime, but also because it had come from a sister who loved her, and because of what that nickel did for her.

Shelly's Mom never got up with the girls to get them ready for school. Almost every night she stayed up very late, sleeping in the next morning, leaving the girls to fend for themselves, any way they could.   Most school days, they never had clean clothes or underwear to wear to school.   They were constantly searching through the dirty clothes basket trying to find something to wear - just one more element which added to their shame and dread of going to school, knowing they would have to endure the jeers and dirty looks of the teachers and the other students, making fun of their dirty, un-ironed clothes.

But as much as Shelly and Marcy dreaded going to school and facing all the taunting of nearly everyone, they dreaded going home at lunch time almost as much. They never knew if there would be anything for them to eat at home or not. The few times Mom did have a bowl of soup or a sandwich for them became cherished moments. At least they could walk back to school with something in their tummy.

Some of the things that make most children what they are, are their adaptability and their resilience. All the taunting of the other children, the gross neglect of their parents, the physical, mental and sexual abuse, all left their own indelible marks upon the girls, marks that would never go away, not in a lifetime. But during all these things, and somewhat in spite of all these things, they managed to survive somehow. As scarred as they were, both inwardly and outwardly, they endured it all, and kept on living, one day at a time. And one of the few and precious memories that somehow kept Shelly going was the fact that, once in a great while, her Mom somehow managed to accumulate just enough money to spare, and she would give Shelly enough change to go to the Warner's Drug Store, across the street from the school, and buy her lunch. She would walk across the street, enter the Drug Store, and wait patiently behind one of the stools in front of the counter until it was her turn.

She always ordered the same thing – a hamburger and a frosted mug of root beer - the best lunch she ever tasted!

But as good as the hamburger and root beer were, a full and happy tummy doesn't offset the dread of knowing she soon had to return to school, and face the cruelty and mockery of the other girls and boys. Back at school, she had only a few minutes to play on the playground, and there were no friends for her to play with, only the hateful stares and ugly whispers to which she had now become so accustomed. She could hardly wait for the bell to ring, signaling it was time to go back inside. She always felt as if she was not worth very much to anyone. Throughout her school years, she never had many friends, and in her little heart she just knew that everyone else was better than her. It was during that time that she began to daydream of someday having a little house with a white picket fence, and a family who would love her.

Shelly's childhood was haunted by many ghosts, some of which were very real to her young mind. The ghastly memory of *"uncle Fred"*, as he was known, was never far from her thoughts and dreams. She was haunted by images of cruel, mocking children, laughing at her and her sisters, pointing and whispering hateful, ugly slurs about them and their Mom and Dad. She endured the trauma of parental neglect and rejection. She lived in an atmosphere permeated with cigarette smoke, loud music, the smell of whiskey, and dirty clothes. She often went to school, and then to bed very hungry. Her days were filled with abject misery, and her nights with deep, dark, gloomy dreams - dreams of the sort no child should ever have to endure. Any bright spots, any happy moments she had, were very few, and very far between. And yet this beautiful little girl, so fragile and frail, survived it all, endured it all, hoping, praying, and believing that someday, somehow, there was a man named Jesus up there in Heaven who was going to make things better for her.

It has often been said that there is a little bit of good in the worst of us, and a little bit of evil in the best of us. Most of us like to believe that is true, at least about ourselves, and about those who are closest to us. Shelly's Mom, Sheila Smith, was no exception. She definitely had her faults, failures and shortcomings as a mother, but when we surround ourselves with those who are basically from the same cut of cloth as we are, having the same basic character, personality and temperament, and many of the same habits, our own faults and shortcomings don't appear nearly as bad as they might appear in the presence of folks more refined than ourselves.

Sheila had her faults, but she also had some positive virtues.

Those virtues were often, (too often,) suppressed and nearly invisible, being ridiculed and/or mocked by some who were less talented that she was. She had a beautiful voice, and loved to sing country music. It didn't take long for her melodious voice to get the attention of many of her neighbors. She had a lot of friends in the neighborhood who would come over when they knew Hank wasn't home. They would all play their guitars and sing along with Sheila for hours out in the back yard. A few of those happier, brighter spots in the girl's lives were those times they could sit and listen to Mom play and sing. These were also the very few times when they were allowed to sit up just a little past their bedtime.

Grandma Johnson did not approve of any of Sheila's acquaintances, calling them white trash. And she never kept her disapproval to herself.   Often, after the neighbors would leave, Grandma would take advantage of the first opportunity to tell Sheila that she was allowing nothing but trash in her house. Hearing this, and living in the same house, Shelly assumed that Grandma was including her and her sisters in that same category – white trash, and that's exactly how it made her feel - like she was trash.

It has also often been said that *"all good things must come to an end."* And in Shelly's troubled childhood, those good things never lasted very long. When the music and the singing ended, the neighbors would often stay a while longer. Everyone would go inside, sit around the table, light up their cigarettes, and begin to talk about their many ailments and afflictions, or about the spirits that supposedly haunted the house. Hearing them talk about all their ailments, Shelly was certain that she probably had the same things, and would probably die soon. According to her Mom, every house they lived in was haunted.   Shelly was indeed scared, afraid to go to sleep without a light on. But unknown to Shelly and her sisters, their Mom had actually gotten into the cult of "*Spiritism*", and believed in the ability of *mediums* to contact the spirits of the dead.

Shelly was constantly fighting with her little sister Beth, who wanted the light turned off in the bedroom. Sometimes Shelly would wake up at night so overcome with fright she couldn't move, knowing a ghost was going to come and kill her before morning. Many nights, after she could gain enough strength and composure to move, she would run to her parent's bedroom, crying and begging to sleep with her Mom.   Her Dad, of course, would get mad because it meant that he would have to go downstairs and sleep on the couch.   One of the scariest episodes in Shelly's young life happened when her Mom actually had some neighbors over to have a séance around the kitchen table, insisting that Shelly join them.

One of her Mom's friends, Sandy, appeared to have gotten in touch with a spirit, and began to speak with her eyes closed. Everyone at the table agreed it was the spirit speaking through her. Shelly was terrified, lying awake and trembling many nights, afraid the spirit would somehow possess her.

Had it not been for the habits and lifestyles of Hank and Sheila Smith, the Smith family could have had everything a family needs, and even a few luxuries beside. Hank Smith made good money at his job. In fact, he made more money than most of his neighbors. In the early 1960's, a blue collar worker who made a hundred dollars a day was considered to be in the "*middle-to-upper class*" of society. But there was never enough money left after Hank's drinking, gambling, and paying for sex from prostitutes. He kept back just enough for Sheila to buy a meager supply of groceries, and her cigarettes. His habits and her habits came first, even if it meant the family had to suffer hunger, and wear dirty clothes to school. On many occasions, there was not even enough money left for Sheila to buy her cigarettes. And when she was without her cigarettes, no one could stay in the same house with her until she got her cigarettes. Her craving for cigarettes was about to become just one more avenue of horror for her girls.

A certain man who was simply known as Rob lived a few houses down the street from the Smith family. Rob was a painter by trade. He was good at his job, and was kept very busy at doing it all over town. He was known for his skill at never dropping a drop of paint on the floor or on any piece of furniture. Whenever he took a painting job, he used "*drop cloths*", or, as he called them – "*paint sheets*".   But Rob, like so many other men with whom Shelly and her sisters came into contact, had a dark side – he was a sexual predator and a pervert who preyed upon little girls. It didn't take long for him to notice the three little Smith girls who lived just up the street. His evil nature rose to the surface quickly, devising a sadistic plan to lure the girls into his house. He knew the habits of Hank and Sheila Smith. He also knew when Hank was not at home. He knew how desperate Sheila Smith could become without her cigarettes, he knew the brand she smoked, and used that weakness to his own devilish advantage. After watching the girls walk up and down the street, his sadistic mind became obsessed with having the two older girls, Marcy and Shelly. He waited patiently for just the right opportunity to get them inside his house. He'd lie awake many nights, gratifying himself, obsessing about having the girls in his bed. He would go for Shelly first.

His plan was laid, and was soon to be executed. He waited for a day when he could see Sheila outside, working feverishly about the yard, cursing under her breath, and glancing up and down the street, watching for anyone who might have a cigarette she could *"borrow"*. He knew she was out of her cigarettes. He grinned his sadistic grin, tucked a pack of cigarettes into his shirt pocket, and quickly walked up to the Smith house. Sheila saw the pack of cigarettes in his pocket. Her craving was so strong she stopped her feverish sweeping, staring at that pack of cigarettes like a child would stare at all the candy in a candy store window. Rob noticed that stare immediately, pulling the pack of cigarettes from his pocket, offering her one.

Sheila Smith had her faults and habits, but she had just a little bit of pride and dignity left also. She was not one to just take a handout from anyone who offered. But now her craving overcame her dignity and pride. She reached out and took the cigarette from his pack. In her pallid face, Rob saw a mixture of fallen pride, and a sense of gratitude. Both would work to his advantage. *"Mrs. Smith,* he began, *I guess you know I'm a painter, and I'm very busy these days, and really don't have time to wash my paint sheets between jobs. I'd be willing to pay you or your girls to take them to the Laundromat for me. It would give the girls a little extra money, and perhaps even teach them the value of a dollar – what do you think?"*

Pretending to be somewhat of a gentleman, he offered Sheila a light for her cigarette, then pulled two more cigarettes out of the pack, handing them to her, anticipating her answer. The expression on her face told him her thoughts were outrunning her tongue. She quickly blurted out - *"Why I don't see any harm in that at all Mr. Rob. When would you want the girls to start?"* His reply was quicker than hers. *"Would tomorrow after school be too soon ma'am?"*

Every week, on Friday, Marcy would take her sisters down to Rob's house. He lived in a little house that sat back several yards from the street. Shelly was now six years old, Marcy was almost eight, and Beth was five. Marcy "*smelled a rat*" from the very beginning. She was not naive. She saw through Rob's scheme. But the money Rob gave them paid for Mom's cigarettes, and she didn't dare say anything, for fear of being punished by Mom, Rob, or both. Rob "*suggested*" that she and Beth take the sheets to the Laundromat, leaving Shelly there with him. The moment the door closed behind Marcy, he would grab Shelly, lifting her up onto his lap. While pretending to hug her and being nice to her, he was fondling her body all over. Shelly sat motionless and stiff, terrified, trying desperately not to cry or show any emotion. She could feel his manhood becoming aroused as he fondled her body. The horrible images of "*Uncle Fred*", leaped into her mind. She thought to herself – "*I must be a very bad girl, and Jesus is never going to love me.*"

Marcy, knowing deep in her heart that something wicked was going on, literally ran back to Rob's house with the paint sheets, praying she was not too late to somehow prevent Mr. Rob from doing more awful things to her sister than he had already done. Upon entering the house, and seeing the devastated expression on her little sister's face, and noticing the bulge in Rob's pants, her heart sank in despair as she quickly grabbed the money from his hand, ushering her sisters out the door. She knew Mom was waiting impatiently for her cigarette money.

Call it fate, call it luck, or call it an act of God, but Marcy somehow managed to persuade her Mom, and Mr. Rob, to allow her to come by herself, and take the paint sheets to the Laundromat. The abuse she knew was being inflicted on her sister was more than she could stand. She loved Shelly so much she was willing to take the chance of being abused herself, rather than see her sister abused any more. Rob, of course, was ecstatic about the proposal, knowing he was about to satisfy his lust with the oldest of the Smith girls. As the deal was struck with Sheila, he walked away, but turned around momentarily toward her, rubbing his crotch up and down, making sure she saw him do it. Unknown to anyone but himself, he planned on luring Sheila into his bedroom also. He was certain he would have little or no trouble in seducing her. He was wrong, and nearly dead wrong. Seeing him arrogantly taunting her, rubbing himself, enraged Sheila. Her first swing of the broom handle would have taken the top of his head off if he had not quickly ducked the blow. The return stroke almost broke his right arm. She was backing him down the street with the broom, swinging at him with all her strength. He got the message. He was not going to be seducing Sheila Smith.

But like all perverted criminals, Rob made mistakes, he miscalculated, he underestimated the wisdom and cunning of a little eight year old girl, Marcy Smith. He also failed to see the love she had for her sister. Marcy took note of everything inside Rob's house, right down to the position of every piece of furniture. She had also noticed the pistol which Rob kept on the nightstand beside his bed. She waited for just the right time to engage her own plan to put an end to his abuse. She took a bath, dressed up in her prettiest dress, dabbing on just a hint of her Mom's perfume. As she stepped inside Rob's house, she could see that he was already aroused, waiting for her. She smiled, as if to indicate she wasn't afraid, even willing, stepping straight up to him, putting her arms around his waist, hating his guts more with every passing moment.

His lustful passion rose to a white hot pitch. He quickly threw her onto the bed, kissing and fondling her body. Utterly consumed in his lust, he closed his eyes, anticipating the sexual fulfillment he was about to experience. In a split second, Marcy grabbed the pistol from the nightstand, pressing the muzzle to his temple, pulling back the hammer with her thumb. In the next split second, Rob was no longer aroused. All his hot passion and lust subsided as quickly as it had risen. Not only was he going to be denied his sexual fulfillment, he had been outsmarted by an eight year old. He was sure his life was about to come to an abrupt end. His sordid past quickly flashed before his eyes. He knew he was about to descend into Hell. Tears filled his eyes as he fell to his knees, begging Marcy for mercy, promising he would never do this to any girl again.

Marcy Smith was mature far beyond her years. With the pistol still cocked, she replied –*"That's right Mr. Rob – you will never touch another girl as long as you live, because you ain't gonna live long."* Rob trembled, closing his eyes, and turning his head, waiting for her to pull the trigger. Leaving him on his knees, she slowly backed out the front door, with the pistol still pointed between his eyes. *"I'm gonna let you live Mr. Rob, but I'm taking the gun with me. I will have it where I can get my hands on it at any given moment. If I ever suspect that you are molesting another girl, I will come here when you least expect it, some night when you're asleep, and I'll blow your brains out. Do you understand me?"*

Rob assured her he understood perfectly. That was the last time Marcy or either of her sisters ever came to his house. Marcy sneaked into her house, hiding the pistol under her bed. That night she fell asleep smiling, looking up toward Heaven, thanking God for giving her the courage to do what had to be done.

Sheila Smith was a beautiful woman, in spite of all the abuse and hard work she had to endure. Her beautiful brown eyes matched her brown hair. She was of average height, with a nice curvy body. She tried to watch her weight as best she could, but after having three baby girls in quick succession, she lost some of her curves, and gained a few pounds. Virtually everyone who knew Shelly's Mom knew she had some very serious mental and emotional issues. Some of her character traits, of course, were inherited, while others arose from the sheer pain and trauma of being abused by her drunken husband. Many times she had endured a severe beating at the hands of Hank Smith, coming home staggering drunk, with nothing better to do than beat his wife to a pulp.

At Shelly's tender age, she had very little, if any, understanding about things like mental illness, and emotional issues in adults. But she certainly felt all the effects of them. She couldn't quite understand the reasoning behind her Dad beating her Mom so severely, and seemingly for no reason. The little bits and pieces of chatter and gossip she often heard from her Grandma Johnson and Aunt Jane, Sheila's sister, when put together, began to accumulate in her young mind, giving her just a little better understanding of why her Mom sometimes did some of the things she did.   When the two ladies would get together, Sheila, more often than not, was the main focus of their conversation, and none of it was positive. Shelly recalled hearing them angrily fomenting their disdain for the way Sheila neglected her house and her children. She also remembered some of the foul names and titles they assigned to Sheila.

Shelia was only seventeen when she married Hank, and both she and Hank knew their marriage was not made in heaven – they married for all the wrong reasons. Neither of them ever really loved the other. Sheila only wanted to get away from her own troubled home, and Hank was infatuated with her figure, her smile, and her willingness to please him. Neither of them knew the first thing about love, tenderness, or commitment. They both knew how to "*make babies*", but neither of them knew how to properly raise those babies. And the babies came quickly. Each successive girl was no more than two years older than the one before her. Sheila Smith had three girls to raise, mostly by herself, without much help from her husband or anyone else.

Hank was a very handsome man, with blue eyes and dark brown hair. He was an extrovert, very outgoing, a people person, who "*seldom met a stranger.*" It seemed he could endear and ingratiate himself to nearly everyone he met, both men and women. He had a slight stuttering problem when he spoke, but Sheila, without any professional training as a speech therapist, somehow worked with Hank, and taught him to speak plainer, even to the point that his stuttering became hardly noticeable, (except when he was drunk).

Shelly was one of those children who never looked forward to seeing her Dad come home. The reason being, of course, she knew her Dad would probably be drunk, and would proceed to beat her Mom. Hank had a temper, and the whiskey only made it worse. And to make matters even worse, when he had beaten Sheila so severely she could no longer stand or fend him off, he then turned to Shelly, beating her for no apparent reason.

Shelly's Mom, with all her own faults and issues, still, in some uncommon way, loved her little girls. Her love may not have been the kind demonstrated by others, but it was real. There were times when she could exhibit a genuine, motherly care for the safety of her girls. But with an abusive husband who held the whole family in constant fear, half starved, and destitute of any hope for a normal life, Sheila had been reduced to a shell of a woman, and devoid of those qualities that make for a happy home. After seeing Hank beat little Shelly mercilessly, she would hide Shelly somewhere in the house, out of his sight, and take his brutal beatings herself. Shelly always wondered why her Dad beat her, but never beat the other two girls. She didn't have to wait very long for the answer. Her Dad told her out of his own mouth why he beat her. His excuse was - the other girls were pretty, and Shelly was ugly, "*because she wore glasses.*" Marcy was her Dad's favorite child, Beth was her Mom's favorite, and neither Dad nor Mom made a secret of it. Shelly simply accepted that she was ugly, and damaged goods, and a bad girl who no one would ever love.

Shelly recalled a few times seeing the "*paddy wagon*" coming to their house after her Dad had beaten her Mom. On one particular occasion, the policeman, after seeing her Mom's swollen face and dried blood, lost his own professional composure, and beat her Dad all the way out the door, shoving him into the paddy wagon. But that was only a short and temporary deterrent to Hank's violence against his family. Not long after being released from jail, his craving for whiskey and beer returned, and his demented need to vent his violent nature erupted again and again. Each time he got drunk, Sheila could expect a severe beating.

But Hank, unlike some other wife-beaters, wasn't content to beat his wife in the absence of the children – he deliberately chose to beat her when he knew the girls were watching. Whatever kind or degree of personal gratification he got out of it, only he and God will ever know. It was just one more horror the girls had to endure. In fact, they became so accustomed to seeing it, and feeling it, they assumed every family probably lived this way.

But in the same way Marcy had stepped in to protect Shelly from Mr. Rob, she again stepped in to protect her Mom from her

Dad. Once, when Hank was beating Sheila in the kitchen, Marcy endured it till she thought he was going to kill her Mom. She grabbed a big kitchen knife from the sink drawer, forcing her body between them, pointing the tip of the knife blade at Hank's stomach, demanding that he stop beating her Mom. Hank, of course, like Mr. Rob, was both surprised and taken off guard by her sudden display of courage. His first thought was to curse and threaten her, and slap her senseless. But Marcy never flinched. She pressed the tip of the knife to his bellybutton, letting him know she was prepared to thrust it in him if he did not stop beating Sheila. The sheer surprise of seeing his little daughter challenge his authority and his strength somehow diverted Hank's attention away from beating his wife for a moment, and that moment was just long enough for his temper to subside. He gave Marcy a hateful, threatening stare, mumbling under his breath, but satisfied that he had sufficiently beaten his wife, "*till next time.*"

Home had never felt safe for Sheila or the girls. For years they had all lived under the constant fear of being beaten. And yet, in spite of all the brutality toward their Mom and themselves, their young innocent hearts still harbored a certain degree of love for both their parents. They honored their father and mother, even though neither of them, from all appearances, deserved any honor. All the beatings, the cursing, the neglect, and even the absence of any semblance of love from their parents never completely took away the girl's natural affection for Mom and Dad. As far as they understood at their tender ages, their family was perfectly "*normal*". They often heard their Dad say to them – "*you girls don't know how good you've got it.*" He was insinuating, of course, that there were other fathers who were worse than himself, and other families even more dysfunctional than his own.

Marcy Smith was a brave little girl, and due to the horrible conditions under which she was raised, her courage was often the only means of warding off hunger and pain for her younger sisters, and herself. Neither of the younger girls quite understood how Marcy somehow managed to take care of them, and they never asked her. They were simply grateful for having one person in their lives who genuinely cared for them, and showed her love by both her attitude and her actions. Whenever there was an occasion they could be together, out of sight of their parents, Marcy became the mother the smaller girls wanted and needed, always doing little things for them – things they never experienced at home.

Marcy, now ten years old, loved her parents, and tried to honor them as well as a ten year old girl knew how. But circumstances often forced her to choose between what she considered the lesser of two evils. Should she obey her parents in all things, while she and her sisters suffered the constant abuse and neglect, or should she take matters into her own hands, and stoop to *"less-than-noble"* practices in order to prevent her sisters from starving, or being beaten, or both? Such choices should never be forced upon a child so young. Marcy fully understood what the consequences would be if she were to be caught doing some of the things she intended to do, but her love for her sisters took priority over her inclinations to honor her parents, and thus began a life of deception, treachery and theft.

Beth and Shelly never bothered to question Marcy as to how she was able to buy things for them. Whenever the rare opportunity came along, Marcy would take the two girls to the bus stop, pay the fare, and take them to the Woolworth store and buy them a good lunch. After lunch she would pay for them having their pictures taken in the little photo booth. The sheer thrill of being away from the horrible conditions of home for a few hours, and having a sister who could buy things for them, were some of the brighter moments in the girl's lives. They, of course, took full advantage of those moments, never questioning how Marcy got the money to pay for it all.

Most of their excursions were to the smaller stores in town, where Marcy mostly bought them candy and soda pop. But with the passing of time, and as her courage increased, Marcy made mistakes – mistakes which would later prove very costly. Having never been caught in her deception thus far, she ventured a bit farther, taking the younger girls to the larger stores, and taking greater risks. Shelly recalled one particular occasion, when Marcy took them to the biggest grocery store in town, and told them to pick out anything, and as much of it, as they wanted. This, of course, was something the girls had never heard in their young lives. They ran happily up and down the aisles, filling their little arms with "*stuff*" – some of which they had never seen or tasted. Whatever looked good to them, they took some of it. Marcy, of course, also helped herself to whatever she wanted also.

The lady at the cash register eyed the girls with suspicion as they piled all their treasures on the moving belt. Their little faces were aglow with anticipation. They were impatient, wanting to get the wrappers off, and enjoy whatever was inside as quickly as possible. The lady rang up each item, asking no questions, until Marcy pulled out a check she had stolen from her Dad's checkbook, and began writing on it. The scowl on her face said all that needed to be said. She ordered the girls to stand still while she called their mother. Hanging up the phone, she threw everything they had placed on the belt into a brown paper bag, tucking the check into her vest pocket. She then marched the girls up and down the aisles, making them put every item back where they had gotten it, then waited for their Mom or Dad to arrive.

The shame and humiliation of having to put everything back, along with the stares and whispers of the shoppers, devastated Beth and Shelly. Marcy remained calm and collected, as if she had done nothing wrong. Before Sheila arrived to pick them up, Marcy reassured the girls that everything was going to be ok. When Sheila arrived, she apologized to the lady at the register, took the check from her, then immediately began cursing, and swatting the girl's behinds as she marched them out the door. The girls rode in total silence, afraid to even glance at each other, knowing the worst was yet to come for all of them.

As soon as they got home, Sheila showed the check to Hank, while glaring at Marcy. She gave Hank the short version of what had happened. Hank grabbed Marcy by her hair, holding onto her tightly as he ordered Sheila, Beth, and Shelly out of the room. He drug Marcy up the stairs by her hair, closing the bedroom door behind them. Marcy refused to whimper or cry. In the downstairs bedroom, Sheila and the two girls covered their ears with pillows, trying to shut out the loud noises coming from upstairs, noises that sounded like a body being slammed into the walls repeatedly.

Marcy was banished from the rest of the family for two days, kept upstairs. No one except Sheila was allowed to take her food and water. When she finally came downstairs, she was hardly recognizable as their sister. This was the only time the girls ever saw their Mom take one of her children into her arms, crying, and offering a few words of comfort. Marcy rejected it all, pushing her Mom away, reaching for her sister's open arms instead. There in the living room, for a few brief moments, two sisters demonstrated their love and compassion for the other sister.

Marcy loved her sisters, and her sisters loved her. They idolized Marcy for her boldness and courage in the face of danger and open hostility. She was the one person in their lives with whom they never argued or fought. Shelly and Beth fought and argued over just about everything. They looked up to Marcy, and wished they could be more like her. In spite of her severe beatings at the hands of her Mom and Dad, Marcy continued to defy them, never letting them believe she was afraid of them, because she wasn't. She had made up her mind that she would somehow take care of her sisters, no matter what it might cost her. She would willingly lay down her life for her sisters. On many occasions the girls were sent to bed early, often without anything to eat. They could hear the laughter and revelry coming from downstairs, as Hank and Sheila entertained friends. They could smell the large pizzas Hank had ordered, as their own stomachs rumbled with hunger. On these occasions, Marcy would sneak downstairs while Mom and Dad were partying with their friends, stealing food from the refrigerator or cupboard to take upstairs for her sisters to eat.

Shelly had several aunts and uncles, who, in turn, had lots of children, giving Shelly lots of cousins, many of whom lived on the same street as Shelly. The ones who didn't live on the same street lived only one or two streets east or west of her house. The ones who lived closest were her Mom's sister, Elizabeth, and her husband Phil. Phil was Hank's brother, which, of course, made their children and Sheila and Hank's children double first cousins. Shelly's Mom and her sister Elizabeth were considered the two black sheep of their family. They were shunned and ridiculed by all the other family members because of the way they lived. Both their husbands were addicted to gambling, alcohol, and extramarital affairs. And both of them regularly beat their wives and children. It had also become common knowledge that Uncle Phil had an affair with a neighbor lady.

The only times in her life when Shelly didn't feel inferior to other children were the times she got to play with her six cousins – three girls and three boys - the children of Elizabeth and Phil. They too had known the pain and shame of having the gas and electricity shut off because there was not enough money to pay the bills. They too had gone to bed many nights hungry and cold. The one big difference between Elizabeth and Sheila was that Elizabeth never let her children go to school wearing dirty, smelly clothes. Being with them made Shelly and Beth feel like equals, neither inferior nor superior in any way. They could all play and talk without either child sensing any shame in the presence of the others.

Uncle Phil's personality could be described in two words – LOUD and LOUDER! He loved to talk, and he insisted on being heard when he did talk. And when he talked, hardly anyone else could get a word in edgewise. As much as Shelly and Beth feared him, they were willing to suffer his manners for a while in order to be with their cousins. Whenever Phil and Elizabeth came over, all the children were soon driven from the house, which was, as it turned out, a blessing in disguise.

One particular evening, as Hank and Phil sat on the sofa watching TV, the subject of another one of Sheila's sisters, Aunt Sue, came up. It happened at the time that Aunt Sue and her husband Tim were going through a bitter divorce. Phil and Tim were two of the small number of men in Shelly's life who had never tried to molest her in any way. To Shelly, Tim was a giant of a man, standing about six feet – five inches tall. Shelly assumed that because he was so big and tall, he must also be very strong. As the conversation continued, and the beer began to have its effect, Hank turned to Shelly, demanding – *"Tell me little girl, if me and your Uncle Tim wuz to get into a fight, who do you think would win?"* Without a moment's hesitation Shelly blurted out – *"Uncle Tim would win, because he's a lot taller and stronger than you."* Hank's face turned blood-red, as he, without a moment's hesitation, grabbed Shelly up from the floor with one hand, slapping her face with the other, then pushed her up the stairs, whipping her bottom with his hand every step of the way. He couldn't bear what he perceived to be a brazen insult to his manhood. In his drunken brain, she had shamed him in front of his brother, and must be punished.

Her tears got her no sympathy, and no mercy. He tossed her onto the bed, cursing her as he left the room, slamming the door behind him. Much later that evening, after the company was gone, he crept quietly up the stairs, stopped outside the bedroom door, putting his ear to the door, listening, to see if Shelly had fallen asleep yet. She was sitting up on the bed, with her head between her knees, sobbing. Hank opened the door, stepping in, halfheartedly demanding an apology from Shelly. But this time, Shelly refused to apologize. At that moment, for the first time in her young life, she found the courage to deny her Dad something he demanded. She rose from the bed, facing him defiantly. He could see the determination and the hatred in her face. For a single moment, she reminded him of her sister Marcy.

Hank Smith had an uncommon way of dealing with his own guilt. No matter what he did, and no matter what he had neglected to do, he always found some twisted form of psychological manipulation which, to him at least, justified his actions. As he had done so many times in the past, he justified his cruelty to his daughter by offering Shelly a dollar, which was his cowardly, sheepish way of saying – *"I'm sorry"*, and at the same time, his way of buying her forgiveness. Each time one of the girls took the dollar from his hand, he felt as if he had fully made amends for his cruelty to them.

Shelly took the dollar, but not for the reason Hank had given it to her. As he left the room, she laid down on the bed, focusing on the dollar for a few minutes. Her aching body hated her father. Her aching heart hated him even more. She began to think – *"there are a hundred cents in this dollar, and I am going to keep it forever, as a reminder of the hundred times Dad has beaten me, my sisters, or my Mom."* But the hundred cents in that dollar would also remind her that she now hated him a hundred times more than she ever had in her life.   But no sooner had those thoughts crossed her mind, she found herself repenting of her thoughts, remembering the words of Brother Parker, who always said – *"we must forgive, and pray for those who despitefully use us."* In that moment, praying for her wicked Dad was one of the most difficult things she ever did, but she did it. Bowing her head, and closing her eyes, Shelly, now eight years young, found the grace to forgive, and to pray for her abusive father. She wondered if Jesus had heard her. After all, she pondered, He probably didn't love her anyway, since she had been such a bad girl.

We've all heard the clichés, like – *"time waits on no man"*; *"time goes faster as we get older"*; and *"children grow up too fast."* For Shelly, time moved at a snail's pace. She wished it would speed up, and her life would somehow take a turn for the better, and the sooner the better. Three more years had now passed, and Shelly was eleven. Nothing had improved. The family was having to move yet again, something Shelly had gotten used to. But in her heart, she wished, she hoped, she prayed that her life could be just a little bit happier, even if only for a few days. She began to think – *"surely things can only get better, because, how*

could they get much worse." She longed to have better and prettier clothes, like most of the other children at school. She wished she could afford a good hot lunch every day, like everyone else. Then, like an answer to her prayers, her aunt Jane and her husband, Don Jaimeson, bought a house just one street over from her family. Shelly's Mom and Dad never owned a house their whole married life, they always rented.

Both Aunt Jane and her husband Don worked at a full time job. That meant they had to have a babysitter for their little boy, Randy. Randy was Jane's son from a previous marriage, making Don his stepfather. They agreed, Grandma Johnson was perfect for the job of taking care of little Randy. But Aunt Jane also needed someone to come once a week, on the weekend, when Grandma wasn't available, and do a bit of dusting and cleaning around the house, so she and Don could have a little quality time together on the weekend. Shelly was perfect for that job. Don had served some time in prison, but served his time, and was released. He got a good job, settled down, and made a good living. He and Jane were so proud of their new home. With both of them working, they could afford brand new furniture, and owned a beautiful new car. Life was good.

Shelly loved going to Aunt Jane's every Saturday. For her, the work was more like play. And having the added responsibility of watching her cute little cousin Randy, now five years old, only added to her joy. And Aunt Jane paid her well for her services. For the first time in her life, she had spending money of her own, money she had earned herself. Also for the first time in her life, she now wore some brand new clothes, new underwear, and pretty shoes. Aunt Jane would take the time after working all day to take her shopping, and help her pick out a new dress, or a pair of nice jeans. It all gave Shelly a sense of pride, accomplishment, and just a little bit of self-esteem –

something she had never had. Between her cleaning and dusting, and Aunt Jane's own tidiness, the house and furniture were kept looking really nice. Shelly also liked the way her aunt would talk to her about things while they were cleaning. She treated Shelly like an adult, giving her respect, and at times, a bit of motherly advice.

And as if things couldn't get any better, Aunt Jane asked Shelly if she wanted to come and live with her and Don, stipulating, of course, that her Mom and Dad had to agree to it first. Shelly's heart leaped into her throat at the thought of asking her Mom if she could come and live with Aunt Jane. But Aunt Jane assured her she would do most of the talking, and was pretty confident she could persuade Sheila to agree. The day came, and Aunt Jane, true to her word, approached Sheila with the proposition. Shelly stood motionless, praying her Mom would say yes. When she saw the little smile on Sheila's face, and heard her say yes, it was all she could do to keep from jumping up and down with joy.

Shelly was so happy living with her aunt. For the first time she could remember, she actually felt special, like she was worth something to someone. She and little Randy slept in the same bedroom. He begged her to read stories to him each night, falling asleep listening to her sweet voice. She adored him, and he loved her. For the first time in her life, there was someone who looked up to her. There was no cursing or swearing in Aunt Jane's home, no alcohol, and no beatings.   Many times she witnessed Aunt Jane and Uncle Don kissing each other tenderly, while holding hands, sitting on the front porch swing. She watched Don teach Randy how to catch a baseball in a little baseball mitt he had bought for him. The many contrasts she was now seeing between her first ten years and her last few months stood out boldly, to say the least. She realized that her family had not been a normal family, and her life had not been a normal life. The happiness she had known in the few months she had been at Aunt Jane's seemed almost too good to be true. She was sure she was going to wake up one morning, and discover it had all been a dream. But until then, she would be grateful, and make the most of her new life. This new life and happiness were not a dream, but another nightmare was looming darkly on the near horizon.

Aunt Jane had suddenly become ill, losing weight and her appetite. She became too sick to go to work. Whenever she tried to eat anything, her stomach would begin to churn. At first she assumed it was nothing but heartburn. The antacid tablets she was dissolving in her mouth didn't seem to help much. Everything she ate came back up. She couldn't sleep because of the terrible burning in her stomach and throat. It was time to see her doctor. Immediately upon hearing her symptoms, the doctor sent her for some tests at the hospital. The test results confirmed what she and Don greatly feared – it was her gall bladder. She would have to have surgery.

She was admitted the next day. She would have to undergo at least two days of pre-op therapy before they could do the surgery. She was severely dehydrated from all the vomiting. The nurse hooked her to an I.V., replenishing her fluids while medicating her stomach. Shelly was devastated, and so afraid she was going to lose her beloved Aunt. The kindly old doctor assured her Aunt Jane was going to be just fine after the surgery. Returning to the house after Jane was admitted, Shelly immediately set about her chores, cleaning the house from top to bottom, making sure everything was in its proper place. She followed her aunt's motto for good housekeeping – "*a place for everything, and everything in its place.*"

The first night of Aunt Jane's absence, after all the chores were done, Shelly sat on the big plush sofa with Randy, watching her favorite show – The Rifleman. The character Lucas McKay, played by the actor Chuck Connors, was her hero. To her, he was the best Dad in the world. Many times in school, she would lay her head on her desk and daydream of The Rifleman riding up to her house, putting her on his horse, and riding off into the sunset. Opposite the big sofa, a few feet to the right side of the TV was a big comfortable chair. That chair was Don's throne, and no one dared be in it whenever he was home.   If there was one man in the world Shelly never suspected of having any sexual inclinations toward her, it was Uncle Don. She trusted him implicitly. Her implicit trust, however, as she was about to discover, had been misplaced. As the show was going off, Uncle Don came down the stairs dressed in nothing but his bathrobe. This, of course, was something Shelly had gotten used to, and thought nothing of it. She had been with Jane and Don for a year now, and he had never made any kind of off-color remark to her, and he certainly had not made any kind of gesture toward her that made her the least bit uncomfortable. But today, his true colors were about to come out.

At the bottom of the stairs, Don hesitated momentarily, glancing at Shelly in a manner she had never seen before. That little grin on his face, and the steady gazing of his eyes sent a shiver up her spine. It was a look she had seen before – a look she recognized, a look she had learned to interpret the hard way. She could tell from the motion of his hands inside the pockets of his robe that he was touching himself. He wanted her attention – and he got it. Shelly quickly glanced away, as the blood rose in her cheeks. She tried desperately to ignore him. But Don was not going to be put off that easily. He walked across the room, sitting down slowly into the big comfortable chair. Shelly asked Randy to go to his room. As she was about to get up and follow Randy,

Don threw back the folds of his bathrobe, spreading his legs, making sure Shelly saw everything. He was naked under the robe, and aroused.

Shelly ran quickly after Randy, closing and locking the door behind her. Randy couldn't understand why Shelly was so upset. She was trembling, partly from the shock, and partly from the rage inside her. This could not be happening to her again. If ever there was a time she wished she could wake up and discover it was all a dream - that time was now. But it wasn't a dream – it was all too real, bringing back all the horrible images of her past in one panoramic view. Don went to bed that night plotting how he was going to get Shelly alone. He knew he had only a few days in which to get what he wanted, and he would have her – somehow. He fell asleep that night dreaming of how it was going to be with an eleven year old. He fantasized about all the things he wanted to do with her, and all the things he was going to force her do to him.

Don got up and hurried off to the hospital early the next morning, stopping to visit Jane for a few minutes before he went on to work. She was so pleased that he would take the time to stop and see her on his way to work. That evening, after work, he stopped and bought her a dozen red roses, holding them behind his back as he entered her room. Jane smiled as he presented the lovely roses to her. He bent over, gently kissing her lips, whispering – *"I love you gorgeous."* What Jane didn't suspect was that, in the back of his perverted mind, he was kissing Shelly, preparing to have his way with her.

"So, how are things going at home handsome?" Jane asked. He assured her everything was just fine at home, replying - *"That Shelly is one heck of a young lady! She can cook pretty good for an eleven year old, and she takes such good care of Randy and the*

house. *You just hurry and get better sweetheart, we all miss you terribly. You don't have a thing to worry about at home. Randy and I are being well cared for."* Jane pulled his head closer, giving him a long passionate kiss before thanking him again for his love and care for her. She couldn't help but notice the slightest blush in his cheeks. He knew she had noticed it, and quickly dismissed himself, telling her he had to stop and get some things for supper before going home.

On the way home, Don stopped at the same flower shop, buying a single red rose. He asked for a long box, and headed toward home. Shelly had never received any kind of flowers from anyone. Don suspected as much, figuring he might stand just a little better chance of seducing her with the rose. Entering the house, he ushered Randy to his room, telling him not to come out until he came for him. He told Randy he and Shelly had some things to discuss. He hurried upstairs to the bathroom, taking a quick shower, splashing on a bit of cologne, and donning his robe. Shelly was in the kitchen doing dishes. She didn't hear him creeping down the stairs barefoot.

With the rose in his hand, he sneaked up behind Shelly, wrapping one arm around her waist, while reaching around her with the rose in the other hand, whispering – *"Hi gorgeous, this is for you."* Taken completely by surprise, Shelly froze. He had her pinned against the sink. She couldn't move. He had her right where he wanted her. He dropped the rose into the sink, wrapping his arms around her in a tight hug, pushing his body against her. When she started to scream, he quickly cupped one hand over her mouth.   Shelly could do nothing to free herself from him. He held onto her, lunging and moaning for what seemed like an eternity to Shelly. Then suddenly he stopped, and walked away, looking back at Shelly, on her knees, sobbing and trembling. As he walked out of the kitchen, he stopped in the doorway, as if he was about to come back. The sickening expression on his face told Shelly this would not be the last time he would try to molest her.

It was Friday. Her Aunt Jane's surgery was scheduled for Monday morning at 10:00 a.m.   Shelly told Don she wanted to go home and visit her family before her aunt's surgery. Don didn't want her to go, but knew he couldn't stop her from going. She saw the lust in his eyes as he gazed at her, ogling her body up and down. She tried to avoid him as much as possible. As she began to pack some of her clothes to walk home, he sat on the big sofa, reaching out his arms to her, beckoning – *"Why don't you come and sit in Uncle Don's lap sweetheart, and we can talk a little before you leave."* Shelly gave him a quick, emphatic NO. *"Ahhh now girlie, don't be that way, you know I could pay you a lot more money than Aunt Jane does if you'd just let me have a little fun."* Shelly dropped her eyes, opened the front door, picked up her bag of clothes, and hurried across the porch. As she was stepping off the front steps, Don stood in the doorway, cautioning her – *"Now you ain't gonna tell nobody about our little love affair, are you honey?"*   Shelly kept walking, never looking back, giving him no answer.

Shelly knew she could never tell her Mom and Dad what had happened. She knew if they found out, then Aunt Jane would find out, and she didn't want Aunt Jane to know right now. She wanted her aunt to have her surgery and get better, then, maybe someday, she would tell her, but not now. But she had to tell someone, and that someone was Marcy. She begged Marcy not to tell anyone else. But when Marcy heard the sordid details, she decided Mom and Dad needed to know. She reasoned with Shelly – *"Now Shelly, if you were married to a scum bag like that, wouldn't you want to know if he had done something like that? And if someone doesn't expose him now, he will only do it to*

another little girl, and then another.   And God only knows how many others he has already molested. We have to stop him now Shelly."

Somewhat against her own judgment, Shelly reluctantly agreed, but only because she respected Marcy's judgment more than her own,   along with the fact that   Marcy had been the only one in her immediate family who had ever really shown any genuine concern for her and her safety. Marcy assured her she would do most of the talking, and would do everything she could to protect her just in case things got ugly. Marcy chose a time when Hank was sober to break the story to him. She also made sure their Mom was present; she wanted them both to hear the whole sordid affair. Neither of the girls was sure how their Dad or Mom would react. They just knew it had to come out, sooner or later, and they agreed – the sooner the better, for everyone concerned.

As Marcy began to tell Hank about what uncle Don had done to Shelly, his face began to turn beet red. Suddenly he stopped her, looking toward Shelly, asking – *"is this the truth Shelly?"* Shelly stammered – *"yes papa, it is all true, every word of it."* Her Dad insisted – *"Well young lady, since it happened to you, I want to hear the story from you, in your own words."* Shelly dropped her head, begging – *"But Dad, I'm so ashamed, I don't think I can tell you all the dirty stuff he said and did to me."*   For once in his life, Shelly's Dad showed some sympathy and compassion toward his little girl. He saw the deep hurt in her eyes, and heard the shame in her voice – she was telling the truth. He rose from his chair in a rage, swearing he would go and kill the low-life pervert. Sheila grabbed his arm, begging him to calm down before doing something he would regret for the rest of his life. And for once, Hank Smith thought things over for a moment, and listened to his wife instead of his own desire to do something foolish. Deep inside, he knew what he had to do. But first, he told Shelly in no uncertain terms that she would never be allowed to work for her Aunt Jane again.

As much as Shelly loved her aunt, and as much as she had enjoyed the time she had spent with her, she knew she could never be in the same house with Don again. Hank Smith did something which was quite contrary to his violent nature – he walked around behind the house, alone, sitting down under the big oak tree, bowed his head upon his knees, silently asking God to forgive him for not being the kind of Dad he could have and should have been to his girls.   And in his own uncommon way, he somehow managed to offer God a moment of gratitude for giving him a wife who, in spite of all her problems, could still sometimes show good judgment, and common sense. He still wasn't quite sure if he could keep from killing Don when he saw him, but he would cross that bridge when he came to it, and he would come to it real soon. He decided to wait until Jane's surgery was over, and she had fully recovered, before approaching Don. He wanted Jane to be there, and hear everything.

In the meantime, Grandma Eloise still came over Monday through Friday, cooking and cleaning, and taking care of Randy. But Randy was now the saddest little boy she had ever known. Jane and Don couldn't understand why their son seemed so unhappy and withdrawn. He had always been so full of life, and energetic. Now he mostly ignored them, his toys, and even his new baseball glove. He refused to play catch with Don. When Jane took him in her arms, asking him what was wrong, he whimpered – "*I miss Shelly, I want Shelly back.*" She assured him she would have Shelly back real soon. Don hung his head, too ashamed and too unwilling to tell his wife, his son, or anyone else the truth. Every day he lived with the horrible fear that

Shelly might tell her folks, and the ugly truth might come out, and he would lose his family, his friends, his job, and maybe even his life. He lay awake at night as words from the past kept ringing in his conscience, words he had heard from an old country preacher, who said – *"remember young man, whatever you do today, you will have to sleep with tonight."* Instead of simply dealing with his guilt, and facing the truth, and confessing what he had done, he began to concoct the story he would tell if he was ever accused. He was sure he could convince everyone that Shelly was a liar.

But the day of reckoning arrived. Sitting on the front porch swing with Jane, holding her hand and telling her how much he loved her, he looked up the street. Suddenly his face turned ghostly pale. He let go of his wife's hand, and began to stammer and curse – *"Oh damn it, there comes the trash of the community."* Jane's jaw dropped in utter shock. She had never heard Don say anything so spiteful about anyone, let alone her own family. She shot back – *"Now wait just a minute my dear man, that happens to be my sister and her family you're calling trash."* Don grunted something under his breath, jumped up and hurried into the house. Hank, Sheila, Marcy, Beth, and Shelly were now entering the front gate.

Hank noticed Don hurrying into the house. He could guess why Don didn't want to face him and Sheila, and especially not Shelly. Hank walked ahead of the others, almost jumping up the steps onto the porch. Without saying a word to anyone, he stomped into the living room, yelling loudly so everyone could hear him – *"Come on out and face me you sorry piece of white trash, let's see if you can handle a man like you handled my little girl."* Jane nearly fainted. No one had ever used such language in her home. And what on earth did Hank mean, claiming her husband had *"handled"* his little girl? Sheila took Jane's hands in hers, and began to explain to her what Don had done to Shelly. Jane shuddered in disbelief, glancing from Shelly to Marcy to Sheila, her mouth open, gasping for breath. Meanwhile, Don came out from hiding with his arms outstretched toward Hank, begging him – "*Now Hank, don't go doing nothing stupid till you hear my side of the story. I swear I never molested her. I swear it on my Mama's grave Hank. All I did was offer her some more work around here, and more money for doing it. Surely you don't think I'd molest a little girl.*"

Hank had his fist drawn back, but dropped it to his side, replying – "*You just admitted it you low down sorry excuse for a man, because no one said anything about you molesting her yet. Now I know you're guilty.*" As Hank made a lunge for Don's throat, Grandma Eloise threw herself between the two men, screaming – "*Now you two just back off and cool down. Hank, I know you're mad, and I know you think you have a good reason to be, but I believe Don is telling the truth. I just don't believe he could do such a thing to a little girl.*" By now everyone else had come into the house, hearing everything that was said. Don made his way around the kitchen table, staying as far away from Hank as possible. He took Jane in his arms, comforting her, asking – "*You believe me don't you sweetheart, you know I could never betray you like that. I love you so much.*" He managed to produce a few crocodile tears, pulling her closer to him. Jane believed him. Turning to Sheila and her family, she looked pitifully at little Shelly, then back to Sheila. After a few moments of tense silence, she said to her sister – "*I think you and your family should leave now Sheila. You are no longer welcome here. If you don't leave immediately, I will call the Sheriff.*"

With no physical proof of molestation, and only the word of an eleven year old child, Hank and Sheila knew there was no use in going to the law for justice. Shelly was now branded as a pathological liar in the eyes of most of her family. The only ones who stood by her and believed her were her Mom and Dad and her two sisters, Marcy and Beth. Once again, the shame and indignity of being sexually abused by one of her relatives overshadowed Shelly's days and nights. And now, to make things worse, the word began to spread that she was an incurable liar.   Shelly's sense of self-worth had nearly disappeared by now. She looked in the mirror each day, telling herself she was ugly. She seldom received any kind or degree of compliment or congratulatory statement from anyone (Marcy being the exception). She was convinced she was a bad seed, a little girl condemned to a life of abuse and exploitation at the hands of anyone who was able to take advantage of her. And yet, somewhere deep in her sub conscience, a tiny grain of hope lay dormant. Those eternal truths she had learned in Sunday School still survived in her memory. She couldn't forget them, and she didn't want to forget them. She still clung to The Golden Rule – treating others as she wanted to be treated. No matter how bad others treated her, she couldn't bring herself to treat them badly – it simply wasn't in her nature.

Seeing Marcy's courage in the face of danger and threatening gave Shelly just a bit more courage than she would have exercised otherwise. She thought – "*if Marcy can do it, I can do it.*" A few weeks later her newfound courage was put to the test. Grandma Johnson asked her to come with her to the grocery store.   In the parking lot she saw her uncle Don getting out of his car.   Shelly knew her Grandma did not believe her story about how Don had abused her. It broke her heart to think her own Grandma whom she loved so deeply would think of her as a liar. Here was an opportunity for her to confront Uncle Don in the presence of her Grandma, and hopefully get the truth out of him. "*Uncle Don, she demanded – "Why are you still lying, and denying what you did to me? Why don't you tell Grandma the truth*

for once?" Don, of course, vehemently denied it all again, stomping away from them in a big hurry. Grandma swatted Shelly's behind, sternly warning her never to bring up the accusation again.

Once again, Shelly's heart sank in despair. She couldn't understand why some of her own flesh and blood either would not or could not believe her. After all, she was only telling the truth, and the kindly old preacher had told her long ago – *"Truth will always prevail in the end."* But right now, it seemed to her, neither truth nor justice had any place at all in the hearts of most grownups. But truth and justice are like a large body of water, dammed up, pressing against their restraining boundaries, just waiting for the tiniest crevice to appear in the dam. And when that tiny opening appears, the water will find its way into that opening, and begin to flow outward and downward, as if it is chasing something or someone, seeking its lowest level. Don had created his own crevice. And now the stream of blind justice had begun to pursue him like a hound from hell. Sometimes the wheels of justice turn slowly, but they turn. In the Holy Bible the rhetorical question is asked – "Can the leopard change its spots, or the Ethiopian his skin...?" This double question, of course, answers itself. The leopard is what it is by nature, and cannot change its nature, or its coat. And so it is with men – they may be able to change their personalities, and they may even improve their reputations, but they cannot, of themselves, change their own character. Without a divine regeneration men will continue to be what they are, and will continue to do what they are accustomed to doing.

And so it was with Don Jaimeson. He was a child molester, and he continued to be a child molester. But like so many others of his kind, he considered himself too wise to get caught. With the passing of time, and having escaped any kind of punishment for what he had done to Shelly, his perverted sexual urges arose in him like a raging fire. He could not subdue his twisted passion for little girls, and other women. When he was not molesting little girls, he was sneaking in the back door of his neighbor's houses, having sex with their wives.

Not long after Shelly went back home, Jane hired another little girl, Carolyn, one of Shelly's double-first-cousins, to move in with her, and do all the things Shelly had done around the house. The fact that Jane hired the little girl gave Don the misguided notion that she trusted him implicitly. He knew her well enough to know she would never deliberately put the well-being of another little girl in jeopardy if she didn't trust him. What he didn't know was that Jane did not trust him like she had before, but was giving him the benefit of the doubt. She reasoned that if he had actually done something with Shelly, now that he had been accused and nearly beaten to death by Hank, he probably would never do it again. But she was wrong.

Jane worked hard at her job, giving her employer an honest day's work for an honest day's pay, every day. When she came home from work, she was always very tired. But she never let her aches and pains get in the way of her family. The needs of her family came first. When she finally got to sleep, she slept soundly, and peacefully. It was often said of her that she could sleep through a thunderstorm. And Don, her husband, knew it better than anyone else. It was just another little tidbit of knowledge he could use to his own advantage.

From the first day Carolyn arrived, Don eyed her up and down, comparing her to other little girls he had molested. She was barely eight years old. He wanted her. And he would have her – somehow, someplace. He waited until Friday night, knowing Jane didn't have to work on Saturday, and usually slept in later than usual. He lay there beside her, waiting impatiently for her to fall fast asleep. When he was sure she was asleep, he slipped quietly out of bed, tiptoeing across the carpeted living room toward Carolyn's bedroom. His heart pounded with excitement, anticipating, imagining how it was going to be with her. He eased her door open very slowly and carefully. The little nightlight plugged into the wall gave just enough light for him to see without tripping over anything. He stood motionless for a few moments, making sure he hadn't disturbed her.

Taking two steps forward he knelt beside her bed, easing his right hand under the blanket, keeping his left hand free in case she woke up and tried to scream. As he gently raised the cover, the dim light barely illuminated her silky smooth skin. He began to fondle her legs, up and down, keeping his left hand hovered over her mouth. Becoming more aroused with each passing moment, he moved his hand upward, feeling every inch of her body. As he touched her chest, she awakened suddenly. He quickly cupped his hand over her mouth. She froze in sheer terror. She could not have screamed if she tried. He somehow sensed her temporary paralysis. He leaned closer, whispering – *"It's alright honey, it's me, Uncle Don. Now if you promise me you won't scream, I'll move my hand, OK?"* Carolyn nodded her consent not to scream. Don pulled the blanket down, exposing her whole body. Taking her head into his hands, he pulled her face toward his, kissing her lips. *"Now remember your promise honey"*, he whispered, as he kissed her body all over, while touching her with his hands. He continued groping her for nearly an hour, then stopped suddenly, reminding her not to scream, and left the room. Ten minutes later he slid quietly into bed with his wife, grinning, congratulating himself that he had not been caught molesting another little girl.

Carolyn, like so many other little girls who are molested by men, felt so dirty and ashamed. She felt as if it was her who had done something evil. And like so many other little girls who have been violated, she was very much afraid to tell anyone, especially an adult. After being molested by an adult, something in her young and innocent psyche told her most adults couldn't be trusted. But she knew she had to tell someone what had happened, and that someone was her cousin, Shelly. Saturday evening she asked Aunt Jane if she could go up the street and play with her cousins for a while. Soon after arriving at the Smith home, she called Shelly aside, a safe distance away from the other girls. As she began to confide in Shelly, she noticed Shelly's face turning red, and her eyes welling up with tears. Shelly let her tell her story, then hugged her tightly, as she, in turn, began to tell Carolyn of her own experiences at the hands of perverted men. The two girls agreed - Don had to be exposed. Perhaps the two of them together could convince their families that Shelly had told the truth about Uncle Don.

Carolyn followed Shelly into the house. Sheila was sitting on the sofa. When she saw the two little girls walk in together, her maternal instinct, and the stern look on the faces of the girls, told her something was wrong.   Shelly was the first to speak. Choosing her words carefully, she began – "*Mom, me and Carol have got something we want to tell you, and it's really bad.*" After listening patiently to Carolyn's story, Sheila told the two girls they had done the right thing in confiding in her. With a motherly hug and a few words of consolation, she sent them outside while she called her sister Elizabeth. After listening to Sheila, Elizabeth was convinced that Shelly had not been lying about what Don had done to her. There was simply too much evidence pointing to his guilt for her to keep denying the cold hard truth. She assured Sheila she was going to drive over to Jane's house, and tell Jane everything. Upon hearing her husband had molested another little girl, Jane confronted him. A big war of words ensued, with Don denying everything. Jane slapped his face, packed her suitcase, and told him he would soon be hearing from her divorce attorney.

Hank Smith decided it was time for him to change careers. One day he came home driving a Mr. Softee Ice Cream truck. Seeing the spotless, shiny new truck with her Dad behind the wheel sparked Shelly's curiosity, and her imagination. As the family gathered around the truck, admiring it, Sheila gasped, asking Hank – *"Oh my God Hank, is this your truck?"* He assured her it was his. Hank, of course, had leased the truck from the Mr. Softee Ice Cream franchise. Shelly began imagining all the ice cream her Dad was going to give her and her sisters. Things didn't quite work out the way she imagined they would.

Hank taught Marcy and Shelly how to operate the ice cream maker in the back of the truck, and to wait on customers. It was hard work, and very hot in the back of the truck. The girls took turns working in the truck, putting in eleven-hour days, five or six days a week when school was out, while Hank sat up front, just driving the truck. Shelly quickly learned how to make change in her head, which turned out to be a good math lesson. The girls also quickly learned some of their neighbors (adults and children,) were not quite as friendly and civil as they appeared to be in school or in church. Many of them were very hard to please, to put it mildly.

Hank sat up front, letting the girls deal with everything in the back, including the complaints and the insults. But it wasn't all negative, for either Hank or the girls. Hank would stop at Shelly's favorite hamburger spot, and buy her a hamburger and fries for lunch. And whenever there was a lull in business, the girls were allowed to eat all the ice cream they wanted. At the end of the day, Hank paid whichever girl had worked that day two dollars.

The free ice cream, the hamburger and fries, and two dollars a day made the hard work, the complaints and insults, and the tiredness in her body worth it to Shelly. But she was extremely happy when the day was over.

Working on the ice cream truck taught the girls some valuable lessons. But it also showed them a little more of the darker side of their Dad. It also provided Marcy with an opportunity to steal money. Hank demanded that the girls give him all the dollar bills, letting the girls keep the change. Whenever Marcy worked the back of the truck, she always kept an extra dollar for herself, giving Hank the rest. Hank never caught on to her thievery, or if he did, he never said anything. Marcy went home each working day with three dollars, a tummy full of ice cream, and whatever change she had received.

Marcy was far more observant than Shelly when it came to what was going on around her. In the same way Hank never caught on to Marcy's stealing from him, Shelly never caught on to her Dad's ulterior motives for leasing the ice cream truck. On many occasions, Hank would tell Shelly or Marcy to stay with the truck and eat all the ice cream she wanted while he went into a certain house to, supposedly, "*take orders*" from the lady of the house for ice cream. But Marcy knew it didn't take more than an hour to take an order. She knew exactly what he was doing. Marcy never said anything to her Dad about his affairs with other women. She used his sins as a means of justifying her own. Slowly, she began to steal a little more, and a little more from him. Marcy sincerely grieved for her Mom because of the things her Dad did with other women, but her Mom never seemed to complain about it as long as she had her cigarettes, and he wasn't bothering her.

Shelly didn't look into a mirror as often as she used to, but whenever she did, she didn't like what she saw. She told herself she was ugly, worthless, insignificant, and just plain bad. She had come to the conclusion that men only molested ugly bad girls, never the pretty ones, like Marcy and her cousins. Shelly, of course, was wrong – men did molest other girls, both the ugly and the beautiful. But in Shelly's mind, it seemed there was something about her, something she couldn't quite define or understand, something that caused perverted men and boys to gravitate toward her more than other girls. As far as she was concerned, it had to be her appearance and her character. Why else, she asked herself, did so many dirty men want to do those dirty things to her? She was only slightly overweight for her age, but she thought of herself as fat, compared to her little slim sister Beth. She also compared her face to Beth's face, telling herself the reason men and boys never molested Beth was because she (Beth), was prettier than her. She lived each day in some degree of fear that the next man or boy she met would, sooner or later, try to molest her. She often wondered – *"Is there any man out there, somewhere, who will ever like me for who I am, and love me, and want to marry me?"* Her answer to her own question was always the same – No. At that age, and having been through what she had endured, she had no way of knowing what God had planned for her destiny.

When summer ended, and school started back, Shelly and Marcy only worked on the ice cream truck on weekends. Some afternoons, after school, Shelly babysat for her other aunt, Elizabeth, who lived a few houses down the street. This was only occasional, because Shelly's cousin Phillip, Elizabeth's oldest boy, who was about the same age as Shelly, did the babysitting most of the time. But Phillip had been offered a job mowing grass for a neighbor – a paying job, at which he could earn some extra money.

Of all her cousins, Phillip was Shelly's favorite. He loved Shelly, and was very protective of her. She felt safe around him, and as she was about to discover, he was one male in whom her trust had not been misplaced.

Another of Shelly's cousins, Nick, fifteen, whose visits to her home were very few and mostly very short, happened to be there the day Phillip was to go mow grass for the neighbor. Shelly couldn't help but notice how he lingered much longer than he ever had before. She was about to discover why.   As soon as the door closed behind Phillip, Nick grabbed hold of Shelly. He began pushing her up the stairs, putting his hands under her top, feeling her chest. As Shelly tried to fight him off, he stopped fondling her, smiling and laughing, telling her he was only playing a game with her. She knew better. She knew what was going to happen if he got her to the top of the stairs, into the bedroom.

She fought him with all her strength, but was no match for him. He continued pushing her up the stair steps, feeling her body as he pushed her. Her resistance was more than he wanted to deal with. He shoved her down on the stairs, determined to rape her right there. As he was about to pull her jeans down, the front door swung open. Phillip had forgotten something, and had come back for it. Shelly screamed. Phillip immediately saw what was happening. Without a moment's hesitation, he leaped up the stairs toward Nick. Nick outweighed him by thirty pounds, and had twice his strength, but what Phillip lacked in size and strength, he made up for in courage and determination. It was David against Goliath. Nick's surprise, coupled with his guilty conscience, temporarily rendered him vulnerable. Phillip took full advantage of that vulnerability.   He grabbed hold of Nick's pant legs, pulled his feet out from under him, and dragged him down the stairs, kicking and yelling. Phillip's grip held firm.

He dragged Nick out the open door, down the steps, into the yard. Somewhere in Nick's cowardly heart, he knew in that moment, Phillip was running on pure adrenaline and courage. And even with his own superior physical strength, he was no match for Phillip's superior courage. The rage in Phillip's eyes said all that needed to be said. Phillip gave him the choice of a fight, or walking away. Nick made the wisest choice of his life – he walked away. Shelly was shaken up, to say the least, but the sheer excitement of seeing Phillip drag Nick down the stairs and into the yard far surpassed her trauma of what Nick had tried to do to her. Suddenly, Phillip was her Rifleman, the man who had rushed to her rescue – her hero!

Phillip had to hurry to get to his grass cutting job, but he took the time to hug Shelly, asking her if she was alright. It was the first time Shelly could recall a boy touching her without putting his hands all over her body. It felt comforting, it felt safe, it felt right. It suddenly dawned upon Shelly – maybe not all boys are dirty after all. But the shame and indignity of what Nick had tried to do to her still lingered. Her sense of her own ugliness and dirtiness came rushing in again. She wept as Phillip left, thinking, "*I'm nothing but trash.*"

Nick happened to be the favorite grandson of the family – admired, respected, and trusted by everyone. Shelly assumed it would be useless for her to tell anyone what he had tried to do to her. She decided to put the matter behind her as best she could. It was just one more unhappy scene that would be added to her nightmares. She was so thankful Phillip had showed up at just the right moment, saving her from another attempted rape. That, in itself, was enough to help her somehow move on, and live, not knowing when or where, or by whom she would be abused again.

She avoided Nick as much as possible from that day on. But avoiding him wasn't as easy as she wished. She and her family often gathered at Grandma Eloise's house for dinners, birthdays or other family functions. Nick was always there, shooting dirty glances toward her, raising his eyebrows, winking at her when no one was looking. Each time he smiled at her, the sordid scene came flooding back to her mind. She could feel his dirty hands groping her legs and chest. She could see that insatiable lust in his eyes. She could sense his perverted certainty that he was going to get what he wanted.   Nick got on with his twisted double life as if nothing had happened, charming everyone with his smile and winsome ways, waiting for his next opportunity – his next conquest.

Once again, Hank decided it was time for a career change. He managed to land a job at the local prison as a prison guard. And once again, for the Smith family, it was time to move into another house. This time they were moving into a bigger house with a winding staircase. It was an old house with a basement. Shelly was afraid to look down into it, let alone go down the steps into it. Shelly and Beth had always shared an upstairs bedroom; Marcy's bedroom was always downstairs. This same arrangement worked out in this house. But the house was much larger than their last one – too large for Sheila to keep it clean. Sheila had not suddenly become obsessed with cleaning, but she at least wanted the girls and the neighbors to believe she was not a total slob. With the girls going to school, and working on most weekends, there weren't enough hands to keep the big house cleaned up. With Hank's new steady income, plus benefits, there was actually a little more money that somehow found its way into Sheila's purse; enough for her to hire Sandy, a friend of hers, to come and clean, dust, cook, and do laundry. Sandy was a single Mom, never married. She was a large woman, very likeable, and easy to talk to. The girls loved her. She became like one of the family. Sometimes she would stay over after cleaning the house, and sleep downstairs with Marcy. Whenever everyone else was asleep, Sheila would often stay up, watching a preacher she liked on TV. Marcy later told her sisters how Hank would sometimes come home late at night, sneaking into her bedroom, waking Sandy, and the two of them would sneak upstairs together. Marcy pretended to be fast asleep when it happened, but she knew what was going on. She tried desperately to keep her Dad's secret rendezvous with Sandy to herself, not wanting to put any more trouble on her Mom than what she already had. But it kept gnawing at her insides. The more she thought about it, the madder she became.   When she could bear it no longer, she went to her Mom, telling her of the many times Hank and Sandy had slipped upstairs. Sheila went into a rage. She and Marcy confronted Hank together. When Sheila asked him for the truth, he cursed, backhanding Marcy across her mouth, calling her a liar, among other things.

Marcy was now fourteen. But to look at her, you would never believe it. To say Marcy was beautiful would be a major understatement.   Her birth certificate said she was fourteen – her body screamed eighteen. To put it mildly, she was quite well- endowed, and well- proportioned in every area, front and back.   She had it all, and in all the right places. She stood about five feet-seven inches tall, with long, flowing, light brown hair, which came down to her waist,   contrasting beautifully with her hazel eyes. All the girls were jealous of her, and all the boys wanted her. When she was around, most of the other girls soon left the area. They didn't stand a chance with the boys with Marcy Smith present.   The boys noticed her, and she noticed the boys noticing her. It might be unfair to say Marcy flaunted her God-given endowments, but she didn't try to hide them either. Marcy took care of herself. She always wore nice clothes, all of which accentuated her curves. She always smelled nice.

When she was out of sight of her parents, she smelled sensuous, erotic, captivating.

She still kept a close eye on Shelly and Beth. She made sure they had something to eat, and something to wear. Her methods of acquiring these things were less than noble, but she didn't care. What mattered was that her sisters weren't hungry or cold. To her, the stealing was a justifiable means to a desired end.

One particular day Marcy took Shelly to the Woolworth store. It was a pretty long walk. Arriving at the store, Shelly was tired, but once they were inside, the sight of all the pretty clothes, jewelry, and other "*stuff*" made her forget all about her tiredness for a while. She was daydreaming as they walked. She sure wished she could have some of those pretty clothes to wear to school. The fact that Marcy always carried big purses never sparked any degree of suspicion or curiosity from Shelly. She simply assumed Marcy liked big purses. Neither Shelly nor anyone else inside the store saw Marcy stealthily dropping things into her oversized purse. After Marcy was satisfied she had taken enough for one day, she handed Shelly her purse, asking her to carry it out the door for her. Marcy quickly ushered Shelly out the door. Now Marcy had two purses, the one Shelly was carrying, and another one on her own arm. Shelly's innocent, unassuming mind still didn't catch on. Marcy hurried her along till she reckoned they were a safe distance from the store.

Marcy told Shelly they both needed to stop and rest a while. Shelly quickly agreed. Then Marcy told Shelly to open the purse. Shelly's eyes lit up with joy as she beheld the beautiful new outfit. Holding it up to herself, she beamed, thanking Marcy for it. It would be perfect for her to wear to school. Then Marcy opened her purse, showing Shelly the contents. Inside were all kinds of clothes, trinkets, and other items. Then it dawned upon Shelley - Marcy had stolen all this stuff from the store. Her beaming smile instantly dropped into a disappointed frown. She started to say something to Marcy, but Marcy stopped her, reminding her how badly she needed those clothes. *"It's OK Shelly,* she smiled, *you have a new outfit, I have some new clothes, and we didn't get caught."* The joy of having a new outfit didn't feel very joyful now to Shelly. In her heart she knew it was all wrong. But Marcy was her big sister, her mentor, her friend and confidante – the one who had always protected and provided for her. She dared not go against Marcy, and try to take the outfit back to the store. A thousand foreboding fears flashed through her conscience. She knew the kids at school would question where she got the outfit, because she seldom wore anything this lovely and new. She would have to lie, and tell them her Mom bought it for her.

Shelly's Dad was enjoying his new job immensely. As a prison guard he got acquainted with the good, the bad, and the ugly. Every day was a new adventure. He witnessed the darkness and debauchery of men who had committed unspeakable crimes, some of whom would soon be executed. There was something deeply saddening about walking another human being that *"last mile"* toward his certain destiny, knowing he would soon take his last breath. The three words that haunted Hank more than any others were – *"Dead man walking."* He witnessed the inhuman brutality some men inflicted upon each other. He also witnessed the inhuman cruelty many of the prison personnel seemed to enjoy inflicting upon some of the inmates. Many nights Hank came home with his uniform soaked in blood – blood that had come from the faces, hands, backs and buttocks of inmates who had been beaten and cut by the guards. Sometimes at home Hank would sit at the supper table, telling his wife and children how he had pulled a prison guard off one of the inmates' bleeding body, staining his own uniform with the victim's blood. Hank Smith had his faults, but he still had a heart that had not yet turned to stone.

There was an unwritten code of authority among the guards. Without any written, formal standard by which to judge the seriousness of an inmate's infractions of their self-made codes, many men found themselves being beaten, and thrown into "*the hole*" at the sole discretion of whichever guard or guards happened to be on duty at the time. Seeing this unwarranted treatment of men, some of whom were barely eighteen, and others who were sick and old, turned Hank's stomach. Whenever he got the chance, and was sure no one was looking, he would make a special trip down to the hole, lighting a cigarette, kicking it into the hole for the badly beaten prisoner. His pack of cigarettes seldom lasted more than a week – two weeks at the most.

The prison had its strengths and its weaknesses. Some of the personnel did things by the book, while others played by "*barnyard rules*". There existed a hierarchy within both the prison staff, and among the prisoners themselves. The prisoners called it the "*pecking order.*" There was also corruption and politics, terms which most inmates considered synonymous. Some of the underlings among the guards could be bribed with five dollars or less. The higher ranking officers demanded more for their goods and services. Among the inmates there was the physical backstabbing; among the staff and hierarchy, the social and political backstabbing.

As is customary in prisons, news of a prison guard with any degree of compassion for the inmates soon spread among them. Hank Smith's name quickly began to be whispered throughout the prison. He was a man from whom they could expect decency and respect. To say they loved Hank might be a bit of an exaggeration. There were a few inmates who genuinely liked Hank, then there were others who gave a stellar performance in pretending they liked him. He was a man they could use to their own advantage under certain circumstances. To put it another way – Hank's good-heartedness could prove to be either a blessing, or a curse, for both himself and the inmates. But Hank was not naïve. He treated the men like he would want to be treated under the same circumstances, but he also watched his back, keeping a watchful eye on the inmates, and the other guards.

Each guard was given a book with ruled sheets of paper. It was used to "*write up*" whoever had broken a rule. Each write up carried a penalty, depending on the severity of the misbehavior. In his career as a prison guard, which lasted only three years, Hank never wrote up a single inmate. It soon became clear to the hierarchy that Hank Smith was not "*one of them.*" He lacked that "*killer instinct*" which, in their thinking, was a required qualification for the job. In their private meetings, many of which were held in hotel rooms with hired "*consorts*", they plotted how they could best get rid of Hank without arousing too much suspicion.

Hank had to carry his write up book with him at all times, in a pocket of his uniform shirt. In order to make it appear to the other guards that he had written up at least a few inmates, he tore some of the pages out. He took those pages home, and laid them on the mantel over the fireplace. He told Sheila she could use them to write up the girls when they broke the rules. He and Sheila agreed that for each write up there would be a whipping from Dad when he got home. Sheila took full advantage of the suggestion. Marcy was the first to get written up, but she didn't care. Each time she got written up she talked Sheila into tearing it up before Hank got home, reminding her that she was Dad's favorite, and he probably wouldn't whip her anyway. Beth received several write ups, but they were also torn up, because she was Sheila's favorite, and Sheila couldn't bear seeing her beaten by Hank because of some insignificant infraction of his rules. Shelly got written up every week for one thing or another. She got a whipping for each write up. She lived in fear, knowing she was going to get a whipping when Hank arrived. The whole scenario was a paradox. Hank couldn't bear seeing grown men being beaten mercilessly for doing things wrong, but he could beat his own children for a minor offense. To add to her woes, Shelly was becoming more outspoken. Each time Mom wrote her up, she insisted it wasn't fair for her to be punished all the time while the other girls had broken the rules, and had not been punished. When Hank got home, Shelly got two whippings – one for breaking the rules, and another for talking back to her Mom.

In addition to his harsh punishment of his little girls, Hank added to the trauma by telling them stories about the brutality that went on in the prison. And he did not spare any of the sordid, gory details. The girls sat in horror as he described how he had seen the blood gushing from the severed arteries of inmates who had been stabbed or had their throats slit with the homemade knives they had fashioned in the prison machine shop. Living as close to the prison as they did, Shelly lived in terror, thinking one of the prisoners might escape, and come and kill her and her family. Each time a car sped by, she ran back into the yard, praying God would protect her from those evil men. Her fear bordered on full blown paranoia. She was fleeing from shadows. The fear became so deep the only way she could express herself was through her tears. For many hours she would sit alone and cry, hoping the tears would somehow alleviate the fear. It didn't work. She had to tell someone. One day while Sheila was taking a nap, Shelly crawled in bed beside her. She lay there till Sheila woke up. Shelly immediately began to tell her Mom about how scared she was, crying – *"Mommy, I need help."* Just telling her Mom seemed to give her some degree of relief. Sheila pulled her close, hugging her, whispering – *"It's gonna be ok honey, Mommy ain't gonna let nobody hurt you."*

It was 4:30 p.m., and Marcy hadn't come home from school. Hank and Sheila were just a bit concerned.   When she arrived, it was in the back seat of a police cruiser. When the officers led her into the house, her smeared makeup made it obvious to everyone she had been crying. Shelly's heart leaped into her throat. She knew Marcy was in big trouble; she only needed one guess as to why. The scene from their day of *shopping* at Woolworth's immediately leaped into her brain.   And here she was, standing in front of her family, under arrest for shoplifting. In her mind, Shelly heard Marcy's last words to her that day – *"we didn't get caught."* Marcy's luck had run out. When the police officer told Hank they had arrested Marcy for shoplifting, Marcy looked straight into her Dad's eyes, waiting for his reaction. To her utter surprise, Hank seemed calm and collected. He shook the hands of the officers, assuring them he was grateful they had brought her home instead of locking her up.

But Marcy knew her Dad. Underneath his cool exterior, a raging volcano was waiting to erupt, and the molten lava of his anger was about to be poured out upon her, the moment the officers left. She pleaded with the officers to take her back to the station with them. The officers glanced at one another; then toward Hank; from Hank to Sheila; from Sheila to the other two girls, then back to Marcy. Somewhere in their experience and training, they had seen other situations quite similar to this one – a child so afraid of the parent they were willing to be detained in a police lock up rather than face the punishment they knew was coming. Hank suspected the officers, like Marcy, could see past his calm exterior. He could hardly wait for them to leave, and they knew it. Knowing there was nothing else they could do for Marcy, they gave her a somewhat pitiful nod, and exited the house. Just outside the door, they hesitated momentarily, as if questioning their own judgment – *"Should they leave this young girl here?"* But knowing the limits of their authority, they shook their heads, saying nothing, walking slowly toward their cruiser.

Peeking out the door, Hank made sure the cruiser had gone out of sight. Closing the door behind him, he grabbed Marcy by her shoulders, spun her around, and began pushing her up the winding staircase, cursing, beating her with his fists with each step. Sheila ran to the kitchen, leaving Shelly and Beth to either run, or stand there and witness the beating of their sister. Beth followed Sheila. Shelly ran out the back door to the back of the garage where she couldn't be seen. All she could do was stand there and weep, knowing what was happening to Marcy. Her heart was breaking, not only in sympathy for Marcy, but also for the fact that she knew Marcy had done what she did in order to provide clothing, shoes and food for her, Beth and their Mom.

Shelly never knew how long her Dad's beatings would last. She sat down behind the garage with her head on her knees, praying this one wouldn't last too long for Marcy. Almost forty-five minutes passed when she finally heard her Mom yell for her to come back into the house.   During the beating, Marcy refused to whimper or cry. She took his beating as if she wasn't feeling the pain at all. She was feeling it more with every blow. Hank was determined he was going to make her scream for mercy. With each powerful blow, she fell backward, getting back up, looking him in the face, not offering to defend herself, and too defiant to acknowledge the pain. She was not going to give him the gratification he craved from beating her. When Hank finally saw he couldn't beat her into submission, he grabbed her by her shoulders again, literally throwing her down the winding staircase.

At the bottom of the stairs, he stepped across her limp body, glaring down at her. As Hank stomped into the kitchen for a bottle of beer, Sheila and Beth helped Marcy to her bedroom. Shelly entered the house hesitantly, glancing all around to see where her Dad was. She didn't dare say a word to him. She ran to Marcy's bedroom. Sheila and Beth had gone into the living room, leaving Marcy alone. Marcy's face and eyes were swollen; she was black and blue all over her body; she was sobbing. The pain was nearly unbearable. Again the hatred she had felt for her Dad before rose inside Shelly's heart. She could almost wish he was dead.

After a few beers, Hank came into Marcy's bedroom, holding out a dollar to her. Marcy didn't want the dollar, and even if she had, she was in too much pain to reach for it. Now she couldn't hold back the tears.   Her hatred of him flared into an uncontrollable rage. She was so choked up with hatred she couldn't speak, but under her breath, in her heart, she was cursing him. Hank could see the hatred in her eyes. Glancing at Shelly, he saw the same bitter hatred. She wished she was big enough to hurt him like he had hurt Marcy. But Hank wasn't satisfied with his humiliation of Marcy yet. Shoving the dollar toward her hand, he began – *"You see this dollar Marcy? If you had only asked me, I would have given you money for clothes and whatever else you wanted. You didn't have to go stealing stuff. Now promise Daddy you will come and ask him if you ever need money again, and promise you won't ever steal again."* Marcy knew her Dad was lying, and so did Shelly. But in order to get him out of her presence, Marcy nodded in agreement. He may have broken her body, but he had not broken her spirit. The next day she limped into another store, stealing more clothing, dropping it into her big purse. Limping into another store, she stole some food items, adding them to the purse. She placed a few small items on the counter, paying for them, congratulating herself that she had again gotten away without being caught. If her Dad was not going to provide for his family, she would, the only way she knew how.

After sufficiently recovering from the worst beating of her life, and all the bruises had finally disappeared, Marcy began taking Shelly and Beth to the local skating rink the girls loved so well. For the girls it was pure fun – a time to be free, and away from the cursing, the drinking and the violence. For Marcy, it was a time to give her sisters that fun and freedom, and to engage in her own brand of fun and freedom. She relished the attention all the boys gave her. In the back of her mind, she often thought – "*I know what these boys want from me is not sacred, but at least they don't want to beat me.*" Marcy's figure, her face and personality didn't just turn heads, they turned bodies, the young, the old, and everything in between. She caused more than a few mishaps. One elderly gentleman, strolling with his wife, turned to stare at Marcy, walking straight into a telephone pole. He received two lumps on his head - one from the telephone pole, and one from his wife's parasol.

Marcy's body made her appear to be a few years older than she was, but she was still a child – a child with a history checkered with experiences no child her age should have to endure. She was forced to grow up too quickly. She was fourteen. She looked like an adult, she talked like an adult, and she wanted everyone else to think of her as an adult. She wanted to make adult decisions and choices, neither of which she was yet equipped to make. Mostly she wanted to be loved. The only real love she had ever known was that of her little sisters.

Until now, that had been enough to sustain her. But she wanted more. She wanted the love and affection of a good man. She told herself she was ready for that kind of love. In truth, she knew nothing about the sacred relationship that exists between two people in love.

But her adventurous spirit longed to be free – free to do as she pleased, and free from the trauma, abuse and violence she had known for far too long at home. She didn't stop to consider her choices might actually take her away from the two persons she loved the most. She never entertained the possibility of being separated from her little sisters for any length of time. And yet the decisions she was about to make would do just that. For Shelly especially, life had been horrible in the extreme. But Marcy knew in her heart it would have been far worse if she had not been there to provide whatever protection and sustenance she was able to give.   She pondered all these things while glancing around the room, soaking in all the attention she was getting from the boys.

While Shelly and Beth were having fun skating Marcy hung out in the room with the jukebox and older kids.   It was there she caught the eye of a nineteen year old Kentucky boy, Buck Jones. The two of them exchanged glances. They each liked what they saw. Marcy had inclinations, Buck had intentions. She would be a prize for him to win. He was infatuated; Marcy told herself she was about to fall in love. Buck played nonchalant, as if he could take her or leave her. He wanted her to be the one to take the initiative. They gave each other just enough body language to let the other know they were interested in each other. All the other girls, many of whom were also interested in Buck, began to slowly drift away, giving Marcy plenty of room to flaunt her features. With each passing moment, Buck's *"interest"* grew stronger. Marcy knew she had piqued his interest. She slowly walked away, pretending to flirt with a few other younger boys. Buck knew the tactic well – playing hard to get, or, as Marcy intended, *not-so-easy-to-get.*

This cat-n-mouse routine continued for about two weekends. But the magnetism between them was too strong for either of them to resist. One night they simply drew near to each other, exchanged a few words of nervous chit chat, then walked hand in hand out to the parking lot of the skating rink. In Buck's car less than a minute, they were kissing passionately. With all the inner strength he could muster, Buck restrained himself from touching her inappropriately. It was no easy task.   It wasn't long until Marcy began sneaking away from home to be with him. She took advantage of every opportunity to spend as much time with him as she could. Sometimes she created those opportunities herself.

One night after the skating rink closed, Buck asked Marcy if he could drive her home. She agreed, but asked Shelly to lie for her and tell Mom she would be coming home with some friends later. Shelly and Beth were to ride with some other friends, so Buck and Marcy could be alone. Shelly never thought she could say no to Marcy, but there was something about Buck she didn't like – she didn't trust him. At her tender age of twelve, she sensed something sinister in him. She was afraid of him, and afraid for Marcy. But how could she betray her most beloved sister's trust after all Marcy had done for her? She carefully weighed her options. Her fear for Marcy's safety and well-being outweighed her sense of loyalty. Something inside her said she should tell her Mom about Buck and Marcy.

To Shelly's great surprise, her Mom didn't react as violently as she thought she would when she told her about Marcy and Buck. When Marcy arrived, Sheila gave her a good scolding, waving her finger in Marcy's face, telling her never to see the boy again. To Marcy, her Mom's words were the equivalent of pouring water on a duck's back – they rolled right off, having no effect whatsoever. Somehow she knew neither Shelly, Beth, nor her Mom would tell Hank, after seeing the brutal beating he had given her before. In this assumption she was right – Sheila didn't dare tell Hank .That night, when she guessed everyone was asleep, she slipped quietly out her bedroom window, meeting Buck out behind their detached garage. At this point in their relationship, Buck had now lost all inhibitions about Marcy's body, and Marcy was willing.

One of Marcy's many chores around the house was taking out the trash. Sheila began to notice lately it had been taking Marcy a lot longer to come back into the house after taking out the trash. In a few weeks she was going to discover why. Sheila's instincts may not have been as sharp as that of some other Moms, but she wasn't stupid. Somewhere in her soul she knew what Marcy was doing, but she chose to ignore it. She was afraid of having her suspicions confirmed, and right now she really didn't want them confirmed.

Shelly wasn't sure how Marcy would react toward her for "*ratting*" on her. She began to wonder if Marcy would ever forgive her. Marcy never said a word to Shelly about it. She passed it over as if it had never happened. She still treated Shelly like she had always treated her – like a little sister she adored. Marcy couldn't bring herself to scold Shelly, or say a harsh word to her. The bond that held them together was much stronger than Shelly suspected. But with Buck in the picture now, Shelly knew she was no longer Marcy's number one. But her love and admiration for Marcy made her willing to accept being number two. Her young heart couldn't help but take notice how when she and Marcy were together, which wasn't as often as it used to be, the subject of their conversations had now shifted from *"sister talk"* to *"boy talk"*. And the boy, of course, was Buck Jones.

The Smith girls all attended the same school. Marcy, of course, was one grade above Shelly, and Shelly one grade above Beth. Shelly had never dreamed of cutting class, something Marcy did every chance she got, and even more so now that she had met Buck. But she wanted to demonstrate to Shelly that she had no grudges against her for having *"ratted"* on her to Mom. She coerced Shelly into cutting class so that she and Shelly could go have some quality *"girl time"*. Shelly was very reluctant to do it, but Marcy persisted, assuring Shelly she would not get her into any trouble. Together they ran and skipped across the open field toward the church. Behind the church ran a little creek, where all the baptizing was done. It was a bright, sunny summer day. It felt good to be away from school for a while, and being with her big sister made it a little more special. Shelly sat on the creek bank, a little surprised when Marcy flipped off her shoes and waded into the creek. Her surprise was heightened when Marcy began searching underneath the water with her hands. Suddenly Marcy came up with two bottles of ice cold Pepsi she had hidden in the creek. There was a bottle opener tied to the neck of one of the bottles. Marcy opened both bottles, handing one to Shelly. It tasted delicious! Shelly smiled, asking herself – *"Is there anything my big sister can't do?"* Shelly didn't know the Pepsi's were bought with money Marcy had stolen from Dad. But it wouldn't have mattered if she had known. The day was gorgeous, she was not in school, she was drinking ice cold Pepsi, and she was with her favorite person in the world. Then Buck drove up to the edge of the creek. With little more than a quick wave of her hand, Marcy was gone, getting into Buck's car. Shelly's heart broke as they drove away. She finished her Pepsi, threw the empty bottle onto the ground, and ran hurriedly back across the field to school.

Shelia's suspicions about Marcy and Buck were not really suspicions at all. Deep inside she knew what they were doing. She simply trained her mind not to dwell upon the images that flashed through it. Her own physical and mental condition was deteriorating with each passing year. The girls were growing up too fast. Sheila realized she had never been the kind of mother she could have been. And whatever kind or degree of motherly authority she may have had over the girls at one time had now disappeared. The two younger girls mostly obeyed her, but their obedience was not based upon that mutual filial love which, in most families, flows naturally between parent and child. More than anything else, their obedience to her rose out of their pity for her.   They didn't obey her because they wanted to; they obeyed her because they didn't want to hurt her feelings by disobeying. Sheila didn't love herself, she was nearly certain her husband didn't love her, and she wondered if anyone did. She wondered if it was too late to find any kind of love in her life. But with what little shred of feminine and maternal dignity she had left, she would strive to at least appear to be a loving mother.

The detached garage out back of the house was never used for its intended purpose, and there was more than one reason for its not being used. Unlike with most other garages, the big garage door faced away from the house, not toward it. Looking out the back door of the house, the back of the garage was all that could be seen. Exiting the garage, the narrow lane was no more than an alleyway, which led to a side street. In order to park his vehicle in the garage, Hank, or anyone else, would have had to take the long way around, and drive up the long alley to the garage. He would also have had to back out of the garage, down the alley, and into the street, not being able to see if another car was coming from either direction. The garage didn't even have a concrete floor – it was dirt. It had one side door. Add to all this the fact that the owner of the house had installed a steel bar and huge padlock onto the garage door, which made it impossible to raise from the inside, making the side door the only entrance and exit, Hank decided parking in the garage wasn't worth the effort. Neither Hank nor Sheila nor any of the younger girls ever went into the garage for any reason. Marcy was the exception.

Call it what you will – maternal instinct, mother's concern, or an act of God, but Sheila decided one evening she had to go out to the garage. Even she didn't know why - she just knew she had to go out there and take a look inside. Marcy was taking absolutely too much time in taking out the trash. Something was going on either inside or behind that garage, and Sheila was going to find out what it was. And when she did, she almost wished she hadn't.   Gently turning the door knob, she swung the side door open slowly, afraid of what she might find. She anticipated snakes, spiders, and/or skunks.

There were two male skunks – both of whom were the two-legged variety, one named Buck Jones, the other Robert Payne. There were also two girls – Marcy and Nicky. Nicky was one of Marcy's friends, Robert was a friend of Buck. Nicky and Robert, of course, were a couple – an un-married couple. The garage had almost all the comforts of a home, a table with chairs, a mirror, a dresser, a big sofa, and a big bed. Sheila's jaw dropped in utter shock.   She demanded an explanation from Marcy. It turned out Marcy had been renting the garage to Robert and Nicky for months, right under the noses of her parents, and they had no idea. This, of course, served a dual purpose for Marcy. The rent money she received from Nicky and Robert gave her and Buck gas money and spending money. It also provided a convenient place for Buck to sneak in and see Marcy. For months he had been pulling into the alley leading to the garage, turning off the engine, and sneaking up the alley to the garage.

The rest is left to the imagination.

Shelia went crazy, ordering everyone except Marcy out of the garage immediately. Buck pretended he was going to stay and defend Marcy, but when Sheila put her hand in his chest, pushing him backward, he knew she meant business. For once in his life, he feared the wrath of a woman – a woman who, at least momentarily, had discovered she was a mother after all. When Hank got home Sheila told him what was going on. Hank grabbed Marcy, doing what he did best, backhanding her across the mouth, cursing her, warning her never to see Buck again. The next night Marcy packed her bags, sneaked out the window, and ran away with Buck to Kentucky.

The despondency into which Shelly sank could not be easily defined. About all she could do was cry. Several factors contributed to her despondency. In her young life, she had never been far away from Marcy. Marcy was the best friend she had ever known, and now Marcy was gone. She just didn't think she could make it in this cruel world without Marcy there to protect and defend her. But she also worried about Marcy. Suddenly she didn't know where Marcy lived, how Marcy was living, or if she was living at all. Her intuitions about Buck Jones were dark, to say the least. Somehow she knew Buck was going to hurt Marcy, in more ways than one. And to make matters even worse, she now had to listen to Hank and Sheila talking about what they were going to do to Marcy if and when they found her. Her little heart learned all too soon what it meant to really miss someone. Hank and Sheila didn't miss Marcy in the same way Shelly did, but they did fear for her safety. In spite of the dysfunctional relationship and unhappy atmosphere that prevailed in the Smith household, she was still their daughter, and they still felt some kind of responsibility for her. Hank vowed he would find her, and bring her back home, no matter what the cost.

Hank Smith may not have been the best of fathers, and he had admitted that fact to himself. But this was a situation in which he had never dreamed he would find himself. He could understand a little immature girl like Shelly running away from home, but it had never occurred to him that one of his older children could hate him so much as to run away from home. But even now, he told himself, it was probably not so much her hatred of him that drove her away, it was more likely her infatuation with Buck.   With that thought still reverberating in his conscience, he hesitated, as the cold hard truth came flooding in like a tidal wave – his daughters hated him. In that moment, an even harder truth gripped his soul like a vice – *"why did his children hate him so much?"* The answer cut his heart like a surgeon's scalpel – they hated him because he had never shown them he loved them. The most cutting question he had ever had to answer now refused to let him go without a response – he tried desperately to evade it by running away like he had done so many times before, but his feet would not move. There was nowhere for him to run. For the first time in his life, Hank Smith shed tears of remorse. He asked himself the question – *"Do I love my children?"* Again the harsh truth stung him. The mere fact that he had to ask himself that question was, in itself, the answer. Somewhere in the scarred cockles of his heart, he did love his children, but now he realized he had failed miserably in demonstrating it. Yes, he loved them, but he had always put his own needs, desires and habits before the needs of his family. Now, in the same way Sheila had suddenly found the inner compulsion to act like a mother, Hank found the motivation to act like a father. He would find his daughter, and he would bring her home, and in spite of all he had done to her, he would find a way to show her he loved her.

Everyone in the Smith family knew Shelly, Beth and Marcy had been virtually inseparable all their lives. Hank used that sisterly bond to his advantage. He began to question Shelly - *"Had Marcy ever divulged to her any kind of information that might give him some clue as to where to begin searching for her?"* Shelly didn't have to hesitate with an answer. She suddenly remembered Marcy telling her she was thinking about running away with Buck to Louisville Kentucky. Until now, Shelly had tried to shut it out of her mind, not wanting to believe Marcy would actually do it. With that scrap of information, Hank began pondering how to get to Kentucky. He didn't have the money, and he didn't have a car that was fit to drive that far.

But unseen forces were at work in Hank's favor. Late one evening he got a call from a County Sheriff in Kentucky. One of his deputies had arrested a certain Buck Jones for driving on a suspended license. He also had a Marcy Smith detained in a juvenile detention center.   Hank choked up, he couldn't speak. The sheriff could hear him sobbing on the phone. With the phone to his ear, and one had covering the mouthpiece, Hank turned to Sheila, still sobbing, managing to tell her – *"Honey, they found Marcy."*   This was a side of Hank Sheila had never seen. Her own heart leaped into her throat. Hank regained his composure enough to talk to the sheriff. What he was about to hear would quickly crush his momentary joy. The sheriff added – *"Mr. Smith, when we brought your daughter in, she was very sick, vomiting and pale. I had her transported to the local hospital. Mr. Smith, your daughter is pregnant."*

Hank turned pale. In a weaker voice than Sheila had ever heard from her husband, Hank told the sheriff he would be down to get Marcy as soon as possible. He hung up the phone, turning to Sheila, taking her in his arms, praying that what he was about to tell her wouldn't send her over the edge. The crushed expression on his face told Sheila everything. Before Hank could say a word, she put her finger to his lips, telling him what he was going to tell her. She put it in the form of a question, knowing the answer before she asked it – *"Marcy's pregnant, isn't she?"* Hank nodded, turned around, pulled a little note from his wallet and dialed the number of an inmate he had befriended in the prison. It was the man who had been severely beaten by one of the guards, until Hank had pulled the guard off him. On the back of the note were six words – *"If you ever need me, call."*

The next day Shelly noticed Hank pacing nervously back and forth across the living room. Instinct told her Dad was waiting for someone to arrive. Soon there was a knock at the door. There stood a huge man, dressed in a really nice suit, carrying a briefcase. To Shelly, his suit looked dazzling, but his face was scary. Before he stepped inside the house, Shelly glanced up the street. There were four strange cars she had never seen before parked beside the curb. Behind the steering wheel of the first car sat one man, well-dressed, wearing a hat. In each of the other three cars sat two well-dressed men, all wearing hats. As Mr. McPherrin and Hank began to talk, Shelly knew Hank wanted her out of the room. She stepped into the kitchen, standing just inside and to one side behind the wall, listening to their conversation. She was shocked, hearing Mr. McPherrin saying to Hank –*"Let me and my boys take care of this Hank. I promise you when we get through with this Buck guy, not even his Mama will recognize him."* Hank countered with – *"No Mason, I appreciate the offer, but what I need is some help in getting her back home - I'll deal with Buck myself, my own way."* Mason opened the briefcase, handing Hank a stack of cashier's checks. Hank stuffed them into his back pocket. He and Mason walked out to the first car. The man behind the wheel stepped out of the shiny new car, handing Hank the keys.   Without a word, he walked back to the car behind him, got in, and drove away. Hank and Mason shook hands. Mason got in the back seat of the fourth car. The three cars pulled away from the curb simultaneously. Of the four cars, the one they left for Hank was the only one with an Ohio license plate. The other three bore New York plates.

When Hank got home with Marcy it was evident she had been crying.   Shelly and Beth both rushed into her arms, their hearts pounding with pure joy that Marcy was home, and she was OK. Marcy was home, but she was not OK. She was as happy to see them as they were to see her, but now things were not the same, and they never would be the same again. Sheila stood motionless, her arms at her side, too choked up to say a word. She wondered if Marcy wanted her to hug her or not. Marcy saw the deep anguish in her Mom's eyes. They both burst into tears as Marcy rushed toward her Mom. Sheila's arms spread wide, as her face broke into a beaming smile. For several minutes the two of them held each other tighter than they ever had before. Without saying anything, each of them knew - all that either of them had ever done to the other was forgiven.

Not so with Hank.   Seeing his little family embracing, with tears of joy on their faces was indeed a scene he had never witnessed. Here was a moment in which Hank could have, and should have, stepped up and joined in his family's moment of joy and gladness. But he let that golden opportunity slip away. The girls and Mom were hugging Marcy, telling her how much they had missed her, and how happy they were to know she was safe. No one was hugging Hank, and no one was thanking him for bringing Marcy home safely. God only knows how, but Hank simply forgot his promise to himself that he would show Marcy his love and compassion. Instead, he approached Sheila with the proposition they send Marcy to a home for unwed mothers. Sheila, for the first time in their marriage, got up in his face, standing firmly, informing him in no uncertain terms – he would not be sending her daughter anywhere. This time, both Hank and the girls were stunned. Here was a frail, sickly, thin woman who had never once raised her voice to her domineering husband. Now she was defying him with the ferocity of a mama bear defending her cubs. Hank, seeing her determination, backed away the same way Buck had backed away from her.

But Hank, true to his word to Mason McPherrin, was determined to deal with Buck Jones, and he would do it quickly. He told Marcy he was going to file charges against Buck for kidnapping and crossing the state line with a minor. Now it was Marcy's turn to get up in his face, and she did. She informed him that if he filed any charges against Buck, she would tell the law Buck had not kidnapped her but she had gone willingly with him. She even added a technicality of her own making, saying Buck had not driven her across the state line – she had gotten out and walked across the bridge into Kentucky. This, of course, was a lie. But Marcy was doing everything in her power to defend Buck against whatever her Dad had planned for him.

It was time for the Smith family to move again. Back to the same street they had lived on before, but a different house. With Marcy pregnant, and no visible means of support, she had to stay with her family. Buck lived with his family in Kentucky. But that didn't stop him from driving to Ohio every chance he got (whenever he could scrap together enough money for gas). He never held a steady job. He was a shiftless drifter, with no plans, and no means of executing a plan if he had one. He lived mostly off the kindness of family and strangers. He was a moocher, with no affinity to hard work. He longed for a hard-working woman who could and would support him and his appetites. He'd stay a while with friends till he wore out his welcome, then go back to his family. And even they soon got fed up with his self-centeredness. Getting his girlfriend pregnant didn't change him one iota. The fact that he was soon going to be a father was of no consequence to him.   To him, Marcy was just one more sexual conquest, by far the most beautiful and sexy trophy he'd ever won.   He never loved Marcy, but she loved him. He never gave a moment's consideration to the child in her womb. He was not ready to be a father, and he was unworthy of the title.

Buck Jones was good at what he did, and what he did was pretend. He pretended to love Marcy. He pretended to be concerned about her and the baby. He had Marcy fooled, but no one else. He made several trips to Ohio, coming to see Marcy each time. Hank would only allow him to stay for a few hours. After leaving the Smith home, Buck would drive across town to the residence of some other girl or woman he had lured into bed before, and sleep with her. From the time he was fifteen till now, his life consisted of one sordid affair after another. Most of his "*conquests*", as he considered them, were either the girlfriends or wives of his so-called "*friends*".

Shelly was elated at the thought of having a little baby around, but at the same time she was deeply concerned about Marcy. Marcy had to quit school, she was too young to be having a baby, and again Shelly's heart broke, having to listen to the unsavory insinuations Hank often threw in Marcy's face. Shelly thought of the many times Marcy had come to her rescue; the many times Marcy had risked her own well-being in order to see that she and Beth had food and clothing; and the many times Marcy had interceded, stopping Hank from beating her worse than he would have if she had not intervened. Her love for Marcy only grew stronger now that Marcy was pregnant. Her little thirteen-year-old heart promised – "*Now it's my turn to take care of Marcy the way she took care of me and Beth.*"

As everyone (except Marcy) had expected, when Marcy went into labor Buck was nowhere to be found. Hank drove Marcy to the hospital, staying close by her side, holding her hand, right up until the time the baby was to be delivered. Marcy kept crying for Buck. At this moment, more than any other, she wished he was there with her. God only knows why and how, but in spite of Buck's sorry treatment of her, she still loved him.

Marcy was fifteen. Neither her body nor her psychological state of development were prepared for this. To say her pain was excruciating would be putting it mildly. Giving birth almost took her life. Hank, pacing nervously in the waiting room, heard her screaming. Suddenly, without warning, all the times he had beaten her flashed upon his conscience. Those images, and the heart-wrenching sound of his daughter's screams stung his conscience like a hornet. He told himself in that moment he would be willing to take all her pain upon himself if it would stop her piercing screams. He had to find some way to salve his conscience a little. He ran to the phone, calling Sheila, sobbing, telling her he couldn't stand knowing Marcy was in so much pain. She was still his favorite – his baby girl. Marcy named her son Buck Jones, Junior. The doctor who delivered him, knowing he was an illegitimate child, and knowing Marcy's age, asked Mary to sign papers, giving the baby up for adoption. Hank, with the baby in his arms, stepped in immediately, informing the doctor - *"She will do no such thing. I will take care of this little boy, and give him my last name."*

Shelly and Beth could hardly contain their excitement, anxiously awaiting the arrival of Marcy and the baby. Hank tooted the horn as soon as he pulled up to the curb outside the house. The world has never seen a man more proud than Hank Smith as he carried his first grandson into the living room. His pride turned to fury as he saw Buck standing beside Sheila. He desperately wanted to beat Buck to death. Handing the baby to Sheila, he demanded – *"And just where were you while your son was being born, you sorry, good-for-nothing piece of crap."* Buck took a step backward, almost hiding behind Sheila, anticipating Hank's fist in his face at any moment. He began stammering, giving Hank some incoherent string of lies. The sordid truth, which Marcy and the whole family would learn later, was that while Marcy had been in labor, Buck had been in bed with another woman.

Some things humans feel and do stand outside the realm of logic and reason, especially to those who are not as immediately connected to the situation as the one who is going through it. Marcy's family could not understand how she could still love a man (a boy in a man's body,) who had openly demonstrated that he didn't love her. Even more inconsistent with their own reasoning was the fact that Marcy was willing to leave the love, safety and comfort (such as it was,) of a family in order to be with Buck. The heart wants what the heart wants, and Marcy's heart wanted to be with Buck Jones. One month after little Buck was born, Hank and Sheila signed papers, giving Marcy legal permission to marry Buck. They were married by a Justice of the Peace in the office of the County Clerk.   Marcy and the baby still had to live with Hank and the family, because Buck had no place for them to live, and Hank would not allow Buck to stay in his home more than a few hours at a time. The tension between him and Buck grew stronger every time Hank saw him. Soon that tension would escalate, and things would get ugly.

Shelly and Beth were invited to a little church down the street from where they lived. They began to attend every Sunday. Shelly was now at the age when she really began to be serious about spiritual matters. Her tender heart yearned to know God personally. Without being told in so many words, she somehow knew that Jesus Christ was the only hope for her and her family. She and Beth were thrilled with their Sunday School teacher, Kate. Kate had a sparkle in her eyes – a real sparkle. To Shelly, her eyes spoke louder than her words. She had a genuine love for the girls, and that love manifested itself in both her actions and her words. They could see Christ in her.   Shelly cherished the warmth she now felt in her heart. Maybe God could forgive her for all the bad things in her life after all. One particular Sunday, listening to the Preacher telling of how Jesus had died for the sins of the whole world, she felt a terrible inner conviction that she was lost, and needed a Savior. With tears in her eyes, she bowed her head, closing her eyes, asking Jesus to come into her heart. What happened next she could never fully define, describe or explain. It was as if the weight of the world had been suddenly lifted from her soul.   She had an inner peace which transcended any joy she had ever known.   Her first thought was to pray for her family's salvation.   Her heart was bursting to tell someone that Jesus had saved her soul. Kate would be the first to hear it. As Kate drove her and Beth home from Church, Shelly found herself praying for total strangers as she saw them walking down the street. She wanted the whole world to know this same joy that overflowed from her heart. She began to tell Kate how she felt compelled to pray for everyone. Kate smiled her beaming smile, telling Shelly God had given her the gift of intercessory prayer.

Shelia's health was continually getting worse. Her body was weakening, and her nerves were shattered. The hard life she had lived had taken its toll, both physically and psychologically. Now she could barely bring herself to step outside the house. Much of her life was now spent in the house, in bed. Everyone noticed the dark circles around her eyes. They also noticed her lethargic behavior. She had no energy, no sparkle, and seemingly not much will to live. She barely ate enough to keep body and soul together. She had a faraway look in her eyes, as if she was somehow detached from present reality, and living in another dimension.

Marcy had no choice but to apply for welfare. Buck had found a job, making minimum wage. But in the same way he had drifted from one woman to another, he drifted from one job to another. For some reason he just couldn't seem to keep a job. Each time he quit or was fired, he came up with another excuse. It was always someone else's fault, not his. Between Marcy's welfare check and the meager handful of dollars he brought home, they managed to rent a house. But in the same way Hank's family was constantly moving, so it was with Marcy and Buck. Marcy's welfare check just wasn't enough to pay the rent, keep the utilities on, feed the family, and furnish Buck with the luxuries he wanted.   Every day brought another fight. Most of their fights only involved a lot of shouting and cursing. A few times Buck resorted to physical violence, but when he did, Marcy fought back. She would be his wife, she would be his lover, and even support his habits, but she would not be his punching bag.

Being evicted from house after house was too much for Marcy to handle. She was constantly leaving Buck, and coming back home to Hank and Sheila. On many occasions, when she came, she brought bags of food and clothing with her. In order to make sure Buck Jr. had milk, diapers, and the necessities a baby requires, and knowing her Mom and sisters were often going hungry, she had resorted to stealing again. Buck kept getting and losing jobs. Being illiterate, he had to take whatever menial job he was offered. A few times he came up with a harebrained idea of how to make more money, quickly and easily. Instead of working steadily and saving his money, he took his own money, and a lot of Marcy's welfare check, put it all together, and bought old cars, most of which were virtually worthless. But being a fairly good mechanic, he took their money, bought used parts from junk yards, patched the old vehicles up a bit, and tried to re-sell them at a profit. As it turned out, he made even less money at this endeavor than he would have made at his last job. Many times he found himself stuck with another pile of junk of which he now had to dispose somehow. Some he had to give away. The only positive aspect of it all was that Shelly got to hold the baby. He had her wrapped around his little finger the first time she held him. She became Marcy's babysitter as often as the opportunity arose, taking him for rides in his stroller and generally spoiling him rotten.

Buck considered himself a *"ladies man"*. In fact, he considered himself God's gift to women. To best describe his appetite for other women - most men, when considering attracting a lady, make sure they have enough money and resources to wine-and-dine her. Buck's definition of wining and dining was taking his wife's money, finding a girl he wanted to seduce, taking her to a secluded spot, and making her a bologna sandwich.

Shelly was now fourteen, and in high school. She told a little white lie about her age in order to get a job at a local hamburger place. She also made one of the biggest mistakes of her life – she quit going to church. But she never quit praying. That was the one thing she couldn't quit doing. But the flame of overwhelming joy she had felt that day in church had subsided from a flaming torch to a flickering candle. Still very young, she had experienced far more than any child her age should ever have to see. She loved the Lord, and had the best of intentions. She knew without anyone telling her that God had a plan for her life. She didn't know what that plan was at the time, but right now she had circumstances to deal with, and necessities which required her full attention and effort. And although some of that flame of joy had subsided, she had not lost the two positive traits she inherited from her Dad – her quick wit, and the ability to make others laugh.

Also to her credit, Shelly had a good solid work ethic. She always gave her best effort. She earned her wages, and had fun doing it. And in her own whimsical way, she made it fun for her co-workers, including the managers. She brought just a little more radiance and sunshine to the place. She got really good at her job, determined she would learn every aspect of it. The managers enjoyed working with her, not only because she worked hard but also because she really enjoyed the work, doing her job in a lighthearted manner that just seemed to make the day go a little better and a little faster. In her first year of working there, Shelly won the employee of the month award several times.   In fact, the manager liked Shelly and her work ethic so much he hired her sister Beth also. Shelly was now sixteen and a half, Beth was fifteen. Both the girls were thrilled to be working together, making their own money, and being able to buy their own clothes and other things they needed.

The high-ranking guards and officials at the prison where Hank worked hit upon what they considered the perfect plan to get rid of Hank. The inmates liked him too much, and most of the guards didn't like him at all. In order to keep working at the prison, the guards had to maintain a certain level of qualification, as mandated by both the prison and the state. Each guard had to pass an annual written examination. He got two chances to get a passing grade.   Hank scored 100% on the test the first time. The chief officer told him he had flunked the test, and would have to take it again.   Again Hank scored a perfect 100%.   He was told he had flunked the test twice, and was no longer qualified to be a prison guard. When Hank asked to see his test results, the officer told him it had somehow gotten lost in the shuffle of all the other tests, and couldn't be found.   He was told to turn in his badge, uniforms, pistol and nightstick within the next forty-eight hours.   Before he left the prison the warden allowed him thirty minutes to say a few goodbyes to a few of the guards who did like Hank, and to one block of inmates. Upon hearing Hank Smith had been *"let go"*, the inmates staged a riot, demanding that Hank be re-instated.   The melee that ensued turned into a bloodbath, with guards and prisoners being severely beaten, bludgeoned, stabbed, and cut with knives and kitchen utensils.   It took every guard on duty using any weapon he could get his hands on to finally quell the riot. The prisoners who were considered being the *"instigators"* of the riot each got his turn in the hole for three days, no lights, no pillow, no cover, no ventilation – one bucket.

The Maffia had long since returned and taken the new car they had loaned Hank when he went to Kentucky to go get Marcy. Now he was back to driving his old clunker. It wasn't much, but it got him to wherever he had to go, and to many places to which he should not have gone. Now he had taken a job driving a cab.   He spent less time at home now than he ever had before. About all he did at home was eat, sleep and use the bathroom.   And now he was dating a divorced woman with five small children. Desperately wanting to impress her, he lavished gifts upon her-necklaces, bracelets, dinners. Between catering to her appetites, and buying toys, dolls and candy for her little girls, she turned out to be a high-maintenance affair, far more than Hank Smith could afford on his paycheck.

Shelly had saved her money from her job, opening a small savings account at the local bank. It wasn't much, but to her it meant a lot, and she was proud of herself for being the first one in her family to have a savings account.   Hank was running out of money every week. All of it was going toward his girlfriend and her kids. But knowing Shelly was working and saving her money, he came to her, asking for money every payday. Now he was not only spending his own money on another family, but taking money from his fifteen year old daughter, and spending that on his girlfriend and her family also. Shelly was afraid not to give it to him, but in her gut she despised him for how he was treating her Mom.

When Shelly had been going to church regularly, her teacher, Kate, had often stressed three things to her class. She told them there were three things every young Christian should get in the habit of doing – reading the Bible every day, praying every day, and staying in church. Shelly had done those three things faithfully for about a year, especially the time she spent in prayer. Now she was sixteen. There were a few things she hadn't tried, and had really never considered trying, until now. She had begun neglecting her Bible, and she quit going to church altogether. She convinced herself that prayer was enough for now; it would sustain her and fortify her against whatever came her way. She was wrong.

Shane Markus, one of the managers of the fast food restaurant where Shelly worked really took a liking to Shelly. On the surface his demeanor seemed perfectly honorable toward her and the other girls. But working in close quarters with several young ladies, in itself, presented – shall we say - awkward situations. To Shane Markus, they presented opportunities to make bodily contact with the girls. It soon became obvious to some of the girls that he was deliberately creating some of those opportunities. Whenever he was fairly certain no one was watching he would sneak up behind Shelly, quickly feeling and pinching her butt. After pinching her butt, he would keep walking toward the kitchen, glancing back at her, winking, as if it was totally innocent - a little game that meant nothing inappropriate, as if being her boss, or, as he considered it, her *superior*, somehow gave him the right to engage in a little hanky-panky.

The open space between the counter and the grille was only about two feet wide; barely enough room for two persons to squeeze by each other without coming into physical contact. This also created opportunities for Shane. If a girl was standing at the counter as he squeezed by her, he made sure his front made contact with her behind. If she was facing the grille, he made contact with her breasts. This went on every day, every hour, several times each hour. Most of the girls, including Shelly, were afraid to report him to upper management, for fear of losing their jobs. Some of them even enjoyed it, but pretended they didn't. The fact that no one had openly objected to his advances and inappropriate contact, as far as he was concerned, gave him the license to not only continue his behavior, but to take it to another level. Unknown to everyone but Shane and one other girl, he was secretly having an affair with one of the seventeen year old girls. He was twenty-five.

One Saturday night, Shane invited several of the employees, including Shelly, to his home for a party. This, of course, was something that just didn't happen to Shelly. She was never invited to parties. To her, it was extra special, being invited to a party by her boss. At her age it gave her a sense of status, being able to mingle with folks older than herself, and being treated like a mature adult; like an equal.   Her personality alone made her stand out from the rest of the more introverted teenagers.   That personality was sometimes misinterpreted by men and boys. To Shelly and most of her acquaintances, she was simply being friendly – nothing more. To several of her male friends, Shane Markus in particular, it said *"I'm available*, or *"I'm willing"*.

The party began innocently enough, with music and dancing, laughter and chitchat; just a few teenage boys and girls having fun with their boss. No one had said anything about a dress code for the party, and as Shane had hoped, the girls showed up wearing tight-fitting jeans with low-cut tops, exposing a lot of cleavage, or miniskirts, exposing a lot of leg. Those who were not as well-endowed as some others had stuffed their bras with padding. Shelly was the exception. Her attire would have been appropriate for a church social, showing as little skin, and as few curves as possible. When Shane concluded that everyone was comfortable with him and each other, he turned the music down a bit, so he could be heard. Asking for their attention, he proposed - *"How many of you guys want to crank this party up a notch?"* A brief moment of silence followed, with each of the youngsters wanting someone else to be the first to respond. One of eighteen year old boys quickly blurted out – *"Hell yeah boss, let's ramp it up."* That was all Shane needed. He rushed into the kitchen, coming back carrying a cooler full of ice-cold beer. Only two of the boys at the party had ever tasted beer. All the others, boys and girls, not wanting to appear juvenile to the others, pretended they had, turning the beer up and guzzling it as if it was something they were used to doing. From their reactions to the taste of the beer, Shane knew immediately which ones had, and which ones hadn't drunk it before. It was Shelly's first time, of course, and to her own surprise she loved the taste of it. Knowing the sad affects her Dad's drinking had inflicted upon her and her family, she once thought she would never touch the stuff. But one beer led to another, then another, and soon she was feeling the effect, and loving the way it made her feel. By the time they took her home she was really drunk. One of the boys drove her home. When she staggered into the house she started getting sick, vomiting on the floor. Hank, hearing her retching, woke up. Seeing her on her knees, too drunk to get up, her clothes drenched in her own vomit, he yelled for Sheila to come help him get her to the bathroom. He lifted her into the tub, clothes and all, turning on the water, as she continued to vomit in the tub. Sheila soaked a washcloth in cold water, wiping her mouth each time she threw up. Hank kept cussing at Sheila, as if she was doing something wrong. She was only trying to help.

The next day, Sunday, Shelly was scheduled to work. She woke up late, and sick. She called in sick – the only time in over two years she had done so. She swore she would never take another drink of beer the rest of her life. But like one of her Uncles had told her years ago – *"Honey, there's two things that are easily broken – promises and pie crust."* Shelly was soon to discover her promise to herself was more easily broken than pie crust.

Unknown to the any of the girls who worked at the restaurant, Shane and another manager – Herb Henderson, were sharing information about them with each other, comparing notes. The two of them often had lunch together at a steak house up the street from their own restaurant. In graphic detail they quietly talked about the girls' bodies, even lying to each other, each boasting that he had stolen the virginity of one of the girls. Herb was telling a half truth. He had engaged in sex with one of the seventeen year old girls, but he had not been her first. Now he wanted Shelly. Shane told him two beers would get Shelly into bed.   By that statement Herb presumed Shane had had Shelly first. Not to be outdone by his associate, he told Shane he would have her next, adding his own lewd comment – *"When I get through with her buddy, she'll throw rocks at you."* Shane chuckled, shooting back – *"We'll see ol buddy, we'll see."*

Herb began arranging another party- this time at his house, with all the amenities Shane told him he would need to seduce Shelly. She loved country music, compliments, funny jokes, and beer. Herb thanked him for the information. As they parted ways, Shane added - *"That's all I can do for ya pal, the rest is up*

to you and your charm. Let me know how long it takes you to get her pants off. Only took me five minutes." Herb grinned, countering – *"It ain't how long it takes to get em off that matters pal, it's how long it takes to get em back on."*

This party began with cold beer for the girls and boys. But Herb was hedging his bet, secretly slipping aphrodisiacs into the girl's glasses, assuming it would greatly increase his chances of getting what he wanted. He wasn't as handsome and charming as Shane, and he was leaving nothing to chance. Before the night was over, he was planning on having at least three of the girls, so he could boast to Shane how he had outdone him. His perverted mind was already anticipating telling Shane how much Shelly had enjoyed it.

Shelly knew she should not have come to the party. Memories of the last one made her stomach tighten a bit. She weighed her options quickly, while remembering how she had enjoyed the fun and the taste of beer. She hadn't had many opportunities to laugh, dance, and have fun with a group of her friends all together at one time. She told herself – *"One more time won't hurt, and I'll be more careful this time."* Herb's house had four bedrooms – two upstairs and two downstairs. As the party progressed, Shelly noticed some of the boys and girls going upstairs, two and two. Having worked with these girls for more than two years, she couldn't believe either of them was that easy to give in to a boy. Something wasn't right with this picture. She sipped her beer slowly, keeping an eye on the other boys, but especially on Herb. With every few minutes she stayed, the more she drank, promising herself nothing bad was going to happen this time. But the alcohol was stronger than her will power. She was getting higher with each glass of beer.

The beer she drank would not have had the same effect had it not been laced with an aphrodisiac.   She couldn't understand why she was having these sudden urges. Her Mom had emphasized one thing more than any other – *"Sex before marriage is dirty, it's sinful, and it will send you to Hell."*   She had not had these kinds of feelings before – not even when she had gotten drunk before.   At this point, she was more drugged than drunk, but didn't know it. She refused the next glass of beer Herb offered her. Now she noticed that she and Herb and one other couple were the only ones in the living room. Herb, assuming Shelly was ripe for the taking, nodded his head toward the other boy, Raymond. It was a pre-arranged signal for Raymond to take his girlfriend to one of the bedrooms, leaving the other vacant for him and Shelly. He approached Shelly cautiously, asking if she liked paintings.

Shelly assured him she loved beautiful paintings. This, of course, was a half-truth on Shelly's part. About the only paintings she had seen were prints of paintings, hanging on the walls of stores and doctor's offices. But she did like them, so she told herself she wasn't really lying. Herb smiled, looking deeply into her eyes, searching for her thoughts. Drawing a little closer, he took the tips of her fingers into his hand, barely holding them. Shelly's heart pounded rapidly. He ran his hands up her arms to her elbows, gently drawing her closer, whispering to her how lovely she looked. So far she had offered no resistance. Herb became more emboldened by the moment, his own heart pounding with anticipation. Believing Shane's lie about having slept with Shelly, his lust imagined how it had been with Shane and Shelly. Now he would show Shane who was the better man. He leaned in slowly, cautiously, waiting for any sign of acceptance from her, hoping she would lean in also. Shelly remained motionless, not resisting him, but neither was she fully accepting his advance. Something inside her wanted him to take here in his arms and kiss her passionately. At the same time something else told her she should not be doing this. Again her Mom's words echoed in her conscience – "*it will send you to Hell.*"

She felt his lips touch hers - so gentle, so innocent, so inviting. For a few moments, time stood still. It was her first real kiss from a man. He took her hand, leading her slowly toward what he thought was the empty bedroom. With every step Shelly questioned what she was about to do. She had been molested, abused, and beaten by men. But no man had actually raped her. Right now she wasn't sure what she wanted. She just knew she was taking a horrible risk. The effect of the drug and the alcohol were slowly wearing off.

As they approached the door of the bedroom, Herb stopped, unbuttoning the top button of her blouse, so sure of himself. Shelly thought she heard noises coming from inside the bedroom – muffled sounds. Herb heard them also. Opening the door, he led Shelly inside. Raymond was standing at the foot of the bed in nothing but his jeans. His shirt was on the floor. His girlfriend was on the bed, drunk and drugged. It was quite obvious what was about to happen. Raymond had taken her to the wrong room. Herb ordered Raymond out of the room, demanding he take his girlfriend with him. She was too drunk to get up, and Raymond was too aroused to let this opportunity get away. Herb was about to close the door and let Raymond rape Lisa when Shelly stepped in. Whatever residual effect the aphrodisiac and beer had on her was suddenly overcome by her adrenaline and her rage.

She shoved Herb to one side, grabbing Raymond's belt, jerking him away from Lisa with all her strength. Holding onto his belt, she pulled him out of the room. He was almost as drunk as Lisa. Falling onto the floor, he lay there, either too drunk or too afraid to get up. Her fighting rage only made Herb want her more. He came toward her, arms outstretched, still believing he could get her in bed. He was wrong. She slapped him hard, kicking his shins, demanding he take his filthy hands off her. He persisted, not willing to let her get away from him. As he reached for her breasts she grabbed his hand, biting so hard the blood oozed out. He started to hit her with his fist, but she ducked, coming up with a steel poker from the fireplace. The sharp point ripped through his shirt, leaving a red and black gash across his chest. Before he could recover from the shock and pain, she pressed the sharp point into his bellybutton, holding him against the wall with the poker. Herb was a pervert, but he was not a fool. He knew if he moved she would shove the poker through him. He surrendered. He knew his bleeding chest and hand needed attention, and soon. The poker had left a deep ugly gash. His shirt was soaking up most of the blood, but he knew if he didn't get to a doctor soon, it would get infected. His concern for his own well-being took precedence over his lust for Shelly's body. Shelly released him from the wall, still holding the poker. She walked over to the phone, calling Marcy to come and pick her and Lisa up and take them home.

Marcy, now eighteen, announced she was pregnant again. Nine months later her second son, Bubby, was born. Hank, Shelly, Buck and Beth were with her this time. Sheila wouldn't come. Less than an hour after he was born the doctor told Marcy and her family the baby would have to be taken to Children's Hospital immediately. Without knowing what was wrong with him at the moment, Shelly began to pray earnestly, begging God to watch over Bubby. As she prayed she made promises to God – if He would make Bubby alright she would go back to church, and strive to be a better person.   As she finished making her promises, her Uncle's words echoed again – *"promises and piecrust are easily broken."*   The waiting in the family waiting room seemed like an eternity.   While everyone else chatted nervously or paced the floor, Shelly continued to pray, paying them no mind. Finally, when the doctor came out of the ER, everyone held their breath, expecting the worst. When the doctor smiled, they all breathed a sigh of relief before he said anything, interpreting his smile as good news. And it was good news. It was just a little fluid in the baby's lungs. He was going to be just fine. While everyone else was thanking the doctor, Shelly was thanking God.

Shelly and Beth started hanging out with their cousin Phillip. Of all her cousins, Phillip was Shelly's favorite. He was always nice, his smile was genuine, and the girls always felt safe with him around. Phillip was the strong quiet type. He never looked for trouble, but if and when trouble came, he ended it quickly and effectively. He did everything in his power to avoid a fight, but after he had exhausted every resource at his disposal, and the other guy persisted, it was the other guy who got the worst of it. Now, everywhere Phillip went, his reputation preceded him. Not many young guys challenged him. He had made a lot of friends, and a few enemies. But even his enemies had learned to respect him. Nobody messed with him.

Phillip believed in upholding his family name, and honoring his parents and other relatives. His love of family was strong and real. And in the same way nobody messed with him, neither did they dare mess with any of his relatives when he was present. This family honor cost Shelly and Beth a few boyfriends when Phillip was around. Many of their would-be suitors steered away from them when they saw Phillip. He would not tolerate any kind of off-color language in the presence of any girl, and especially not around his cousins. Phillip didn't just talk the talk, he walked the walk. His personality matched his character. What you saw was what you got – every day. As Phillip himself would say – "*I ain't no saint, but I know right from wrong.*"

Shelly's promises to God and herself were slowly receding to the back of her mind. The crisis was over, Bubby was ok, and she was still a teenager in high school, and she loved to party and drink.   She was being drawn to it like a moth to the flame. She had experienced her first passionate kiss, and now she wasn't as certain as she had been before as to how far she was willing to go. She was looking for love, but deep inside she knew she was looking in all the wrong places. And now Beth was going with her. And to make matters worse, Shelly knew she couldn't hold her liquor. It only took a couple beers or a couple shots of liquor to send her into party mode. Now that she and Beth were hanging out with Phillip a lot more, he sometimes joined them at some of the parties. Phillip didn't drink. He confessed he had tried marijuana a few times, but he absolutely did not like the taste of alcohol. Neither did he like the effects of it. He had seen too many lives destroyed by it. He never condemned others for drinking, but he just decided he could live without it.

Phillip loved his cousins, and enjoyed their company. Shelly always had a way of making him laugh when no one else could. She was easy to be around. But Shelly had changed in some way that worried Phillip. It seemed she was just a little too comfortable with the boys now. He also noticed the way boys looked at her, as if she was an easy score. Shelly didn't realize it, but she was getting a reputation also, and it wasn't exactly that of Snow White. With Phillip close by she knew she would be protected from the worst of the boys. He would never let any physical harm come to her. Phillip could protect her body, but he couldn't protect her heart and mind. And neither could he dissuade her from going to some of the places she gravitated toward.

It seemed to him the kind of boys she was drawn to be the ones she should have been avoiding. But he kept his thoughts to himself. She was his cousin and his friend. There were some life lessons some young girls and boys were set on learning the hard way.

Shelly was in high school, hating every minute of every day. Graduation could not come soon enough. That dreaded sense of inferiority that had plagued her all her life wouldn't go away. In her mind, everyone else was so much better than her – girls and boys. She never considered herself as being pretty, let alone beautiful. She even thought of herself as being ugly. She could not have been farther from the truth. She was a beautiful young lady, with long, flowing, dark brown hair, and a figure that drew every bit as much attention as Marcy, or any other girl, for that matter. Now she was about to meet a few of Phillip's other friends who lived on the wealthier side of town – the other side of the tracks – the rich folks. She presumed they would all be somewhat snobbish and uppity, and would look down their noses at her. To her great surprise, none of them did. They greeted her graciously and treated her as an equal the first time she met them. Soon her sense of inferiority began to wane a bit. She found herself really liking most of them - one boy in particular – Matt.

Shelly didn't know it at the time, but Matt had both a drinking problem and a drug problem. But for now he seemed really nice. She felt safe and comfortable with him, especially knowing Phillip was close by. One evening they were at the home of one of Phillip's rich friends, shooting pool down in the basement. To Shelly's pleasant surprise, Matt was there. But in the same way Shane and Herb had discussed Shelly to each other, Matt, behind Shelly's back, and without Phillip's knowledge, had been telling the other boys he had *"bagged"* Shelly Smith. The other boys, of course, were thrilled, listening to him boast of how he had easily seduced Shelly. They wanted details, and Matt produced those details vividly, describing Shelly's body in lurid terms. One of the boys who had only met Shelly once couldn't quite recall meeting her. Matt refreshed his memory, laughing – *"Yeah, you know her, Phillip's cousin, the little hot one with the great stacks, beautiful legs, and shapely caboose."* Everyone got a good laugh out of it, slapping Matt on the back, congratulating him on *"bagging"* the hottest one.

Tonight, as Shelly mingled with the girls and boys, Matt seemed to be deliberately avoiding her. She didn't understand why. He had been so nice and gracious before. Then she saw him staggering. He was so messed up on drugs and alcohol he couldn't hit the cue ball. Phillip suddenly remembered an errand he had to run, announcing he would be back a little later. Before leaving he asked Shelly if she would be ok here with these guys. It was probably the alcohol doing the talking instead of Shelly's own confidence, but she assured him she would be fine. Surely, she thought, these guys would not do anything stupid, knowing Phillip would be back soon. As soon as Phillip closed the door behind him, Matt, for no apparent reason, came toward Shelly grinning, waving the end of his pool stick around in circles. Suddenly he began to whack Shelly's legs with the pool stick, laughing, as if it was some kind of game. Shelly started backing up, toward the stairs, trying to make him stop hitting her. When the other boys saw the fear and hurt in Shelly's eyes, they joined Matt, surrounding Shelly, each of them striking her legs with their pool sticks. Then just as suddenly as they had begun hitting her for no reason, they stopped hitting her, going back to their pool game as if they had done nothing wrong.

Shelly had no way to get home until Phillip returned, so she was forced to remain there until he arrived. She desperately wanted to tell him what his friends had done to her, but as she pondered that idea, she concluded it would be in Phillip's best interest, and hers, not to say a word. She knew if she told Phillip he would most likely beat Matt to death. But looking around the room, she also calculated that Phillip would be heavily outnumbered here, and would probably get beaten up if he were to challenge the whole gang. Her jeans concealed the bruises the pool sticks had made, so she knew Phillip couldn't see them. For now, it was best that she just suffer in silence.

The next day, as Shelly was getting dressed in the bathroom, she saw, and felt, the ugly bruises on her legs. Her legs were covered with bruises from her thighs to her ankles. Marcy came upstairs, and without knocking, barged into the bathroom. Seeing the bruises on Shelly's legs, she assumed the worst. To her, those kinds of bruises on a girl's legs meant that she had not only been beaten, but in all likelihood, beaten and raped. Marcy's went into a rage, demanding that Shelly tell her what had happened. Until now, Shelly had always fully confided in Marcy, sharing all her secrets with her. But in the same way she knew what Phillip would have done, she also knew Marcy's wrath. She was not going to get Marcy, Phillip, or anyone else involved this time. She didn't want to lie to Marcy, and she knew Marcy would not believe her if she said it was an accident. So, for the first time in her life, she simply faced Marcy, telling her it was none of her business. Marcy was already mad, but now she was even madder. Being the big sister, and having been so close to her younger sisters for so long, and having been like a mother to them, she reckoned it was not only her duty, but somehow her the right to be involved in their personal lives.

Marcy had never seen this side of Shelly. Suddenly she was no longer the shy, submissive, insecure little girl she had known. It seemed as if something drastic had happened overnight –

some mystical metamorphosis that had transformed Shelly into a defiant, self-reliant, courageous young lady who could, and would, stand on her own two feet. Marcy quickly put her finger in Shelly's face, letting her know she was going to tell Mom about this.

Shelly really didn't care if Marcy told Sheila, but she told herself Marcy was just getting even with her for telling Mom on her for letting Buck drive her home that first time. Marcy didn't know exactly what to expect when she told her Mom about the bruises on Shelly's legs, but she was determined to tell her anyway. Sheila listened, but it seemed to Marcy as if she was talking to a lamp post. That faraway look in Sheila's eyes gave the impression she hadn't heard a word Marcy said. Sheila had heard every word, but her physical and mental state just would not let her deal with it right now. It was as if she was looking past Marcy, hearing, but not quite understanding what she was saying.

At this point in their lives, Shelly and Beth were pretty much on their own. They lived in the same house with their Mom, but it seemed as if Mom wasn't really there. Hank was seldom seen anymore. Once in a while he came by to say hello and goodbye, or maybe sleep for a night or two, and he was gone again. Sheila spent most of her time in bed. Hank, having spent nearly all his money on his girlfriend and her girls, would leave a couple dollars on the mantel for Sheila to buy her cigarettes and food. It was never enough. The two dollars paid for Sheila's cigarettes, but nothing else. The little store down the street allowed Sheila and the girls to buy small amounts of food and other necessities on credit. Sheila survived on a can of vegetable beef soup and a cup of 7Up every day. Supper consisted of TV dinners, with Beth eating most of them.

Whenever Marcy came over with the boys Beth and Shelly knew she and Buck had been fighting again. Shelly had learned long ago how mean and ugly Buck could be, especially when he had been drinking, and tonight he had been drinking a lot; she could smell it when he stomped into the house. Buck went straight for Marcy, swinging his fists and cussing her. Some of the blows missed, but a few of them landed. Marcy swung back, landing a few of her own punches. But she was no match for Buck. He was like a raging bull, and he was not a small man (physically). Shelly rushed toward them, forcing herself between them, trying to separate them, screaming at Buck, telling him to get out of their house. Buck landed a hard right to Shelly's left jaw, nearly knocking her off her feet. She was sure he jaw was broken. While Buck was momentarily off balance, Marcy grabbed the first thing she could get her hands on – a statuette weighing about three pounds. Swinging at his head with all her strength, she nearly knocked him unconscious. With the little bit of consciousness he had left, he got the message, staggering out the door. He knew Marcy loved him, but he also knew she would kill him if he pushed too far. For now, he'd had enough. Shelly and Marcy, both looking more like victims than victors, hugged, congratulating each other on their victory over a more powerful foe.

Neither of the girls knew in what mental or emotional state they might find their Mom on any given day. They had now come to expect just about anything except the happy, smiling mother they once knew. There had been a time when Shelly could, with relative accuracy, interpret the varied expressions on her Mom's face, along with her body language. But now it was nearly impossible to discern what was going on inside Sheila's head and heart. On the surface it appeared their roles had been reversed. Each of the girls seemed to be more of a mother to Sheila than she was to them. But in spite of her mood swings and sometimes unintelligible behavior, Sheila could still, in her own way, express herself whenever the situation demanded that she do so. Often – far too often, her tears said more than her tongue. When the tears appeared, Shelly knew there was a crisis.

Shelly saw those tears as soon as she came home from school. Sheila was sitting on the couch, sobbing. Shelly sat beside her, taking her hand, asking what was wrong. Between her trembling lips and sobbing she somehow managed to tell Shelly that Hank was with Marcy at the hospital. Marcy had taken a whole bottle of pills, attempting to commit suicide. Shelly, of course, in her mind, saw Marcy lying dead in the hospital. Now, Sheila accurately interpreted the expression on Shelly's face, quickly adding that the doctors were able to pump Marcy's stomach, saving her life. Shelly's own emotions swirled like a tornado inside her. In the same moment, she was grateful that Marcy was alive, grateful that Hank was with her, and hating Buck Jones with every fiber of her being for what he was doing to her sister. Again she wondered how and why a beautiful, intelligent girl like Marcy could still love, and stay with a monster like Buck. She could not imagine her life without Marcy. But right now, her Mom needed her as much, if not more, than Marcy did. Mother and daughter simply sat there holding onto each other as if each of their lives depended upon the other. Shelly knew her Mom loved all her girls, she just wasn't able to express, or articulate that love the same way other mothers could.

Hearing the front door creaking open on its rusty hinges, they jumped up from the sofa, running together into the front room. Hank had Marcy's arm around his shoulder, supporting her as she half stumbled toward Sheila and Shelly. Shelly grabbed her first, holding onto her as tightly as possible without breaking her ribs. She'd never seen Marcy so pale and weak. Already fearful of the answer she would get, she asked where the boys were. Marcy was too weak to answer. Hank confirmed Shelly's fear – Buck had taken the boys to Kentucky again. It was his dastardly way of hurting and punishing Marcy even more every time they had a fight.   It was times like this that Shelly wished Marcy had never ever met Buck. And the thing that was the farthest beyond her comprehension was the fact that she knew Buck would be back, he would apologize, beg Marcy's forgiveness, and Marcy would forgive him and take him back as if nothing had happened.

Hank had seen enough. No, he had seen too much, and now he was going to do something about it. He had every intention of beating Buck Jones to death the next time he saw him. Each time Marcy let Buck come back, he would deliberately stay away from Hank as far as possible for a long time. But with the passing of time, when he figured everyone's temper had cooled enough, he ventured back onto the Smith's property. Each time he saw Hank, he gave him a wide berth, sensing the anger and hatred that had been building up inside Hank for a long time. He couldn't look Hank in the eye. Around Hank, he had that look of the proverbial *"sheep-killing dog."*   And now every ounce of Hank's pent up wrath was about to be unleashed – all at once. This time Hank was waiting for him.

Hank and Buck were pretty close to the same height and weight, and in a fair fight, no one in his right mind would have placed any bets on which man would win. One man was as big as the other, and each was as mean as the other. But Buck didn't know how strong or how quick Hank was for his age. He knew Hank would kill him if given the opportunity, and that knowledge, in itself, kept him at a safe distance from Hank as long as possible. He sometimes pondered the dark notion of killing Hank first. But as mean and as devious as Buck was, and knowing Hank actually wanted to kill him, he knew he couldn't avoid Hank forever. He knew if he didn't go to Hank, Hank would bring the fight to him. Either way, a confrontation was inevitable. In most cases, in a fair fight between two men of equal height and weight, the outcome is mostly dependent upon the skill, the cunning, the stamina, and the determination of each man. But sometimes none of these are the deciding factor. Sometimes the sheer degree of hatred of one man for the other determines the outcome. And sometimes one of them fights dirty, taking whatever advantage he can find.

They met in Hank's front yard. Hank made sure of that beforehand. He wasn't going to let Buck inside the house where he might get his hands on a weapon of some sort. He didn't want to fight Buck in close quarters. From all appearances, the only weapons either man had were his bare knuckles. Sheila, Shelly, Beth, Marcy, Bubby and Buck Jr. stood on the porch, watching. Sheila and the girls knew it would be useless to try to stop it. As Buck came through the front gate Hank met him, calling him a few choice names, and using expletives that would make a drunken sailor blush. Buck responded in kind, calling Hank a low down dirty dog, among other things. Buck was the first to feel the business end of Hank's fist, right between his eyes. He felt like he had been kicked by a mule. Buck went down like an empty sack. Hank, and everyone else, thought the fight was over. This fight was so quick and easy for Hank, he suddenly lost his desire to kill Buck. He reckoned he had demonstrated to Buck and everyone else that he was the better man. He was confident that Buck had no more fight left in him.With Buck lying on the grass, moaning and trying to recover from that first punch, Hank turned to walk up onto the porch. Buck reached into the back pocket of his jeans, coming up with a thin sharp blade. Seeing Hank's back turned, he lunged forward, intending to cut Hank's throat from behind.

Shelly screamed – *"Dad, look out, he's got a knife!"*

Still only half conscious, Buck knew he had only one chance of survival. If he missed his target, Hank would not be so foolish as to turn his back again. It was kill or be killed. Shelly's scream saved two lives that day. If Hank had not turned when he did, the sharp blade would have sliced his brain stem in two. Facing Buck, the blade sliced Hank's lower lip in half, horizontally, from left to right. Buck reeled backward, staggering, falling into the fence. Hank fell onto the porch, bleeding profusely from his lip. Sheila ran into the house, grabbing the cleanest towel she could find, pressing it to Hank's bleeding lip. Marcy ran toward Buck, screaming at him. She turned to make sure Hank was alright, helping Buck up from the ground. When she was satisfied Hank was ok, she shoved Buck toward his car. She was still yelling at him as the two of them drove away. At least three emotions now gripped Shelly's heart – fear, helplessness, and hopelessness. And like so many times before, there was only one way for her to express what she felt- she just stood and cried, watching Buck's car go out of sight.

After Hank and Buck kind of got each other out of their systems, there was a brief period of calm around the Smith household, but it was only the calm before the storm. Shelly had an old car that she drove to work and to school. She would be graduating soon and she could hardly wait. Hank had promised a new car to the first girl who graduated high school. Shelly believed him.

One evening after another one of Marcy and Buck's cussing and shoving fights, Marcy, as was her custom, came over to her Mom's house. She didn't have to say anything, because everyone knew what had happened. This had now become like a ritual – another fight; another visit from Marcy; another fight, another visit from Marcy. Seldom could they go more than two weeks without a fight. And each time Marcy came, everyone knew Buck was soon to follow; and when Buck followed, another fight ensued. Now Shelly was the one who was fed up with it all. She knew she couldn't fight Buck the way Hank had, but she could fight him another way. She was sick and tired of seeing Buck hit Marcy. When she heard Buck's old car pull up, she grabbed Marcy's arm. The two of them ran toward Shelly's old car. Shelly was determined that this was one time Buck was not going to beat Marcy. As she and Marcy hurriedly got in the old clunker, they each locked the doors. Shelly didn't even look to see if anyone was coming up the street. She just turned the wheel and pulled out into the street.

She was praying that Buck wouldn't follow them; that his anger would subside; and maybe he would go home and cool off; and maybe Marcy would be spared at least one beating at his hands. Buck was not so easily dissuaded. His anger only increased, not only toward Marcy, but toward Shelly also. He pursued them. Shelly saw him in her rear view mirror. Now she had no choice – she had to evade him somehow. She didn't know where her sudden surge of adrenaline and courage came from, but she would later attribute it to Jesus watching over her and Marcy. She knew if she stopped, Buck would start beating Marcy, and maybe even her, now that she had defied him again. With one quick glance at Marcy, raising her eyebrows as if asking for Marcy's approval, but not her permission, Shelly slammed the accelerator to the floor. As far as she was concerned right now, there were no red lights, and no stop signs; she totally ignored both.

Buck had at least five different forces working against him – fate, fury, frustration, females and a Ford – Shelly's Ford. Fate has a way of interfering with men's fury without them realizing what's happening. Buck was furious at his wife for no good reason, furious at Shelly for interfering in his affairs, and totally frustrated that he was being outsmarted by two females, and being outrun by an old Ford.   Shelly kept taking side streets and alleys, dodging street signs and fire hydrants. Marcy was hanging on for dear life, just knowing they were both going to die in an awful wreck. Finally, Shelly's female intuition kicked in. She pulled out onto the main highway where she knew the traffic would be much heavier. Buck was still in hot pursuit. Shelly quickly pulled over to the side of the highway. She waited for Buck to pull in behind her. As Buck started toward them, she and Marcy jumped out, waving their arms, with Shelly facing one direction and Marcy the other, screaming – HELP, RAPE, RAPE, RAPE!   Other motorists quickly began to stop on both sides of the highway, rushing toward the two girls. Buck saw what was happening. He ran quickly back to his car, jumped in, and squealed the tires getting away from the scene. Seeing the girls were safe, the crowd soon dispersed. Shelly and Marcy thanked all of them for stopping. Shelly drove around for a while until she thought it was safe for them to go home.

They say bad news travels fast, and the news about the big fight between Hank and Buck was one that was hard, if not impossible, to keep a secret. To this day, no one really knows how Phillip found out about it, but when he did, he took matters into his own hands. He knew that sooner or later his and Buck's paths would cross. He started coming over to visit Shelly more often. No one really knew why, but Hank and Sheila were Phillip's favorite Aunt and Uncle. Shelly already knew she was his favorite cousin. Hearing what Buck had done to Hank enraged Phillip. He was going to teach Buck a lesson he'd never forget.

Since his fight with Hank, Buck had avoided Hank like the

plague. He knew Hank didn't come home often, since he now had another "*home*" where he spent most of his time. About the only times he ever came to the Smith's home now were when Marcy would leave him after another fight. Virtually every family within ten blocks of the Smiths, in any direction, had now heard, and many had seen, some of the fights that took place there. But Buck Jones had a weird way of telling and showing folks how he felt about them. Not only was he a brutal, merciless wife-beater, a shiftless, no account father, and a dimwit; he was also very spiteful. At the low risk of exaggerating slightly, there were probably only three persons on earth who loved Buck Jones – Marcy, his mother, and himself. And of the three, he probably loved himself more than the other two put together.   He was a narcissist to the largest degree. He knew he had very few friends, and most of those only tolerated him because of what they could get from him – he could fix their cars and trucks when they broke down. Buck never really had a deep abiding love for Marcy. It would be unfair to say he hated her, but everyone who knew him and Marcy, judging from what they saw and heard, would most likely come away with that opinion. He didn't hate Marcy, but he hated her family – every one of them, and he made no secret of it. Whatever he could do to cause them pain and suffering, no matter how rude, underhanded, or callous it might be, he would do it. But there was no love lost. They hated him just as much as he hated them. But because they knew Marcy loved him, they also sometimes tolerated his manners.

One of the many spiteful ways in which he would torment them was by deliberately coming over to their house unannounced, (without Marcy's knowledge, of course), and just hang out, either in the yard, or on the porch, or even inside the house, acting as if he was one of the most beloved members of the family, knowing all the while he was totally despised. Buck had learned to invent, and display several different personalities. He could turn one personality on and another off instantaneously. If someone who didn't know him were to visit his home, he could convince them he was the most loving, caring, and nurturing Dad they'd ever seen. But the moment they left, he could turn around and beat his wife senseless for no apparent reason. Many times, in the Smith's home, he would offer to wash the dishes for Sheila. Many times he volunteered to work on Hank's vehicles without taking any pay for his labor. If he had the money, he'd go and buy pizzas for some of the parties Shelly and her friends attended. As Shelly herself once commented – "*If you were stranded in the middle of a desert, Buck would ride a bicycle out there to help you if necessary.*" And on the surface, it all appeared to be very real and sincere. Only God and Buck knew for certain how much of it was real, and how much of it was fake.

It was one of those days he had nothing better to do than to try to spite his in-laws. He'd go and visit them. But to his everlasting regret, he chose the wrong day – the day Phillip was there. Buck had heard of Phillip's reputation as a tough hombre. But since he and Phillip had never tangled, and since he, in his own mind, had soundly defeated Hank, and since he now had this sense of invincibility, and since he never left home without his thin sharp blade in his back pocket, what could possibly go wrong? Everything went wrong. Phillip was waiting for him, and Phillip was ready for him. Phillip sat in a chair on the porch, leaned back against the front of the house. Buck was about to bypass Phillip, totally ignoring him, as if he wasn't there. Phillip allowed him to get as far as the front door.   Before Buck made it into the house Phillip grabbed him, slinging him out into the yard. For a moment Buck hesitated, asking himself if he should stand and fight, or run for his life. But this was one of Marcy's relatives, which, by itself, gave him the right to hate Phillip. And now he screwed his hatred up to the highest notch. Phillip never hesitated, coming on without breaking his stride, straight at Buck. He backed Buck into the street.

Now a crowd had gathered, surrounding the two men. Buck had no choice but to stand and fight. He was both bigger and heavier than Phillip, but he was much slower. He began to circle to his left, hoping for any opening in which to get in the first blow. Phillip watched his eyes closely, closing in suddenly. Phillip struck like a coiled rattlesnake. A straight left jab from the shoulder, a wicked left hook to the jaw, and a right cross to the other jaw sent Buck sprawling, face down on the asphalt. Phillip and everyone else saw the imprint of the knife in Buck's back pocket. He had just enough composure left to reach for it. That was his last mistake. His first, and biggest mistake, was hurting one of Phillips relatives. Some of the other young men started to jump into the fray, but Phillip stopped them. He put his foot on Buck's wrist, preventing him from pulling the knife out of his pocket.   Reaching down with his left hand, he pulled the knife out himself. As Buck rolled over Phillip waved the knife in his face. Buck trembled, as the fresh memory of Hank's gushing lower lip flashed upon his conscience.

Phillip threw the knife across the street into the woods. Glaring down at Buck, he took a step backward, challenging Buck to get up and fight like a man. Buck was foolish in many ways, but not totally stupid. Phillip kicked him in the teeth, daring him to get up. Buck wiped the blood from his mouth with one hand, raising the other hand, surrendering to Phillip. Phillip humiliated him a bit farther, reminding him he wasn't so tough when it came to fighting a man as he was at fighting a woman. Before walking away, Phillip issued his last stern warning to Buck, telling him if he ever laid a hand on Hank or Marcy again, his next beating would be far worse than this one.

The warning was effective as far as Hank was concerned, but not for Marcy.

Hank was still in a relationship with his cousin's ex-wife, Barb. Supporting her expensive appetites and the needs and necessities of her five little girls continued to be a heavy burden on Hank's wallet, not to mention his nerves. Shelly wasn't sure if her Mom even knew what was going on. It would not have mattered one way or the other if she had known.   Sheila no longer cared what Hank did. It was as if he didn't really exist anymore. He was someone she once knew, but who had now become a stranger. She still spent most of her time in bed. She was afraid to venture outside the house. But one encouraging ray of hope for Shelly about her Mom was that she noticed Sheila had begun to pray a lot lately.   Shelia's sister Elizabeth had begun to stop by regularly to check on Sheila, but each time she came by it seemed another little piece of her heart had been cut away. Seeing Sheila in this condition was almost more than her own heart could take. She silently blamed Hank for everything that was happening to Sheila and her family. Elizabeth had the best of intentions for her sister, and truly wanted to help her in any way she could. She tried to encourage Sheila to fight her fears, fight her depression, fight her emotions, and fight Hank if necessary. But seeing the emptiness in Sheila's eyes, she silently acknowledged – Sheila had no fight left in her.

To accurately define and describe Sheila Smith's mental and emotional state at this point in her life would require the expertise of several professional persons, including medical doctors, psychiatrists, psychologists, therapists, counselors and others. But to say the minimum, her depression was severe, and her withdrawal from other people and the things around her was highly visible. But with all of that, there was something else, something which many of these same professional persons often either overlook, or deliberately neglect. Sheila Smith was not only exhibiting symptoms of mental and emotional disorders, her very soul was troubled – she had a spiritual problem. She still listened to one TV minister in particular, and she loved what she heard. The simple and sincere way in which he presented the Word of God touched her deeply. But he said something she had never heard any other preacher say. In fact he seemed to contradict what many other preachers seemed to imply.

What she had heard from most other preachers was to the effect that Jesus Christ is the one and only answer to every single problem that humans can have, whether mental, emotional, spiritual, financial, physical, or any other type, period. But this preacher was saying that Jesus is not the one and only answer to *every* problem, but He is the answer to mankind's *biggest* problem – the problem of sin.   He was implying that there are some problems which men and women have that other men and women are able to fix, but that there is one problem which God, and He alone, can fix. The more she listened to him, the more sense he made. Sometimes it seemed as if he was speaking directly to her, as if he somehow knew and understood her situation perfectly.

Hank made one of his rare visits to see Sheila. But he hadn't come to see Sheila, he had come to humiliate her, only what he had to say went far beyond humiliation. Sheila, and the little piece of paper that said he and Sheila were married, were standing in the way of his happiness. He wanted to marry Barbara. But Barbara wanted to marry Hank more than Hank wanted to marry her. That couldn't happen, of course, as long as he was still married to Sheila. But instead of coming right out and asking her for a divorce, he took a more indirect route, telling her he was going to have her committed to a mental institution. His twisted and self-serving reasoning was that it would be in everyone's best interest, and it would appear more humane and benevolent to have Sheila committed first, then proceed with a divorce. And he was saying all of this in front of two of his girls, Shelly and Beth! Both the girls leaped to their feet at the same time, getting up in his face, emphatically telling him he was not going to have their Mom sent anywhere. They further emphasized that they were going to tell Marcy about his little plan, and together, the three of them would see to it that Sheila would not be committed to any institution.

Shelly didn't know for certain where her own fears and weaknesses stemmed from, she only knew she still had plenty of both. At seventeen she still couldn't go upstairs by herself at night.   Neither could she stay in the house alone, day or night. This house, like all the others they had lived in, according to Sheila, was haunted. And Shelly was afraid of ghosts. There were no locks on any of the doors, and Hank had never bothered to install any, because he couldn't afford to buy the locks. The owner of the house pleaded the same excuse, claiming he didn't have the money to put locks on the doors. The girls never felt entirely safe, and Sheila couldn't have stopped an intruder if he were to walk in. But in spite of her sickness and frailty, the girls took whatever little comfort they could from her for no other reason that the fact she was their mother, older and wiser than them, and would, no doubt, defend them to the death if the situation ever called for it. With Hank gone most of the time, Shelly slept with her Mom. She felt just a bit safer there than anywhere else in the house.

The glorious and long-awaited time had come for Shelly to graduate from high school. It was glorious for more than one reason. She hated every minute of it, and now it was going to finally be behind her. And now she could just picture herself behind the wheel of that new car her Dad had promised to the first girl to graduate. Her new car turned out to be another old clunker; the only thing Hank could afford. The car didn't even have an engine when Hank bought it. He got it from an old friend who was about to sell it for scrap. Finding an engine that would fit in it, he paid another friend to install the engine. One of the many hard lessons Shelly had learned from her Dad was that when her Dad said he was going to get her something "*new*", he never meant "*brand new*", off the showroom floor, he meant "*new-to-her*".

But another even harder lesson she had learned from him was that if and when he did actually follow through on a promise, he never intended to fully keep that promise. The car he bought and patched up for her wasn't really hers. It was hers only when Hank didn't need it. The rest of the time it was his; just like the old Ford had been. But she loved the new car, and as long as she was behind the wheel, it belonged to her. The freedom of driving around town uninhibited and unrestricted, knowing she'd never see the inside of a classroom again was exhilarating. It was those times, out there by herself, doing as she pleased, that defined happiness for Shelly. But happiness for Shelly was just one of the many fleeting ghosts who came and went quickly.

Late one Saturday night the phone woke her up. It was Hank. He was drunk, and not only drunk, but laughing hilariously. She waited impatiently for him to tell her whatever it was he had called about, and the hour at which he called told her it was not good news. He and Barb had been out cruising around, bar hopping. He had wrecked the car; it was totaled. Shelly said nothing. Her tears said all that needed to be said. She knew Hank would never buy her another car. She just couldn't understand why he thought the whole thing was so funny. Her silence was intended to send Hank a message, but Hank, as always, wasn't listening. She hung up the phone while he was still laughing. She went back to bed crying.

In the same way Buck Jones invented ways to vent his spite upon Shelly and her family, Hank seemed to be forever searching for new ways to vent his cruelty to them. And he succeeded. Rushing into the house one Saturday afternoon, he threw the five report cards of Barb's five girls onto the coffee table in front of Shelly and Beth. *"Look at these,* he demanded, *all of these girls are smart, all of them make straight A's, and all of them are on the honor roll, because they have a mother who is smart, and cares about their education, and helps them with their homework."* The inference, of course, was quite clear to Beth and Shelly. Their Dad thought of them and Sheila as being stupid and unconcerned. They both knew that, had it not been for their own initiative and hard work, neither of them would have been able to go to school at all, let alone graduate. Once again, their own father had made them feel like trash.

Shelly, knowing beforehand that her own family had made no plans to celebrate her graduation, took matters into her own hands. She and her best friend Katie, who was graduating with Shelly, along with a little financial contribution from Beth, had rented a hotel suite for the occasion. They were going to have a party with some friends immediately after graduating. Shelly wished her Mom could come to her graduation, but she knew Sheila was in no condition to attend. At her graduation itself, the only family members were Hank, Beth and Marcy. Barb, Hank's girlfriend, who considered herself part of the family, wanted to come to the graduation, but Hank knew better than to let her come. He knew his girls would probably kill him and Barb both if she showed up with him. The embarrassment and humiliation would have been more than they could have endured. For once, Shelly was glad he had used better judgment, and left her behind.

When Shelly's name was called, she walked up the steps onto the stage with as much pride and dignity as a lady receiving a doctoral degree. She had done it; she was the first in her family to receive a high school diploma! Beaming with pride, she took the diploma from the principal, tossed her tassel to the side, and strutted to the end of the stage, almost dancing down the three steps onto the gym floor. Hank and her sisters gave her a round of applause. In the parking lot, Hank slipped Shelly a card with fifty dollars inside, hugging her sideways, asking – *"So, where does my proud little girl go from here?"* She told him she was going to a graduation party with some of her friends. Hank invited himself and Barb to the party, telling Shelly – *"Well, honey, we'll be there."* Shelly was devastated. She knew she was on the horns of a dilemma. It would be horrible enough for her to endure the embarrassment of having him and Barb at the party in front of her friends, but she could not endure the thought of Beth having to endure it also. She decided she would spare Beth the added humiliation – she would leave her behind.

Katie, knowing Shelly's family had made no plans to celebrate her graduation, asked her own parents to invite Shelly to go with them to a restaurant for dinner before the party. Katie's parents said it was a great idea. Arriving in front of the big restaurant, Shelly gasped. She had never seen anything as fancy as this. And she was even more impressed with the inside. Everything was perfect. All the tables were elegantly set, and perfectly spaced. Adjacent to the dining area was the ballroom, adorned with crystal chandeliers, a full orchestra, and marble floor. The sheer elegance of the place took her breath away. For a brief moment, she was Cinderella, being twirled around the ballroom by her handsome prince. It was an evening she would forever cherish, and never forget.

But now it was back to the real world – the world she was used to. And it was time to go to the party. Shelly was so delighted that Phillip was there, along with Matt and several more of Phillip's friends. Hank and Barb hadn't come yet, and Shelly was hoping this would be one of those times that Hank would be himself, and break his promise.   But her gut told her they would be there, sooner or later. Hank and Barb came to the party, but not to celebrate Shelly's graduation. Hank was broke, and he and Barb wanted to do a little partying of their own. As Shelly mingled with her friends, Hank found a chair in a corner. Barb, pretending she didn't want to trouble anyone by asking them to bring her a chair, sat in Hank's lap. But as if that weren't humiliating enough, Hank motioned for Shelly to come over to where they were sitting. He didn't hesitate at all, telling Shelly he really needed that fifty dollars back. Shelly slapped the money into his open hand, walking away, disappointed that he would do that, but also glad that he and his girlfriend were leaving. Suddenly, her craving for cold beer kicked in. She was going to get drunk.   She just didn't care anymore.

Upon the advice of her TV minister, Shelia started having a Christian counselor come to the house and talk to her. Shelly was just a bit skeptical at first, but gave the man the benefit of a doubt, praying he might be able to help her Mom somehow. But her skepticism was more than just a bit of doubt in the man's ability to help her Mom, she simply did not trust men at all. A strange man she had never met, or even heard of, coming to see her Mom, in the absence of her Dad or any other member of the family just didn't sit well with Shelly. To her happy surprise, however, she could see a visible, positive change in Sheila after only a few sessions with the counselor.

Beth had also noticed a slight change in Sheila's attitude lately. It wasn't anything to make the girls shout for joy yet, but now, in their Mom's eyes, they were seeing a tiny glimmer of hope.

Sheila had not stepped outside the house in more than a year. The house, from everyone else's perspective, had become Sheila's prison. To Sheila, it was her only refuge from all the overwhelming horrors of the outside world. In her mind, Hank was now a non-entity. His few and sudden appearances were just that – appearances, apparitions. To her he was this shadowy phantom who suddenly appeared, then left just as suddenly, and each time he left, a few dollars magically appeared on the mantle over the fireplace. One can only imagine the horror that gripped Beth's heart, coming home from school, and finding Sheila was not there. She dropped her books on the floor, running frantically from room to room, from top to bottom, searching every closet, looking under the beds, searching the bathroom, screaming – *"Mommy, Mommy, where are you?"* With each room she searched, and not finding her Mom, she just knew she was going to find Sheila dead in the next room, probably from suicide.

Beth ran out the front door screaming and crying, running down the street from house to house, asking if any of the neighbors had seen her Mom. Finally one neighbor, Mrs. Spurlock, calmed Beth's fears, telling her she had seen Sheila walking around the neighborhood earlier that morning. She and Beth walked hurriedly back to Sheila's house. Sheila was sitting on the sofa, smiling, watching her favorite preacher on TV. Beth's joy and relief cannot be described in words alone. Hugging her Mom tightly, she asked quietly – *"Mom, where have you been? I was so scared."* Sheila held her daughter close, replying - *" I just went for a little walk honey.*

My counselor said it would be good therapy for me to venture outside for a while. And you know what? He was right. I feel a lot better now."

College had never been in the picture for Shelly, but some of her friends told her that her high school diploma would help her get a better job. They were right. Dressing up in her nicest clothes, she applied for a job at the bank. She noticed the gentleman conducting the interview had roaming eyes. He asked if she had a high school diploma. She had it with her. She was hired on the spot as an encoder. Leaving the bank all smiles, she wondered which factor had contributed the most in landing this job – her diploma, or her dimensions.   Not wanting to flatter herself, she concluded it was a little of both. She didn't know it at the time, but not only had her dimensions contributed somewhat toward her new job, they had also gotten the attention of her future husband, who happened to be walking down the same street as Shelly approached her car.

Shelly's paycheck from the restaurant provided her with not much more than the bare necessities of life. She could afford to buy decent clothes, but not the nicer attire she would need, and want, to work in a bank. At her interview she had noticed that none of the ladies working there wore casual clothes, but mostly expensive slacks or knee-length skirts or dresses. They were all very professional-looking. Her savings account had dwindled considerably. She and Beth were now the breadwinners at home. Together they bought all the food, and paid all the bills. Shelly never had to spend much on her drinking – the boys she hung out with kept her in beer.   Once again, Marcy took matters into her own hands – literally. Knowing Shelly needed nicer clothes for her new job, Marcy acquired them for her, using her *"five-finger discount."*   Shelly asked no questions, and offered no objections.

She showed up at the bank looking every bit as lovely and professional as any of the other ladies. In fact, she turned some heads. Having thought of herself as poor, ugly white trash from the poor side of town for so long was something not easily dismissed. But now, working beside these classy ladies in a friendly environment, and making more money than she ever had before, it made her feel like maybe she was worth something after all. And for the first time she could remember, even Hank paid her a compliment, praising her for landing a job that paid decent money, and would no doubt lead to a great career.

With the counseling Shelia was getting, and the medications the doctor had prescribed for her, her mental, emotional and physical health seemed to be improving almost daily. She still had a long road ahead of her, but she was far better now than she had been in years. Her counselor, Reuben Chandler, who she had now come to know as Brother Chandler, was more than just a counselor; he had become her friend, one who genuinely cared about her and her family. Somewhere in every counseling session he'd had with Sheila, he made it a point to ask her about her relationship to God. And he never failed to share with her his personal testimony of how Jesus Christ had changed his own life. It soon became evident to Sheila that Reuben was different from any other person, man or woman, she had met so far. His total honesty, sincerity, and transparency made her feel perfectly as ease with him. He allowed her to talk to him, and he listened. Not once did he ever insinuate or suggest a condemning attitude toward her. But when he did speak, Sheila was willing to listen, because he had something to say – something that made sense. And the one thing, more than any other, which spoke to Sheila's heart and to her situation, was that God was speaking through Reuben, revealing to her what her deepest need really was – the need of a spiritual re-birth.

There in her living room, one afternoon, with Reuben by her side, Sheila Smith bowed her head, asking the Lord Jesus to forgive her of all her sins, and to come into her heart. And He did.

Beth still worked at the fast food restaurant where she and Shelly had worked together. Shelly really missed working with Beth and her friends. And as much as she enjoyed working at the bank now, it did have at least one negative aspect for her – she had too much time on her hands, too much time to think, and for Shelly that was not a good thing. She was eighteen now, and much more mature than she and been a year ago. But from her childhood traumas she had carried a lot of emotional baggage with her into her adolescence. With too much time to think, her thoughts drifted in the wrong direction, back to her childhood, and the days and nights filled with horror, hunger and pain. Dwelling upon some of the more sordid scenes, she sometimes went into panic, sitting at her desk. She was still afraid of the dark, afraid of being alone, and afraid of dying in some bloody, horrific manner.

She still slept with Sheila at home. But the bathroom was upstairs. To get to the bathroom she had to go through the bedroom where she and Beth had slept when they were younger. Off to one side of the bedroom was another much smaller room with a window with no curtains. Shelly always dreaded walking past that room at night when the moon was out. The light of the moon filtering through the dirty window cast an eerie glow into the room, across the narrow hall, and into the bedroom, but not all the way to the bathroom.   Sitting on top of an old dresser was a large poster. No one had even bothered to take the poster out of its original white plastic covering. The moonlight, shining upon the plastic covering, and barely showing the outline of the poster itself, could play tricks on a child's imagination, especially a child who was already frightened. It was a young woman who climbed the stairs that night, but a little child who hesitated at the top of the stairs, quickly finding the light switch, turning on the light. Even with the light on, Shelly still dreaded going past that little room. Her fears mounted with each step toward the bathroom. The moonlight cast its eerie glow upon the big poster. Shelly gasped at what she thought she saw. Staring out at her through the plastic of the poster was the face of an evil spirit. She froze in sheer terror. She thought her heart had stopped beating. Her next thought told her she must be possessed by the evil spirit. Her scream pierced the night like the cry of a banshee.

She ran down the stairs screaming. Hank was there on one of his rare visits, talking to Sheila. As Shelly stammered, trying to tell them what she had seen, Sheila ran to her, hugging her, holding her close, trying to reassure her that everything was alright. Hank, glancing from Sheila to Shelly, remarked – *"You make me sick Shelly, you're just like your Mom."* With that, he left Sheila and Shelly standing there. Shelly begged her Mom to please help her pray the evil spirit out of the house. Sheila was willing to do whatever it took to calm her daughter's fear. She lit two candles, handing one to Shelly. Together they climbed the stairs slowly, holding each other's hand, each of them carrying a lighted candle. At the top of the stairs Shelly hesitated again, not wanting to go near that room. She stood trembling as Sheila squeezed her hand, and began praying out loud, asking Jesus to banish the evil spirit from her home.

Something about the humble, sincere manner in which her Mom talked to Jesus touched Shelly's heart. She spoke to Him as if He was her dearest friend, standing right there with them. Shelly's fear vanished as suddenly as it had come. She was not possessed by an evil spirit, she was loved by an awesome God, and a loving Mother. The fear of being possessed was gone, but the hurt of being abandoned by her Dad in a moment when she needed him the most had not gone.   Hank Smith harbored a loathing for people who were either sick or fearful. To him, sickness and fear in others were both weaknesses, and he despised weakness of any kind. He was quick to condemn it in others, but unable to recognize it in himself.   The following day Shelia got Shelly an appointment with her counselor, Mr. Chandler.

Hank never talked to anyone in his family about what went on between him and his girlfriend Barb, and no one ever asked, because no one cared.   He still came and went like he had ever since he had started seeing her. Each time he came home, he left a few dollars on the mantle, as if that somehow still made him the man of the house, and gave him the right to come and go as he pleased, and still continue his affair with another woman. But his relationship with Barb was not as great as he pretended it was. Now she was pushing him to divorce Sheila, and marry her. The pressure was becoming heavier and heavier with each passing day. The rare visits he made to Sheila's house sparked just a bit of suspicion with Barb. She began to accuse him of going home to sleep with his estranged wife, then coming back to her. And now he had run out of explanations. There was only one way to relieve the pressure – he'd get drunk again.

What neither Sheila nor Barb knew was that Hank was cheating on them both, every chance he got, and driving a cab created a lot of chances to do it. He was still sleeping around with the wives and girlfriends of his friends and co-workers, while juggling back and forth between Sheila and Barb. Sheila, of course, would not allow him to touch her, let alone get in her bed. But alcohol has its own code of ethics. It makes men laugh, it makes men cry, it makes men do stupid things they would not do otherwise. That's why they call it *"spirits"*, because once it takes control of a man's brain, it talks to him, like an unseen spirit, telling him what to do and where to go. Tonight the *"spirits"* were telling Hank Smith to go home to his family, which, on the surface, sounds like a good thing. But when the demon spirit of whiskey does the talking, it means the one to whom he is talking is not in control of all his faculties. He really doesn't mean to do what his brain is telling him to do. He is only obeying the voice of the *"spirits"*.

Hank half stumbled into the house. The first person he saw was Shelly. In broken English he asked her to call Barb and tell her he didn't want to be with her anymore. Shelly had mixed emotions about doing it, but to pacify him she picked up the phone and dialed Barb's number. She told Barb exactly what Hank had instructed her to say to her. Barb nearly exploded, demanding she put Hank on the phone immediately. Hank groaned as Shelly handed him the phone, disappointed that Barb had not accepted Shelly's speech, and now he would have to face the music himself. He tried to cover the earpiece so as to prevent Shelly from hearing Barb's loud voice. Shelly wasn't trying to hear the conversation, because she didn't care what it was about. Hank and Barb talked a few minutes, then Hank hung up the phone, dropped a few dollars on the mantle, and stumbled out the door to his car.

A few days later Hank returned, sober, and with a lawyer. He let his lawyer do almost all the talking for him, while he stood there sheepishly listening, staring at the floor. He couldn't look any of his family in the face. The lawyer stood over Sheila, reading the papers to her. Shelly was eighteen now, and Beth was sixteen and a half. Neither of them could make much sense of the mixture of English and Latin the lawyer was using to tell Sheila what the papers contained. But the one part they all understood was that Hank wanted a divorce. Sheila couldn't wait to sign the papers. What she didn't know was that she was not only granting Hank a divorce, but she was also signing away all rights to child support and alimony.   With her signature on the papers, Hank stepped over to the mantle, making sure the lawyer saw him, leaving eight dollars on the mantle. He and the lawyer hurriedly said goodbye.

Later, when Sheila received a large manila envelope full of papers from the civil court, she had Marcy come over and read them to her in the presence of Beth and Shelly. The language was quite clear to everyone now. Sheila and the girls would have to fend for themselves. Sheila wasn't nearly as upset as the girls thought she ought to be about it. She calmly reminded the girls that this really didn't change anything as far as their finances were concerned, because Hank had never supported his family before, so the only thing these papers did was to make it legal. But Beth's heart was broken. She had gotten used to seeing her Dad come and go, and she knew he was fooling around with other women. But to her, this was the lowest he had ever gone – deliberately and totally abandoning his wife and children, and tricking his wife into signing papers, officially legalizing his abandonment of them with them looking on, oblivious to what he was doing.

Hank moved all his belongings out of the house this time, moving in with Barb. He still dropped by occasionally, always leaving a few dollars on the mantle for Sheila's cigarettes. But the thing that really cut to the heart of the girls was the fact that Hank was now providing Barb and her five girls with all the things he never provided for his own flesh and blood. He provided his new family with food, clothing, shelter, toys, and an education, things his own family had to obtain any way they could, and a lot of that came by way of Marcy's "*ingenuity*".

But often, when we think matters couldn't get any worse – they do! Sheila's sister Elizabeth and her family had been evicted from their home for non-payment of rent. With nowhere else to go, cousin Phillip moved in with Shelly, Beth and Sheila, while Elizabeth, her husband, Phillip Sr., and her other children moved in with Marcy and Buck.

Having seven additional persons move in on such short notice naturally presented several problems for everyone, especially in the mornings, when more than one person needed to use the bathroom at the same time. There was Marcy, Buck, their two children, Elizabeth, Phillip Sr., and five of their children, making a total of eleven persons in one house. But family is family, and Marcy was determined to make the best of a bad situation. She could never turn anyone away from her door, family or otherwise. Phillip Sr. was a construction worker whose livelihood depended upon the weather and the economy. When he worked he made good money, and when he made good money, he gambled, losing most of his wages. Between his sparse income and Buck's odd jobs, there was no way the two of them could adequately support their respective families. Marcy and Aunt Elizabeth took matters into their own hands. Elizabeth served as Marcy's lookout while Marcy shoplifted from one store, then Marcy served and Elizabeth's lookout while Elizabeth stole from another store. Between the two of them, they furnished their own families, and Sheila's family with food, clothing, school supplies, toys, feminine necessities, and other necessary household items. The two of them had an agreement that if one of them got caught shoplifting, she would take the rap, and not implicate her partner. This, of course, served a dual purpose – only one would go to jail, while the other could continue to steal on her own.

Marcy was the first to get caught. Marcy didn't know it at the time, but virtually every store in town now had her on their "*watch*" list. Her description had been passed around from store to store, warning store managers and other personnel to be on the lookout for her. With her stunning figure and beautiful appearance, she was easy to spot. Some days, of course, were more "*profitable*" than others, and Marcy had quickly taught Aunt Elizabeth which were the best days of the week to go shoplifting. They had developed a set of verbal and hand signals between them to signal to each other when no one was looking. They pretended to be total strangers, walking about six feet apart along the aisles. Elizabeth kept an eye on the end of the aisle and the mirrors, while Marcy, using Elizabeth as a shield, quickly dropped items into her oversized purse. After stealing whatever she thought she could get away with, Marcy would signal to Elizabeth by zipping her purse shut. Then they would both pick out one or two cheap items which they would pay for at the checkout counter.

This system worked quite well for several months. When they were satisfied they had stolen enough stuff to last for a month or two, they would take a short break from stealing. But sometimes Marcy, being a little too sure of herself, would venture out alone, leaving Elizabeth to tend to all the children at home while she "*shopped*" for some "*specialty*" items, like new drapes, pillow cases, and silverware. Without Elizabeth to shield her, she got caught stealing three times. She was arrested three times, and three times she was let go without any punishment. It turned out that Hank, her Dad, having worked inside the criminal justice system, had some "*connections*" in high places, one of which was a certain Judge. On the third offense, the Judge sternly warned Hank and Marcy that this would be the last time he would be lenient with Marcy. Hank took the Judge seriously; Marcy didn't.

Buck and Uncle Phil were both running low on cigarettes, and there was not enough money between them to buy a single pack. All Buck had to do was show Marcy his nearly-empty cigarette pack, and she was off to the store with her big purse. Without Elizabeth as her lookout, she quickly stuffed two cartons of cigarettes into her purse. The store manager saw her in one of the large opaque mirrors hanging in a corner. Marcy zipped her purse, picked up a toothbrush, and headed toward the checkout. When she laid the toothbrush on the counter, a policeman came through the door. The store manager nodded toward Marcy's big purse. Opening the purse, he asked Marcy if she had a receipt for the two cartons of cigarettes. Marcy held out her hands for him to cuff her, smiling as the officer quoted her rights to her. She was sure her Dad could get her out of trouble one more time. Hank called the Judge, asking him to be lenient with Marcy one more time, but this time the Judge refused, reminding Hank that he had been too lenient with her already, and may have even contributed to her habit by his leniency. After pleading *"no contest"* to the charge, and receiving a good tongue-lashing from the Judge, she was sentenced to six months incarceration in a Women's Workhouse.

While in the workhouse, Marcy made friends easily, mostly with the male guards, and for more than one reason. Not only did they admire the way she filled out her clothes, they soon fell in love with her cooking also. It soon became obvious to the other women that Marcy was receiving *"special treatment"* from the guards. Most of them assumed it was because the guards were receiving *"special treatment"* from Marcy. Their definition of special treatment, of course, meant that Marcy was probably giving sexual favors to the guards. Their assumption, however, like most assumptions, was false.

Marcy's six-month absence created some major difficulties

for her family, and for Aunt Elizabeth's family. Elizabeth was too afraid to continue shoplifting without Marcy. This, of course, meant that both Buck and Phil had to step up and do whatever was necessary to provide food and shelter for two families. They began actively searching for work anywhere they could get a day's work. Elizabeth took care of all the children, only visiting Marcy whenever Buck or Phil was home to watch the children. Thankfully, Carolyn was now big enough to do a bit of cooking, babysitting and housecleaning.   It was very difficult for Shelly to visit Marcy in the workhouse. Although it was called a workhouse, to Shelly, it was a women's prison.

Six months of being cooped up inside four walls can seem like a much longer time for some folks, but not for Marcy. For her, the time flew by. She kept busy every possible moment. When she wasn't cooking or serving, she was cleaning or doing laundry, or making new friends. After everyone got to know her better, she became a source of comfort, laughter, and companionship to nearly every person she met. There were a few, however, who were impossible to get close to, no matter how hard Marcy tried to befriend them. Six months of being cooped up inside four walls for shoplifting would probably have cured most women of the habit, but not Marcy. Two days after being released from the workhouse, she and Aunt Elizabeth were right back at it again, partners in crime, just like old times.

Phillip had a lot of friends, boys and girls, most of whom were around his own age. Some of them attended a place known only as the Worship House. Phillip had gone with them a few times, and was now attending regularly.   Knowing Shelly was going through a rough time, he thought it might be beneficial in some way for her to visit the Worship House with him, and meet all the other girls and boys. On her first visit, Shelly was quite impressed with the size of the crowd of young people. Phillip introduced her to all the ones he knew. Shelly quickly made friends with two of the girls. She couldn't help but notice that many of the young people were actually living there, in the Worship House. It was sectioned off into several bedrooms, a large kitchen, an even larger dining room, a huge sanctuary, and one office, which was always locked, and restricted to everyone except one man - Stuart. Stuart was the founder, proprietor, and final authority to whom all questions and issues ultimately came. He had his own private plane, in which he traveled from one Worship House to another. Shelly soon learned there were scores of these Worship Houses scattered across several states, all of which were under the exclusive control of Stuart.

There was not a lot of high pressure put on visiting youngsters to actually join the congregation, but there was plenty of gentle persuasion. Under the direction of a designated leader, designated by Stuart, the young people were sent out into the city and county, wearing badges bearing the slogan – "Get Smart-Get Saved". Every individual was encouraged to walk up to total strangers, and "*evangelize*" them, telling them about Jesus, and how to be saved. So far their method was working quite well, with their numbers swelling weekly. Shelly and Phillip only wanted to enjoy the company and fellowship of all the other young people, but not necessarily get too deeply involved with their religious activities just yet. And for the moment, there seemed to be no real pressure for them to join in. Shelly was more open and receptive to the teaching than Phillip, because Phillip, for the most part, just wanted to meet beautiful girls there.

All the studies were centered around Jesus Christ and His Words. While on the premises, all other chit chat was to be kept to a minimum. They were to focus on God, prayer, and the Bible. There was no degree of physical contact allowed between boys and girls. A few of the prerequisites for joining included, but were not limited to – moving into the Worship House; keeping a steady job; buying your own food and other necessities; abstaining from all secular activities that did not involve God in some way - including going to movies and bowling, and sending a portion of your salary or wages to Stuart every month. Shelly had some serious reservations about committing to the group, but at the same time, she reasoned that maybe she actually needed some imposed restrictions on her life – perhaps it would teach her more responsibility, and help her to more readily accept a little accountability also. She decided she would stay a few nights, and just see how things went. She also considered that maybe this was where God wanted her to be right now.

In the meantime Phillip started bringing another new friend, Tony, over to their house. Shelly noticed five things about Tony the first time she met him – his big "*afro*" hairdo, his skinny frame, his shyness, his permanent smile, and his long green army coat. It turned out Tony didn't live very far from Shelly. He worked full time at the Catholic Church where he and his family attended faithfully. He made no secret of the fact that his parents were devout Catholics.   Shelly was not attracted to Tony in any way at all – there simply was no "*chemistry*" between them. But both Shelly and Beth, now 18 and 17 respectively, were, to put it mildly, "*feisty*". They were also very well-built. Like her sister Marcy, Shelly was well-endowed by her Creator in all the right places. Beth was slimmer than Shelly, but every bit as lovely. Whenever one of them walked by, no red-blooded boy could keep his eyes straight ahead for very long. And now they were simply in the mood for a bit of feminine flaunting, flirtation, and fun, all of which was intended to see which one could most easily turn Tony's head. Of the two, Shelly was definitely the most outgoing and feisty.

At that time, miniskirts were all the rage, and as some of Shelly's and Beth's male friends often commented as they were walking away – *"Them gals sho nuff know how to make a skirt look good."*

Sometimes Tony would come over when Phillip wasn't there. It was during these times when Shelly and Beth (but mostly Shelly) would use their God-given endowments to engage Tony's attention. Shelly still worked at the bank, where she was allowed to wear slacks, dresses, or skirts. Miniskirts were not encouraged, but neither were they entirely prohibited, so long as the bank manager determined that the girls wearing them were not *"showing too much leg".* Coming home from work, and seeing Tony there, she and Beth wasted no time in playing their little game. They both pretended to really like Tony, but they also pretended to be fighting over which one of them was going to sit with him.   Tony had no idea what they were doing, or if he did, he did a good job of pretending he didn't.   The girls, without coming right out and saying so, were acting as if they were interested in a boyfriend/girlfriend relationship with Tony. Shelly, of course, took the bolder initiative.

Sporting her favorite miniskirt in front of Tony, she deliberately passed in front of him as closely as possible without actually coming in contact with him, making sure he got a full view of her legs. For Tony, there was no escape – he was being intimidated by the wiles, and the wiggles of a woman. And just when he thought he could not be more embarrassed, Shelly turned suddenly, parking her pretty packaging in his lap. With her legs crossed, and her arm around his neck, she whispered – *"Call your Mom and tell her you're bringing me home for supper."* The heat from Tony's red face would have warmed half the city. For a moment, half of him was in Heaven, and the other half in Hell.

No girl this gorgeous had ever been this close to him, and no girl had ever embarrassed him this much.

With the passing of time, and a few more visits from Tony, Shelly began to have real feelings for him. He had recovered somewhat from the shock of her sitting in his lap, and now they both silently agreed that it had been just a flirtatious joke between friends. But now there was some genuine chemistry between them, and both of them felt it, in their hearts. Everyone knew that Shelly was Phillip's favorite cousin, and neither of them tried to make a secret of it. But once in a while Phillip, just to show Beth that he liked her too, would ask her to come along with him and some of his friends, whether it was just a joy ride on the outskirts of town, or a trip to the mall. This time it was to the mall, and Tony also tagged along for the ride. Sauntering around from one shop to another, Beth saw the most beautiful dress displayed in a store window. She stared at it a long time, knowing she could never afford a dress like that, but still imagining herself in it. Tony saw the look in her eye, but said nothing.

One Saturday morning Shelly and Beth heard a gentle tap on the front door. Then they heard rapid footsteps on the front porch. Hurrying to the door, they saw a gift-wrapped package on the porch. The tag had Beth's name on it, but there was nothing to indicate who it was from. Opening the box together, they pulled out a beautiful light-brown, long-sleeved dress with flared cuffs and a pattern of tiny flowers. Shelly knew Beth didn't have a boyfriend, and she knew the dress could not be a gift from their Dad. There weren't many candidates left – in fact there were only two – Phillip or Tony. Beth, of course, knew exactly who had bought the dress for her – Tony. She began to tell Shelly about her trip to the mall with Phillip and Tony, and how Tony had seen her staring at the dress. Shelly's heart sank.

She knew that if Tony had feelings for Beth, and Beth for him, then she didn't stand a chance with Tony. Beth was reading Shelly's thoughts. She quickly assured Shelly that she had absolutely no designs on Tony. Shelly thanked her for that assurance, but now longed for that same assurance from Tony – that he had no designs on Beth. With each visit from Tony, she now began to act more like a lady in love than a girl with an infatuation. Tony got the message, loud and clear.

Shelly still attended the Worship House fairly regularly. It was a place where she could find both fellowship and solitude. This time the place was abuzz with excitement. Some of the girls gathered around Shelly, excitedly telling her they were going to Pennsylvania to see and hear Stuart himself. Shelly wanted to meet this Stuart face to face. She decided she would go with them. Both Tony and Matt offered her their sleeping bags, because everyone would be sleeping on the floor of a huge warehouse. She took both bags, but fully intended to sleep in the one Tony gave her. Arriving in Pennsylvania, the place was packed with people from all over the country. There was barely enough room for another sleeping bag on the floor. When Stuart walked in the whole crowd applauded and cheered, chanting his name. It made Shelly very uncomfortable. It seemed to her these people were almost worshiping Stuart. His charismatic personality and eloquent oratory did nothing for her spirit. She was glad when it was over, and she missed Tony desperately. They had not become a couple yet, but right now he was the only man in the world she wanted to be with.

She was glad when they loaded up the van and headed back home. She thought of Tony the whole trip back to Ohio. Tony was still very shy around women, but now he found himself far more comfortable being around Shelly than with any other female.

But he was still too afraid of saying or doing the wrong thing to approach her with his feelings. When they were apart he thought of everything he wanted to say to her, but when they were together he couldn't say it. Shelly waited patiently for him to come out of his shell. Finally he decided he would show her how he felt instead of just telling her – the first chance he got. That chance came one day when Shelly and two of her friends were driving Tony home from Shelly's house. Shelly and Tony were in the back seat. Tony had his arm around Shelly's shoulder. Suddenly, without any warning or words, he turned toward her, pulling her closer to him, planting a passionate kiss on her lips. It was shocking, to say the least, but the most pleasant shock of her life. They were a couple now. They went on dates as often as possible.

Shelly invited Tony to go with her to the Worship House to meet everyone. Tony was Catholic, and cared nothing for the manner in which these folks immediately tried to convert him. One night when Shelly was there without Tony, he called, asking for Shelly. The young lady who took the call told Shelly she should not be talking to Tony, let alone dating him. She said Tony was a wolf, who was trying to steal and destroy God's sheep. With that Shelly knew it was time for her to leave the Worship House. She was not giving up Tony for them, she did not like the way they tried to control her life, and she did not appreciate them calling Tony a wolf. That gut feeling she had experienced when listening to Stuart in Pennsylvania had been a warning. She now realized she had been involved in a cult which worshiped its self-proclaimed prophet instead of God. She thanked God, and Tony, for showing her the truth.

It was all Shelly could do to continue working at the bank. It was too quiet, and too professional for her. Around the other ladies, most of whom had a college degree, fancy clothes, and husbands who picked them up in fancy cars, her feelings of inferiority and insecurity all crowded in on her. At work they were constantly bragging to one another about their fancy homes, their expensive furniture, and their high-yield investments. And Shelly noticed the only times they did their boasting was when they knew she was listening. They were deliberately trying to degrade and debase her. Many of them made it a point to remind her that, compared to their own lucrative careers, her menial job as an encoder was beneath them. She knew that all of them knew she was from the poor side of town, and they never let her forget it. Sometimes she just wanted to cry. Other times she wanted to run away. One day she did just that. Telling a co-worker she had an emergency at home, she clocked out and drove home, panic-stricken every mile of the way. Arriving home, she went straight to the nearest corner of the room, where she sat down and cried till Sheila found her there. Sheila came to her, putting her arms around her, asking her what was wrong. Shelly tried to explain her fears and emotions to her Mom, but she just couldn't find the words to express what she was feeling inside. At a few minutes past 9:00 a.m. the next morning she called the bank, telling them she would not be back to work.

Shelly had quit drinking just before she met Tony. She was afraid to drink anymore. She was afraid to do a lot of things. She was afraid to confide her fears to Tony, thinking he would not understand. But she wanted him to know. She wanted the man she loved to know everything about her. It took some doing, but she prayed for the courage to tell Tony everything. To her pleasant surprise, Tony listened to every word, holding her hands in his, smiling, and assuring her that what she had told him didn't change his feelings for her at all – he understood. She felt as if a heavy boulder had been lifted from her heart. It was difficult for her to accept, but for the first time in her life she was in a real relationship, with a real man, who had real feelings for her, and accepted her for who she was.

Some men don't really become men until late in life, while others never grow up into manhood. Far too many are still boys walking around in men's bodies. Tony Davidson was a man - a good man with a heart of gold at the age of seventeen. He couldn't bear seeing others suffer when he had the means to relieve their suffering, if only a little, or for a short time. He was the man who would literally give you the shirt off his back if you needed it. And without being told, he knew Shelly and her family were suffering financially. He was by no means rich, and sometimes had to deny himself many of the luxuries other men could easily afford. But whatever he had, he was willing to share, especially with anyone he knew was trying to do their best with what they had, and not looking for a handout. He knew Shelly and her family had it rough financially, especially with Shelly's Dad only stopping by once in a while, and leaving a few dollars on the mantle. And now, with Shelly temporarily unemployed, the family was going without food and other necessities in order to pay the rent. And now they were behind on that also. Tony didn't want to embarrass Shelly by asking if he could help her and her family financially. He knew what her answer would be. Seeing the few dollars Hank would leave on the mantle from time to time, he began to secretly add some money of his own to the money on the mantle. It didn't take long for Shelly and Beth to catch on to what he was doing. As the amount of money increased they knew their Dad never left that much. The moment Shelly figured out what Tony was doing, she took the money to him, telling him she knew it was him who was leaving the extra money, and demanding that he take it back. Tony refused to take the money, explaining to her that he felt some kind of responsibility to help them. Shelly could read him like a book.

It wasn't responsibility that made Tony do what he did – it was his love for Shelly and her family. Shelly took the first job she could find, as a waitress in a restaurant.   She made more in tips than she made in wages. Now, between her and Beth, they somehow managed to get by without being evicted from their home.

Shelia's condition, physically, mentally and emotionally was steadily improving. She was now able to go for longer walks around the neighborhood, sometimes even stopping to chat for a few minutes with a neighbor. But she still couldn't bring herself to mingle with a group of more than three or four persons. Now it was time for Beth to graduate from high school. More than anything else in the world, she wished her Mom could be there to see it. But she quickly dismissed the notion, knowing Sheila wasn't quite ready for a crowd that size. As she left home to go to the graduation, Sheila gave her a big hug, not saying anything; her own heart was aching, wishing she could somehow find the courage to conquer her fear of crowds, and attend Beth's graduation. Beth just smiled at her Mom as they each nodded to the other, the little nod conveying all that needed to be said – they both understood why Sheila couldn't go.

As the graduation ceremony proceeded, Sheila sat on the sofa at home, crying, totally frustrated, and angry at herself for not having the courage to go to Beth's graduation. It was just one more special event in the life of one of her children that she would have to miss.   One by one the names were called in alphabetical order, as the students marched proudly across the stage, receiving their diplomas and flipping their tassels from right to left. Shelly, Marcy and Hank watched with anticipation, waiting for Beth's name to be called. Finally the moment arrived. As Beth took her first step up toward the stage, two voices called out her name simultaneously – **_Elizabeth Smith_**!   Every head in the auditorium turned to see Sheila, standing just inside the entrance, her eyes focused on nothing but her daughter, reaching for her diploma. The expression on Beth's face at that moment defined joy better than any dictionary ever could. There was no girl in the world any happier than Beth Smith. She ran from the stage, running straight to her Mom. Mom and daughter held each other in a tight embrace, tears of joy streaming down their faces.   After a long embrace, again they nodded to each other, which was their way of saying everything without saying anything. Knowing this was very hard for her Mom, it was the best gift her Mom could ever give her. Beth was still her "*baby girl*". By now, Shelly, Marcy and Hank had made their way to where Beth and Sheila were standing, each of them giving Beth a big hug. Sheila and Hank refused to make eye contact.

As it had been with Shelly's graduation, so it was with Beth's – her family couldn't afford to throw her a party, or take her out to dinner in celebration of her accomplishment. But in Beth's heart, she'd had the finest graduation ceremony any girl could hope for. Shelly grieved for the fact that they couldn't afford Beth a party, but there was nothing she could do.

Tony was now spending more and more time at Shelly's house. They spent every possible moment they could spare with each other. Their relationship was growing stronger, and their love for each other was growing deeper with every passing day. With Phillip living with them, Shelly was a bit surprised that he hadn't objected to her dating Tony since he had been so protective of her before. But Tony wasn't like most of the other guys he knew. He trusted and respected Tony, and it was quite evident that he and Shelly were deeply in love. And besides, Shelly was old enough to make her own decisions.

Little by little, Shelly and Tony kept filling in little details about their past to each other. Neither of them deliberately pried into the other's past, but they both voluntarily confided in each other.   Shelly wanted Tony to know the whole truth about her past, hoping that doing so would not change his opinion of her, but if it did, then he would have the option of accepting her with all her baggage, or walking away.   Tonight she told Tony about Matt, including the fact that Matt had kissed her once, but quickly explaining that Matt was drunk at the time, and how the kiss had made her sick to her stomach. Tony just laughed it off as nothing. But then Shelly decided to tell him about the incident with the pool sticks. Knowing Tony's mild manner, she didn't think there was any harm in sharing it with him. Tony listened quietly, showing no emotion whatsoever as Shelly described the incident.

One night Phillip came home with Matt behind him. It was obvious Matt was drunk again.   Shelly was sitting on the couch with Tony, his arm around her shoulder. Matt stumbled over to the couch, plopping down on the other side of Shelly, putting his arm around her also. Shelly froze instantly. Matt was feeling the back of Tony's head, thinking he was feeling Shelly's hair. It would be the last time he ever touched Shelly. Tony grabbed his arm, roughly slinging it off Shelly's shoulder. No one said anything. Matt got up and walked into another room. For now, that was the end of it, nothing bad happened. Tony was very quiet, and no one ever knew exactly what he was thinking. What he was thinking was that he didn't want to beat up a man who was drunk, and incapable of defending himself in a fair fight. He would wait till Matt was sober.

A week later, Shelly, Tony and Sheila were sitting in the same room when Phillip came in with Matt again.   This time Matt seemed sober. Tony didn't say a word, keeping his eye on

Matt the whole time. Matt walked into the kitchen, picked up the phone and was talking to someone. Matt was just over six feet tall, Tony was five feet – nine inches. Without a word to anyone, Tony jumped up from the couch, walked into the kitchen, and proceeded to tap out Morse Code on Matt's face with his fists. Matt back-peddled, but Tony closed in. Every punch landed. Matt's face was now a bloody mess. He never stood a chance against Tony's rapid punches. Phillip and Shelly ran in to try to stop the one-sided match, but Tony was already satisfied that Matt had had enough. He finished him off by shoving him out the back door, into the yard, on his rear. Both Phillip and Shelly were somewhat in shock. They had never seen this side of Tony. They never dreamed he was capable of this degree of violence. There was a short silence, with Phillip and Tony nodding to each other in mutual respect, each man hoping he would never have to tangle with the other. Tony put his hands in the pockets of his long army coat, and walked away, saying nothing to anyone. Shelly ran back into the house, grabbing a towel, coming back to wipe the blood from Matt's face. Later that same night, when Tony presumed Matt would be gone, he came back to Shelly's house. Shelly asked him why he had beaten Matt so severely. Tony, in his quiet manner, replied – *"I don't like him, and I don't like what he did to you."* After they kissed good night, as Tony was walking away, Shelly watched him out of sight, thinking – *"He really does love me, and I love him."*

The landlord had made several visits to the front door, asking for the rent money: money that Shelia didn't have. When Shelly saw him drive up, she would answer the door, telling him she would have her Mom call him. She didn't know what else to do. They were on the verge of being evicted. Through one of the neighbors, Shelia heard about some flats that might be available to rent only one street over from where they now lived.

She and Shelly walked over to the office of the caretaker, asking him if he had a flat empty. To their mutual gladness, he had one available, straight across the street from Marcy and Buck. Looking inside the flat itself, they were both thrilled with the place. The whole area impressed Shelly as being much more cheerful than the dull, spooky, drafty old house they now occupied.   Of all the houses they had lived in, this last one was the one Shelly hated the most.

The flat was much smaller than the big house, but it was actually the perfect size for them. Beth loved the place as much as Sheila and Shelly. No one expected any help from anyone else as far as coming up with the money for the deposit and the first month's rent. Pooling all their money together, Shelly, Beth and Phillip managed it. But to their utter surprise, Hank himself chipped in enough to buy a few groceries after the rent and deposit were paid. It was one of the happiest days of Shelly's life. She didn't know which gave her the most joy – moving into the newer, more modern apartment, or leaving the moldy, dilapidated house. She never wanted to see that house again if she could possibly avoid it.

Shelia continued to improve. She was getting out of the house more, and walking down the street to her Mom's house (Grandma Eloise,) having coffee with her nearly every day. Shelly still retained a few of her fears, still sleeping with her Mom. She often wondered if she would ever be "*normal*".   Her constant prayer was to have just a normal life, without any phobias to haunt her. Her most cherished source of comfort and happiness, of course, was Tony. She wanted to spend the rest of her life with him, and the sentiment was mutual. They both knew they were too young, but they also knew they were going to get married. They both knew it would not be a big fancy wedding.

They didn't have that kind of money, and neither did either of their families.

Beth had landed a fantastic job, making big money. She immediately began buying brand new furniture for Sheila, along with whatever else her Mom wanted or needed, and had money left over. Now they didn't need Hank's few dollars anymore. Whenever Hank was in the area, he always stopped by Marcy's house. Now, with Sheila and the girls living across the street, he would walk across the street, saying hello before leaving.

One day Hank came running into the house, gasping for breath. Sheila and the girls could see he was very angry. He had been over to Marcy's house. Marcy had a black eye. But he hadn't seen Buck, so he assumed Buck had beaten Marcy, and had either left hurriedly, or was hiding somewhere in the house. He told Sheila and the girls they had better be prepared to come visit him in prison, because this time he was going to kill Buck. They knew he meant it. Beth started crying with fear, as Sheila tried to reason with Hank, begging him not to do something stupid. *"Hank, she urged, if you kill him you will not only destroy your own life, but Marcy's too."* But Hank was livid with rage – he refused to listen to either of them. Running back across the street, he barged into the house, demanding that Marcy tell him where Buck was. Marcy simply motioned with her head, toward the stairs. Hank leaped up the stairs, taking two steps at a time, screaming Buck's name.

Buck came wobbling out of the bedroom, holding his chest. He was bloody from head to toe. His face and chest were covered with blood from the deep scratches from Marcy's fingernails. Looking closer, Hank saw the stab wounds where Marcy had stabbed him with a knife. Hank himself didn't know where his sudden change of heart came from, he just knew if he didn't get

Buck to a hospital soon, he would bleed to death. Yelling for Marcy to grab some towels, he helped Buck down the stairs. Marcy handed the towels to Hank. Hank told Buck to hold the towels tightly over his wounds while he drove him to the hospital. After Buck recovered from his wounds, Hank swore he'd never say another word if or when Marcy and Buck got into another fight. He knew now that Marcy could, and would, take care of herself. In fact, he actually felt a little pity for Buck, considering the shape he was in.

Shelly thoroughly enjoyed meeting Tony's parents, Paul and Mary Davidson. There was something that just drew her to them like a magnet. She admired the way they loved and respected each other, which was something she had never seen between her own parents. Their lives were structured, but not mechanical. They lived by certain principles, some of which were self-imposed, and others taught by their Church. There were five children – Tony, three brothers, and one sister, who was the youngest. Both Paul and Mary were older than Shelly's Mom and Dad.   Paul, after having served in the Navy, and becoming part of the elite group – The Navy Seals, became a policeman for a few years, then went to work for the local Conservatory.   Mary, who was seven years older than Paul, was an accountant. Not long after they began raising a family, Paul was diagnosed with heart disease. Then things got worse – he began having heart attacks, which forced him to quit working altogether. It couldn't have happened at a worse time, because Mary was pregnant with their last child-their daughter. Like so many other working families, they went through some very rough times, but they went through them together, loving and supporting each other, each doing everything he or she could to make the other happy.   Many times, when other couples, who were also struggling with their own problems, asked Mary or Paul how they coped with all the adversity, the answer was always the same – their love for one another, and their faith in God.

Mary Davidson was a strong, no-nonsense woman who always spoke her mind. She was never deliberately harsh or unkind, but neither did she pussyfoot around a question or an issue. When asked for her opinion, she would give you an honest answer, which sometimes could be painfully honest.   Strongly suspecting, but not knowing for certain that Shelly was pregnant, she constantly reminded Tony of how the Catholic Church frowned upon pre-marital sexual activity. But neither did she hesitate to tell them both they were absolutely too young to think about getting married.

Tony and Shelly still spent every possible moment they could with each other. Whenever they weren't working, they were in each other's arms. Tony was strong, quiet and handsome, and Shelly was still turning heads wherever she went. A bit of jealousy on both their parts was inevitable.   Tony knew better than to try to forbid Shelly from socializing with her friends, but it was quite evident he wanted her all to himself, all the time. He really didn't have anything to worry about on Shelly's part though, because not long after she and Tony became a couple, she had deliberately refrained from a lot of socializing with her friends in order to be with him. Whenever Tony openly demonstrated his jealousy, which was more than a few times, Shelly smiled inwardly, interpreting his jealousy as a token of his love for her.

Desperately wanting to have a place of their own, they saved every penny they could save, which was not easy, given the fact that Shelly had to contribute most of her wages to the support of her own family. Their impatience grew even worse when each time they thought they had saved enough to rent a place, the owner of the apartments where Shelly lived would raise the rent, or the cost of utilities would go up, or both. It seemed as if all the forces in the universe were working against them. Two of those forces lived across the street - Marcy and Buck. Only now, as if things couldn't get any worse, the apartment next door to Shelly and her family had become vacant. Marcy and Buck moved into it. The thin wall that separated the two flats made it impossible to ignore the loud fights in which Marcy and Buck engaged almost daily.

Late one evening, while Sheila was boiling water for her final cup of coffee, she, along with Tony and Shelly, heard Marcy screaming for help. Shelly and Tony ran out the door, telling Sheila to stay put. As Tony stepped inside the apartment, Marcy immediately commanded him to grab the two boys and take them to Sheila. She knew if she didn't, Buck would run off to Kentucky with them after the fight. Tony scooped the two boys up in his arms, and was turning to leave with them when Buck sucker-punched him in the mouth. Under any other circumstances, Tony would have beaten Buck to a pulp, but wanting to get the boys to safety, he let Buck have that punch – making a mental note that he and Buck would meet again, and under different circumstances. With his lip bleeding, he got the boys over to Sheila's apartment. Marcy, knowing what Buck was capable of, told Shelly to go back home, assuring her she would be alright now that the boys were safe. Shelly left reluctantly, but remembering how Marcy had stabbed Buck before, she took Marcy's advice.

This time Buck was determined to beat Marcy into submission, to teach her never to fight him back again. This time he would make an example of her. Marcy somehow managed to get away from him long enough to make it out the front door, and over to Sheila's apartment. Tony and Shelly were upstairs in the bathroom, where Shelly was helping Tony stop the bleeding from his lip. Buck kicked the front door open, cursing and demanding they tell him where Marcy was. Marcy was halfway up the stairs.   Buck bounded up the stairs after her. Catching her by the back of her jeans, he pulled her down on the steps and started pounding her in the face. Marcy reached backward, picking up a big metal hair dryer that was lying on the steps, beating Buck in the head with it. Shelly ran out of the bathroom ahead of Tony, rushing down the steps, and began kicking Buck in the head while Marcy pounded his head with the dryer. The heavy metal hair dryer got Buck's attention. He stopped beating Marcy long enough to stand upright, trying to recover from the blows to his head.   Sheila came out of the kitchen carrying a pan full of scalding hot water. As Buck turned back to start beating Marcy again, Sheila threw the whole pan of scalding water all over him. Now it was Bucks turn to scream, and scream he did. Shelly and Marcy shoved him down the stairs. As he hit the bottom, Sheila whacked him over the head with the steel pan. He ran out the front door screaming in pain, as the blisters from the scalding hot water raised up on his skin. Tony stood at the top of the stairs, holding a rag to his lip. Looking down upon the situation, from all appearances, the ladies didn't need his help. Marcy and the boys stayed the rest of the night with Shelly and her family. No one heard from Buck for a few days after that. They assumed he was somewhere licking his wounds.

It turned out that finding an apartment they could afford was the easiest part for Shelly and Tony. Finding furniture they could afford was more difficult. Tony wanted Shelly to have the best, but right now he simply couldn't afford it. Shelly assured him she didn't have to have anything fancy. To her, *"things"* were not what mattered right now. They were together, in their own place, about a mile away from the never-ending drama of

Shelly's family, and a few months away from becoming parents. With what they had in the way of material things, and the love they had for each other, they called it their home.

Tony's parents, (especially him Mom,) were worried for Shelly and the baby. More than once she had stressed to them that they were both too young to be getting married, let alone having children. Between Shelly's nerves and being pregnant she was not able to work, so Tony worked two jobs to be able to support them. With Tony being only eighteen he was only able to get minimum-wage jobs. Even working two jobs, they both knew he wouldn't make enough to cover the hospital and doctor bills. Marcy had heard of an agency in town, funded by the government, which helped low income families with high medical bills. She took Shelly to the agency to fill out an application for the assistance. Once again, Shelly was so grateful for her sister, the one who was always looking out for her.

The stress of working two jobs was taking its toll on Tony, both physically and emotionally. To relieve some of that stress, he turned to drinking.   The stress relief, of course, was short lived. It helped him relax for a while, but at the same time, it was becoming a habit – one that he could neither afford nor break. Shelly hated him drinking, especially after knowing what it had done to her, her Dad and Buck. She had been hoping and praying that she and Tony would have a home totally free of alcohol. But now that alcohol had found its way into their home, it brought with it all the little demons that follow it through the door. The first time Shelly confronted Tony about his drinking, an argument ensued. He insisted that he was quite capable of handling it. He gave no indication that he was going to give it up. If it can be said that anything good came of it, Shelly was thankful that Tony's drinking didn't turn him into the monster her Dad and Buck portrayed.

She knew Tony would never hurt her physically, no matter how drunk he got. Her fear was not for herself, but for Tony.

One justification Tony proposed for his drinking was that one of his friends, Billy Samson, who along with his pregnant wife, Debbie, drank also. They lived next door to Tony's parents. Tony pointed out to Shelly that Debbie didn't mind her husband drinking at all, and joined him in it. Shelly didn't know if Tony was merely using Billy and Debbie as justification for his own drinking, or if he was insinuating that she should join him in his drinking, which would give him even more justification for it. She was determined to abstain from it, especially now that she was pregnant. The Samson's not only enjoyed drinking together, they loved playing cards along with it. They began to invite Tony and Shelly to come and join them. When they arrived, Billy said he needed to run to the store real fast, to pick up some snacks for all of them, asking Tony to go with him. Something in Shelly's gut told her Billy was up to no good. She desperately wanted to trust Tony, but with Billy around to influence him, her trust was tainted with a drop of suspicion. As Billy and Tony were heading to the door, she begged Tony not to be drinking. Tony promised he wouldn't.

Shelly knew the store they were going to was only a few blocks away, and it should have taken them about fifteen minutes to get there and back. After half an hour went by Shelly knew they were out drinking somewhere. An hour passed, then another. Shelly was really getting upset by now, but Debbie just laughed about it, saying she was glad to be rid of her husband for a few hours. When they finally pulled up in the driveway, Shelly went out to the car. As soon as the two men got out of the car, she could tell they had been drinking. They were both laughing at each other as they stumbled from the car. Shelly was crying, and yelling at both of them, scolding Tony for breaking his promise, and scolding Billy for driving drunk. Billy started cussing Shelly, telling her to shut up. Tony was drunk, but no so drunk as to allow anyone, friend or otherwise, to talk that way to the woman he loved. He put his hand on Billy's chest, pushing him backward, warning him not to open his mouth to Shelly again. Billy got the message. Shelly had now walked over to Tony's parents' house, and was sitting on the porch, weeping. Paul came out and quickly sized up the situation. He got in Tony's face, telling him he had no business being out drinking, and certainly no business upsetting his pregnant wife this way. This time, Tony got the message. Tony didn't say much on the way home, feeling a bit ashamed that he had exposed Shelly to this unnecessary trauma.

The mile of city streets that separated Shelly from her former residence and the ongoing drama of it turned out to be more than a single blessing. The loneliness of being at home with Tony working two jobs was more than she could tolerate. And being pregnant, she was always craving something. Now she gained a lot of weight. She still had a lot of phobias. She worried about everything – the baby, the bills, Tony, Marcy, her Mom and a score of other things and persons. Most of her fears reached way back into her childhood; memories that came creeping into her dreams like ghosts, haunting her. Many times at night Tony would hear her tossing and turning, mumbling unintelligible words. Sometimes when he reached over to touch her, intending to comfort her, she would fly awake suddenly, screaming.

Walking the mile from her apartment to Grandma Eloise's house, or to her Mom's was great therapy, both physically and emotionally for Shelly. She loved to stop along the way and listen to the birds singing in the trees that lined the median between the sidewalk and the street. There was something cheerful in the way the birds seemed to be communicating with each other. Sometimes she almost imagined they were singing to her, taking her mind off all the darker things for a while.

Of all the things she craved, ice cream was the one thing she craved the most - vanilla ice cream with chocolate fudge topping, which helped explain the seventy pounds she had gained. You may call it fortuitous circumstance, you may call it coincidence, but whatever it was, Shelly was eternally grateful that Tony's brother John worked at the local Dairy Queen. After leaving work Tony stopped by the Dairy Queen, bringing home one bucket of ice cream, and another bucket of chocolate fudge topping.

Somehow time seemed to speed up for Shelly. The sheer anticipation of having a baby of her own made the moments fly by. Her thoughts developed into images – what would the baby look like? Would it be a boy or a girl? Would he or she favor her more than Tony? And would the baby be healthy and whole? She pictured a son, with Tony's hair and eyes, cradled in her arms, precious and warm. And she and Tony would be the most loving parents a child could hope for, and give him all the things they never had.

When her labor first commenced, Shelly immediately asked Tony to take her to her Mom's house, where she would remain until it was time to go to the hospital. She knew her Mom would know what to do in an emergency. Arriving at Sheila's apartment, the pains increased only slightly, then quickly subsided. This continued throughout the day. Shelly began to convince herself that this was going to be easier than she expected. Her pains were noticeable, but not excruciating. But when it came time to leave for the hospital, the pains had increased in intensity and frequency. As soon as she arrived at the hospital, the nurses checked her vital signs. Her blood pressure was extremely high. When the doctor himself checked her, he immediately recommended chemically inducing her labor to speed up the process. The pain was coming harder and faster now.   Remembering the Lamaze classes she and Tony had attended together, she began to do the breathing exercises, which, of course, were supposed to lessen the pain just a bit.

It was storming outside, and the pain was getting worse. Tony kept a close eye on the monitors, not liking what he was seeing. Hank and Marcy rushed into the waiting room, drenched from the heavy rain.   One of the nurses told Tony that some of Shelly's relatives were out in the waiting room, wanting to know about Shelly's condition. Shelly granted him permission to leave her for a few minutes, begging him not to be gone long. As he entered the waiting room, Hank and Marcy immediately bombarded him with a barrage of questions, none of which he could answer. He told them he had to get back to Shelly. The worried expression on Tony's face told them more than any answers he might have given them. They stopped asking questions, and started praying, silently. Tony glanced from Shelly's face to the monitors. He didn't like what either was telling him. The baby's heart rate was really high, and Shelly, without seeing the monitors, didn't like what Tony's expression was telling her. Tony let go of her hand, telling her he needed to talk to one of the nurses about something. Shelly simply nodded her agreement. When the nurse looked at the monitor, she called for the doctor. One look at Shelly, and another at the monitors, the doctor ordered Tony out of the room – he and the nurses had to prepare Shelly for a C-section. Tony ran straight to the men's bathroom, locking the door behind him, and falling on his knees, begging God not to let anything happen to Shelly and the baby. Marcy tried to force her way in to see Shelly, but the nurses restrained her. When Hank told them he was Shelly's father, they allowed him to go back to the delivery room. Shelly was screaming when Hank walked in. It was the first time in his life he had felt this kind of fear, and this degree of helplessness.

The moment Little Tony was placed in her arms, Shelly's pain, her fear, her worries, all disappeared, at least for a time. The tears of joy she cried in those few moments somehow replaced and nullified every tear of sorrow she had shed in her life. Here was a miracle; a living miracle; her miracle. In that moment – that sacred moment, not a single sordid event from her past, nor all of those events put together, could overshadow the blessedness that was hers. It has often been said that sometimes silence speaks louder than words: this was one of those moments. The blessedness of a newborn baby lying in the bosom of his mother is impossible for an artist to paint, and equally impossible for any poet's pen to describe. It must be felt, in the heart. Seeing his son for the first time, Tony's heart pounded with pride, gratitude, and love. In that moment he became more of a man than he had ever been. His prayer in the bathroom had been answered. Hank, staring into the face of his daughter, holding her first child, couldn't say a word for a few moments. His heart softened just a little, watching Shelly gently stroke the baby's tiny nose with her finger. Marcy's smile said all that was in her own heart. Not wanting to appear to be the most sentimental one in the room, she held back her tears, pointing her finger at Shelly, demanding – *"You ain't having no more babies young lady, this was too hard on you."*

The minor complications following the birth kept Shelly in the hospital for seven days. When the doctor was satisfied that she and the baby were both strong enough to go home, he dismissed her. Tony's Dad gave them a baby bed that had been passed down from his Dad. Tony's grandfather, his father, Tony, and all his brothers and one sister had slept in it at one time or another.

There were still visible teeth marks on the wooden parts of the bed from where the many babies had bitten them while teething.   Shelly and Tony were grateful to have it.   Before Little Tony was born they had bought a lot of used clothes for him from a second hand store. Marcy organized a baby shower for Shelly, from which she got a lot of new clothes for the baby. Aunt Elizabeth proved to be a real blessing also, coming over and helping take care of the baby, and doing nearly all the housework and cleaning. Having the baby had left Shelly much weaker than she had anticipated. Everyone could tell she wasn't quite ready to do everything that needed to be done and care for the baby too.

Shelly was so thankful for her aunt Elizabeth. She took care of the baby as if he was her own. One look at little Tony, and it was love at first sight for Elizabeth. Tony was still working two jobs, coming home nearly exhausted from work, but he would still get up at night and tend to the baby just to give Shelly more rest till she got better. Finally, when everyone was convinced that Shelly was ready to do it all on her own, Aunt Elizabeth reluctantly went home. Shelly couldn't thank her enough for all she had done for them.

Tony's hard work and dedication didn't go unnoticed. Hank recommended Tony to his company, as a cab driver. As it turned out, Tony was assigned to a contracted route, picking up school kids and driving them home. And when he wasn't doing that, he could work pretty much as many hours as he wanted. He made more money driving a cab than he had at both his other jobs combined.   Shelly had taken a job as a babysitter for another couple. With their combined incomes they were able to buy a little house.   But being young, and a bit overzealous to have their own house, they didn't stop to consider how small the house was.

It would have been just right for the three of them, but they weren't thinking ahead, to a larger family. Tony's Mom strongly objected to them buying the house, but Tony was adamant about it. Someone Tony knew, a realtor, somehow arranged for Tony to buy the house with no down payment. To Tony, it was just too good a deal to pass up at the time.

Paul and Mary loved little Tony as much as any grandparents can love a grandchild. Shelly made sure they got to see and hold the baby as much as possible. Now, they were about the only ones she trusted to babysit him, other than Aunt Elizabeth. Mary had been losing weight, and getting sick to her stomach a lot lately, but she ignored it as much as possible, attributing it to "old age". She wanted to enjoy spoiling her grandson every moment she could.

It was New Year's Eve, and Tony's brother Frank invited them to a get together at his wife Mindy's brother's house for a party.   Shelly tried to graciously refuse the invitation, knowing there would be a lot of drinking at the party, and she didn't want to expose herself or Tony to the temptation. Tony finally persuaded her to go, promising her he wouldn't get drunk. The house was nearly packed with guests when Shelly and Tony arrived. Several tables were full of snacks and desserts.   The floor of every room was lined with coolers, all filled with cold beer, on ice. When Shelly and Tony walked in, everyone was already drinking. Shelly refused every beer that was offered to her. Tony accepted the first one, and helped himself to several more.

Shelly didn't see a lot that really interested her, but engaged in a little cordial conversation with some of the ladies her own age. Finally, after becoming somewhat hungry, she spied a plate of brownies on a table. She noticed they were a bit thicker and heavier than any brownies she had eaten before. Tasting one, she decided it wasn't bad. Sitting on one of the sofas in the living room for a while, she began to feel really funny, like no sensation she'd experienced before. It got so bad she got scared, trying to tell Tony she was sick, but Tony was just drunk enough to hear only what he wanted to hear. He was thoroughly enjoying himself, and didn't understand half of what she was trying to tell him. He shrugged it off, telling her she was going to be just fine. Shelly went out to the back porch, where she quickly sat down. She was shaking and crying uncontrollably. Another one of Tony's brothers, Frank, saw her and knew something was wrong. Coming over to her, he asked her what was wrong, assuming she had either drunk too much, or that something she had eaten had made her sick. As Frank was trying to calm Shelly, Tony came out the back door, looking for Shelly. Frank told him Shelly needed to go to the hospital. Tony insisted that she was going to be ok. As Shelly continued to tremble and cry, Frank and Tony each put one of her arms around their shoulder, helping her walk down the street to Frank's house. Lying on the bed, Shelly tried desperately to calm herself, but to no avail. Now she was really scared, afraid she was going to die. She tried to close her eyes and go to sleep, but just as she was about to drift off, she would quickly snap awake again. Her fear was becoming unbearable. She told herself she had to get some sleep, and when she woke up, it would all be gone, but it didn't work. This was only the prelude to another living Hell into which she was now about to descend.

With a new baby, a job, a husband and a house to tend to, Shelly had decided she didn't have time for the counseling sessions with Mr. Chandler. She didn't tell Mr. Chandler what she was thinking, but she had also reached a level of self-confidence. In her mind, she was a grown woman now, and not an irresponsible little girl. She told herself she didn't need the counseling anymore. But the incident at the New Year's Eve party had frayed her nerves. Someone told her she had eaten a brownie heavily laced with marijuana. Now she was afraid to eat much of anything, and she trusted no one.   The fear of eating had become so intense, each time she looked at a plate of food, to her, it was the equivalent of stumbling upon a coiled rattlesnake. The very thought of taking food into her mouth gave her flashbacks of how she had felt at that party. But knowing she had to eat something in order to survive and take care of her baby, she forced herself to eat a slice of cheese, washing it down with a full glass of water. This became her diet for about three months. During that three months, she lost sixty pounds.

Everyone on both sides of her family noticed the change in Shelly, both the physical and the emotional change. Everyone, including her in-laws tried to convince her she needed to eat in order to survive. Tony, more than anyone else, was really worried about her now. But no amount of persuasion from anyone could get her to eat a plate of food. She still cooked for Tony, and kept her little house as clean as a pin, but she never sat at the table with him. Finally, after realizing her family was suffering as a result of her fear of eating, she decided to go back into counseling, only with a different counselor. For the first time in her life she heard the term *"panic attack"*.   She had no idea what a panic attack was, and no idea how to deal with it. All she knew right now was that she was afraid to live, and afraid to die.

The counseling wasn't going nearly as well as it had with Reuben Chandler. Each time Shelly showed up for counseling, she had a different counselor. And it soon became evident to Shelly that some of these counselors were woefully unqualified to be counselors. One counselor in particular, a very heavy gentleman, told Shelly all she needed to do was relax, and everything would be fine. While demonstrating a relaxation technique, using breathing exercises, he fell asleep in his chair. Shelly listened to his snoring for a few minutes, chuckling to herself. As he snored, he almost tipped over. He snapped awake just as Shelly was walking out the door, laughing at him. Overcoming her fear of eating would be a long and arduous journey for Shelly.

Little Tony was almost two when Mary, Tony's Mom, was diagnosed with stomach cancer. It had advanced to the stage at which all her doctors agreed she had little, if any chance of surviving. They stopped just short of telling her family she was terminal. But Mary already knew. But she was a fighter. She was determined not to just roll over and die. She would fight to live till her last breath. She would enjoy every day of her remaining life as best she could, and she would enjoy her family every possible moment she could. Tony was heart- broken, not willing to accept that his Mom was going to die soon. Shelly and Mary had become as close as any mother-in-law and daughter-in-law could be. They each demonstrated their love for one another in deeds, and not in words alone.

Mary always considered herself as being *"from the old school"*. She held to her old-fashioned values, and lived by her old-fashioned principles. She also held too many of the old-fashioned traditions and sayings she had heard while growing up, one of which was the saying – *"give me my roses while I live."* And Mary interpreted this saying both literally and figuratively. The implication of this saying, of course, is that no one can either see or smell the flowers we   bring after they have died, and neither are they able to enjoy the benefit of a good deed, no matter how well-intended it may be.   Only the living can enjoy the beauty and fragrance of a rose, and only the living can benefit from our kindnesses. Mary's favorite flowers were carnations. On many of her visits to Mary and Paul, Shelly stopped by the little flower shop on the way, carefully picking out the prettiest and freshest carnations she could find to give to Mary. The beaming smile on Mary's face was all the thanks Shelly needed.

The chemotherapy treatments made Mary very sick.   Her condition was deteriorating rapidly. Marcy and Shelly joined forces, cooking for Paul, and cleaning Mary's house for her. Mary ate very little now, dropping more weight every week. She spent most of her waking hours on the big sofa, resting. She and Paul still had two children at home, John and Marie.   John's high school graduation was about three months away. Marie, now sixteen, had two more years of school ahead of her. As sick and as weak as she was, Mary insisted on being at Little Tony's second birthday party. Tony, not wanting to accept his Mom's impending death, found himself on his knees a lot now, praying for her as he had prayed for Shelly and the baby. But this time, God was going to say no to his request.   Seeing her weak and emaciated frame, he somehow knew this would be the last birthday party his Mom would ever attend. He could see the pain in her eyes.

The love Paul and Mary shared was the deep enduring kind of love which so many artists, poets, novelists and Hollywood producers have tried to reproduce on canvas, on paper, and in films, but can never quite capture perfectly. Her life was his life, her joy was his joy, her pain was his pain, and as was about to be clearly demonstrated, her death would be his death. The pain in his own eyes was all too visible, as he watched his beloved wife slowly slipping away.

One day while Tony and Shelly were visiting, Mary, lying on the couch, beckoned for Tony to come and sit by her. Her voice was so weak Tony had to lean downward to hear her. *"Tony, she whispered, do you know how much I love you?"* Choking up, Tony managed to answer her – *"Yeah Mom, I know – all of us know how much you and Dad love us."* Mary managed a weak smile, adding – *"I'm dying Tony, and I want you to promise me you will quit drinking, and raise your family proper."* Unable to speak now, Tony nodded his promise to her, taking her frail body in his arms, afraid to hug her too tightly, then gently lowering her onto the sofa. One month later, God took Mary home. Exactly one month later, on his birthday, Paul rejoined his beloved Mary. Her life was his life, her joy was his joy, her pain was his pain, her death was his death. To employ a paradox, the children were forced to bear the unbearable – the death of both parents in a single month.

Tony, of course, was devastated. Shelly couldn't, and didn't want to imagine the grief which the Davidson children were going through. But reflecting upon the lives of Paul and Mary, and how close she had been to both of them, she could look upon their passing with no regrets as far as her own relationship to them had been in life. They knew Shelly loved them, and she knew they loved her. And she had borne them a beautiful grandson, who they had both loved dearly, and who both had thoroughly enjoyed spoiling as best they could for two years. They had both died knowing Tony and Shelly loved each other, and that Shelly wanted the same happiness for their son and grandson as they had wanted.

Shelly's eating disorder affected her in more ways than one. No amount of counseling could fix her problem. It was hot healthy food she needed. But her fear, for now, was greater than her food intake. She kept losing weight, and being sick. And now she was pregnant again. Her doctor was genuinely concerned about her weight loss, and her eating disorder.

After confirming her pregnancy, he graciously reminded her that she needed to eat more, not only for her own sake, but for the sake of the baby in her womb. Some days she really didn't feel like getting up off the couch, but knowing she had no choice, she somehow found the strength to do those necessary things a mother has to do. To her credit, Shelly seemed to be able to find somewhat of a silver lining behind every dark cloud that overshadowed her life. She was so grateful for a loving and understanding man like Tony, who loved and supported her no matter how dark the situation became. She was also grateful for a little boy who was so smart, well-mannered and easier to care for than most little tykes his age.

When Tony came home from work he would help her cook, clean, and help out with whatever needed done. Three months into her pregnancy, Shelly woke up one morning, looked out the window at the sunshine, looked at her little boy sleeping peacefully, rubbed her belly, and made a decision, all on her own, with no counseling and no coercion from anyone. She was hungry, and she was going to cook some breakfast, and eat it, just that simple. She realized in a single moment that all her fear of food had been ungrounded. Yes, someone had slipped marijuana into some brownies, and it had almost killed her, but no one would slip anything harmful into the food of a pregnant woman – would they? And an even more compelling argument, the one that broke her fear, was the fact that the little one inside her needed nourishment, and that's what mattered more than anything else. After a single hot meal, she felt better – both physically and emotionally.

Tony found a bigger house in an upscale area not far from where they lived. With the money Tony's parents had left them they were able to meet the required down payment on it. Growing up, Shelly never dreamed she would ever live in one of the nicer houses, many of which were less than a mile from where she had lived.   The demographics of every area where she had lived so far could be summed up in two terms – "*poor*", and "*declining*".   The moment she looked around this new neighborhood, she immediately felt out of place, as if she didn't belong here. Their new house was as modern and lovely as any other, but their car was woefully inferior to the newer ones in every other driveway, and their furniture, and their clothes, were all second hand.   Shelly noticed that almost everyone around them wore "*designer*" outfits, or big name brands. None of the neighbors made any effort to welcome them to the neighborhood. In fact, no one really seemed to acknowledge their presence. All the looks, the stares, the whispers, and the glaring absence of any sign of neighborly kindness made Shelly feel like she had felt so many other times in her life – like she was trash. But again she found that little ribbon of silver in the cloud – she had Tony, Little Tony, and a tiny little person inside her, all of whom furnished her with enough happiness to overlook everything else, and get on with her life. And besides, she reasoned, with her nerves, she really didn't care for much socializing anyway.   She was eating better, and becoming healthier all the time.

Tony was having a hard time dealing with the loss of his parents. They had been the glue that held everything together in his family. Their strength of character, their guiding principles, and their love for each other had been the foundation and the stability upon which he and his siblings had relied all their lives. And now they were gone. He missed his father, whose strong leadership had taught him to be a man, and he missed the gentler teaching of his mother, who had taught him to be a gentleman.   Now he was twenty-one, with a woman, a child, and another child on the way.   But he had a weakness – one which, at the moment, he could not conquer.

Maybe it was a temporary lapse in memory, or maybe it was an irresistible temptation, but he told himself he had to have something to take the edge off his grief, and that something was alcohol. With the first drink, he saw his mother's face, and heard her plea, begging him to quit his drinking. But he was sure his Mom would understand his insurmountable sorrow if she were here. He drank another beer, and the effect of that one justified another, and another.

Having learned some invaluable lessons from the birth of their first child, Shelly and Tony were better prepared for this one. As the time drew near she went to the hospital early, where she was prepped for another C-section. This time Shelly was put to sleep. Both she and Tony were hoping for a little girl this time, but mostly they wanted a healthy baby. Baby James was born exactly nine months from the day Tony's Mom passed away. He was a beautiful, healthy boy. Shelly couldn't help but notice he was a lot shorter in length than Little Tony. During her three day stay in the hospital, Tony only came to see her once. It was the same hospital where his Mom had died, and he just couldn't deal with the painful memory. Shelly was hurt, but tried to understand. She was missing Little Tony so much she couldn't wait to get back home. She seemed to recover from this surgery more quickly than from the first one, but her doctor sternly warned her not to do too much too soon, until she was completely healed. That, of course, was easier said than done with two infants to care for, a house to clean, and a hungry man to cook for. And this time, Tony wasn't as much help as he had been with the first baby. As soon as he got up from the supper table, he would drive over to his brother John's house (the house his parents had owned,) where he and several of their friends got together to drink and play cards, leaving Shelly to tend to both the children and everything else by herself.

Women in a relationship with men know things the men never suspect they know, and Shelly knew that she and Tony were slowly, but surely, drifting apart. The signals were all too visible. Tony's kisses were shorter and less passionate. When he was home, he seemed preoccupied with something other than her and his children. He now spent more time with his brother and his friends than he spent at home. But more than anything else, he couldn't maintain eye contact with her now. She recalled something Rev. Parker had said many years ago, about the eyes being the windows of the soul. There was something missing in Tony's eyes – that bright sparkle she used to see when he would take her in his arms; and the long, slow passionate kisses that used to be the prelude to their long intimate nights. With all these signs, Shelly jumped to the same conclusion to which most women jump – he was seeing another woman! And the proverbial "final nail in the coffin" that convinced her he was seeing another woman came when Tony came home from work one night and announced that he was moving out, and moving into his parent's house with John.

Of all the devastating traumatic events in her life, this was the worst. Never in her most horrible nightmares could she imagine life without Tony. And now he was leaving. And again, she felt there was something dreadfully wrong with her. He had probably met another woman far more beautiful than her – a woman who had no emotional hang ups and fears like she had. Now the man she loved was making her feel like so much trash. With tears she begged him not to go, but her words fell upon deaf ears. As he walked out the door, Shelly's heart sank in despair. It seemed as if her whole world had just fallen apart. The only way she knew how to cope was to turn to her children and the house. She began to do everything in a frenzy. She was like a mechanical robot, rushing to get everything done without realizing she was doing it.

She couldn't stop working in the house, doing everything twice just to stay busy, and keep her mind occupied.

Tony was so distraught over losing his parents he became fixated upon them. They were all that consumed his thoughts, nothing else. He stayed away from Shelly and the boys for almost a week, trying to drown his sorrow from a bottle. In the meantime, Shelly was doing too much too fast, and it caught up with her – she was physically and emotionally drained; then the panic attacks set in again. With her last vestige of sanity she called 911. The Emergency Squad team was able to get her calmed down enough to avoid a trip to the hospital, but sternly advised her to follow up with her doctor the next day. The doctor told her the same thing the paramedics had told her – she needed to slow down, and get some rest.

Tony, realizing his mistress-alcohol was not the answer to his grief, decided it was time to be a man, and go home to his family. Shelly welcomed him with a happy heart, and open arms. With Tony back home to help with everything, including the boys, she began to heal rapidly. She had now gotten acquainted with some of the ladies in the neighborhood by way of their children. Everyone noticed their kids were drawn to Shelly like a magnet, and she to them. Some of them asked her if she would babysit their children while they worked.   Shelly accepted the jobs immediately.   It felt so good to be trusted with the children of ladies she considered far better than herself. It gave her just the measure of self-esteem she needed right now. Perhaps she wasn't so trashy after all. And besides the self-esteem that came with being trusted with the children, all these ladies paid her quite well for her services. Now she could help Tony pay the bills.

Tony's cab driving job was rewarding in many ways. Not only

did he make good money at it, but he thoroughly enjoyed cruising all over town, learning all the streets, and meeting new people every day. Then there was the school trip he picked up every day, which paid more money than any of the other trips. Tony was about to learn why it paid more. He was also about to learn why he had gotten the run in the first place, when it should have been given to one of the other drivers who had more seniority than him; that reason being - no one else wanted it. The school where he picked up the children was in a bad part of town; so bad in fact, the windows of the school had steel bars protecting them from vandals, thugs, thieves, and from some of the students themselves. Tony always arrived a little early, leaning back in the seat, relaxing for a while before the kids came out.

He saw a young man walking toward his cab. As the young man approached, he nodded. Tony, thinking he was nodding to him, waved at the guy. The nod was both a distraction, and a signal – a distraction to Tony, and a signal to the man's accomplice on the other side of Tony's cab. It distracted Tony just long enough for the accomplice on the other side of the cab to sneak up and open the door. It was too late for Tony to escape from the car. The two men proceeded to beat him with their fists from each side. As they beat him, they kept demanding that he tell them where his gun was. Tony didn't have a gun, and in this case, it was a good thing he didn't, because if he had, someone would have been killed. Trapped inside the car, Tony had little chance of defending himself against the two attackers. It was broad daylight, with people walking right by, seeing Tony being beaten and robbed. No one stopped to intervene, no one called the police. The two men beat Tony severely, taking all his money, ripping off his shirt pocket and the back pocket of his jeans, which held his wallet, leaving him with his face swollen from the beating. When he arrived at home, Shelly, seeing his swollen eyes and lips, knew what had happened. She begged him never to go back to driving the cab again. Tony quickly agreed.

During the time it took for all the swelling to go down in Tony's face, he couldn't look for another job. It was also during that period the payment on their mortgage went up considerably. The loan company had set them up with a variable interest rate, and now the rate was almost double the original rate. With only Shelly's income from babysitting, there simply wasn't enough money to pay the bills. As a result, they were now falling behind on the house payment. They both began to realize that, barring a miracle, they were going to lose the house.

Chad and Beverly Martin, who attended a very large church in Bedford City, had become good friends with Shelly and Tony. Finding out that Tony needed a job, they recommended him to their church as a groundskeeper and general maintenance man, a job at which Tony had a lot of experience from working at the big Catholic Church before. With Chad and Beverly's recommendation, Tony was hired immediately. And not only did the job pay well, it also came with great benefits, including life and health insurance.   But as great as the new job was, it was too late for them to keep from losing the house. They were too far behind to catch up now. They had to find another place to live, and soon. Tony found a two bedroom townhouse for rent, owned by another couple who attended the same church where he now worked. When Tony took Shelly to see the place, she said she felt like they were moving to another country, because it was so far away from any of her family.

The townhouse was a lot smaller than their house, but that turned out to be a blessing for Shelly; she didn't have as much housecleaning to do.   But it was taking her longer to adjust to this new place than it had in any other place they had lived. She didn't know anyone in this neighborhood, there was no family close by, and her panic attacks were more frequent. It didn't take long at all for Tony to make new friends; most of the couples enjoyed sitting outside on their porches or balconies, drinking beer and socializing on weekends, which made Tony fit right in. Seeing that it was taking Shelly a while to adjust, he took it upon himself to introduce her to some of the ladies who lived close by. She became especially fond of one lady in particular, Trina, a divorcee, who like herself, had panic attacks regularly. It seemed that having someone who was going through the same things – someone who could relate and understand, somehow made things just a little bit easier to cope with.

Shelly's driver's license had been revoked when she was seventeen due to an accident in which she was at fault, having no insurance, and no money to pay for the damages to the other vehicle. Now she had to walk wherever she went, because there was only one vehicle, and Tony had to use it to go to work.   Not only did Tony have the only vehicle, he also had the checkbook – he handled all the bills and managed all the money. If Shelly wanted to buy anything, she had to ask him for the money to buy it. She felt like a child begging for an allowance. It was demeaning and degrading for her to go to him and ask for money. She and James walked Little Tony to school in the morning, then walked him home in the afternoon. When she could spare the money, on the way home she would stop in at the little convenience store next to the school and buy the boys a bag of candy. It touched her heart each time the boys reached into the bag and offered her a piece of their candy; they were both such little gentlemen.

As much as Shelly loved being away from the constant drama and fighting she had endured when she lived close to some of her family, there was still a loneliness that made her miss them, although she stayed in contact with Marcy on a daily basis via the phone. Marcy kept her up to date on current family "*events*". She also called her Mom Sheila once in a while. When she asked her Mom how she was doing, she always got a somewhat different story than the one she got from Marcy. Sheila, not wanting to worry Shelly, always assured her that she was just fine, but when she spoke to Marcy, Marcy told her the truth – Sheila was not as well as she claimed to be.

Not long after she and Tony moved into their townhouse, Tony's brother John, his wife Kelly, and their son, John Jr. moved into a three-bedroom townhouse across the lot from them. Their being there gave Shelly a bit more comfort, just knowing she had a relative close by. She seldom heard from her younger sister Beth now that Beth had gotten married and was working full time. She and Kelly had become close friends soon after they first met. Now that they lived this close to each other, they took turns visiting each other on a daily basis. Another good thing that came out of them being close was the fact that their little boy, John Jr., and James were about the same age, giving James a friend he could play with.

Shelly's Mom Sheila was still seeing her counselor regularly, and on the surface it appeared that she was improving, emotionally and physically. When in the presence of her counselor, she appeared perfectly sane and stable, but as soon as the counselor left, she would recede into gloom, paranoia, and outbursts of rage. She still had issues which her counselor knew nothing about, one of which was her inability to manage money. She received a disability check every month, but instead of paying her rent and other bills responsibly, she spent most of that money at yard sales, buying things she didn't really need. Each time she received an eviction notice, the girls would have to chip in a little each month in order to prevent her from being evicted, and neither of them could really afford to keep bailing her out on a monthly basis. Finally they decided it was time to take decisive action. They would have her evaluated by clinical psychologists to determine her competency to manage her own affairs. The girls agreed that if she were to be found incompetent, then one of them would be appointed as her legal guardian, with power of attorney to manage her finances, and prevent her from being evicted from her house. Sheila, however, somehow managed to convince the psychologists and psychiatrists that she was mentally competent to manage her own affairs. And so the vicious cycle continued.

Sheila simply refused to accept responsibility for her actions. Whatever happened as a result of her irresponsibility, she found someone else to blame, and Shelly was her choice of a scapegoat. When her utilities were shut off, she blamed Shelly; if she got another eviction notice, it was Shelly's fault; if she didn't have the money for groceries, Shelly was somehow to blame. It didn't matter that Shelly lived miles away, and had absolutely nothing to do with her Mom's affairs, Sheila would call Shelly, screaming at her on the phone, telling her she had gotten another eviction notice, insisting it was Shelly's fault. Sheila didn't realize what she was doing to Shelly. As Shelly silently listened to her Mom's accusations, it took her mind back to that dark period between the time Hank had come to the house with his attorney, and the divorce itself. During that time, Hank and Sheila never spoke to each other, but used Shelly as a liaison between them. Instead of talking to each other, whatever Hank and Shelia had to say to each other was relayed through Shelly, back and forth. And what they each had to say to each other was not really *to* each other, but *about* each other, and none of it was pretty.

Neither of them had stopped to consider that what they were

doing was affecting Shelly more than themselves, inducing her panic attacks.

In some ways Shelly and her sisters were relieved, and maybe even a bit happy, when Sheila met, and eventually married Mick Ryerson. Mick and Sheila had a few things in common, but they also had some essential differences. As for their similarities, both had virtually the same mental and emotional issues, both loved listening to country music, and they seemed to be genuinely in love.   Mick was good *to* her, and he was good *for* her. But the one big difference (and the one for which the girls were the most grateful,) was that Mick was far more responsible in financial matters than Sheila. He paid the rent on time; he paid the other bills on time, and made sure that Sheila had whatever she needed or wanted.   And the one asset which endeared him to Sheila more than any other was that he did whatever she told him to do - no questions asked.

On the negative side, however, Mick often either refused, or simply neglected to take his medications. And when that happened, he was hard to live with. As long as he was on his medications he was a perfect gentleman, but one day without his medications and he could become quite overbearing, telling everyone around him, including any children that might be present, what to do, and how to do it.   Shelly never cherished the idea of having her children around Mick, but if she had no other choice she made the visit as short as possible. She knew Mick was harmless, but she didn't want her children exposed to his harsh language.

Almost all the people who lived around Tony and Shelly were single, and almost all of them enjoyed drinking on the weekend. One exception was Trina, who had a lot in common with Shelly, including panic disorder. Trina and Shelly didn't drink at all, but they didn't mind socializing with those who did. And then there was Lisa - single, sexy, sassy, sultry, sensuous Lisa - the blonde bombshell of the community, with the face of a goddess and the body of a legendary Hollywood movie star. She had the body, and she flaunted her body, wearing outfits that left very little to anyone's imagination. Most other women envied her, and quite a few both envied and hated her, especially when she sunbathed in a two-piece bikini in front of their husbands and boyfriends. Lisa loved to watch the other ladies turn green with envy when she came walking toward the pool, laying aside her skimpy towel, revealing an even skimpier bikini. Gazing at her bronzed body, the few men who were married suddenly forgot their wives' names, while the single guys who had girlfriends forgot their girlfriends were lying beside them.

Shelly tried desperately to refrain from judging anyone by their appearance, and Lisa was no exception. As long as Lisa was sober, she posed hardly any threat to anyone's marriage, but after a few drinks, she turned into a tiger that was hard to tame, flirting with any and every male who came within arm's reach, whether married or single, old or young. The alcohol not only loosened her tongue, it also loosened all her inhibitions. This, of course, led to some heated exchanges of name-calling and outright violence between herself and the women whose husbands and boyfriends she flirted with, and between the men and women themselves. Shelly never suspected there was anything going on between Lisa and Tony, mostly because she trusted Tony implicitly. And besides, she and Lisa had become good friends - so good in fact that Lisa had begun to come over and visit often, even staying for dinner. She and Shelly had some long and meaningful conversations. But today Lisa was drinking, and making eyes at Tony, and Tony was drinking heavily, making her even more attractive in his eyes.

He was totally ignoring Shelly.

Lisa stretched her well-tanned body out on one of the lounge chairs by the pool, donning her expensive sunglasses and rubbing scented lotion on her long silky smooth legs. Shelly got up and went into the kitchen to bring back some hot dogs, chips and sodas. She was gone about ten minutes, just long enough for Lisa to take off her sunglasses and make eye contact with Tony, curling her finger, beckoning him to come over to her. Tony, taking an extremely foolish and costly gamble, walked over and sat down beside Lisa. When Shelly walked out of the kitchen, Tony had his right arm and hand on Lisa's left leg. Shelly calmly set everything down on a nearby table, walked over to Lisa's right side, and sucker-punched her really hard on the side of her head, nearly knocking her off the lounge chair. Lisa was too shocked and in too much pain to do anything. Tony got up and began cursing at Shelly, shoving her backward. Shelly pushed back. After a few minutes of cursing and shoving, they both decided this was the wrong place and time to settle this. But it was by no means the end of their fight.

Tony's drinking binges became more frequent, and now he also began staying out later and later. Each hour he was gone doubled Shelly's anxiety. She knew she was on the verge of another panic attack, and there was nothing she could do to stop it. Not long after they had moved in she had Tony install extra locks and deadbolts on both doors. She was afraid someone would break in on her and the boys. And now she was afraid Tony would be too drunk to drive home, or maybe he had gotten into a fight and was hurt, or maybe he had a bad wreck and was lying in a ditch somewhere. And the panic set in. Sometimes when the panic reached a certain level, she would hurriedly grab the boys and rush over to Trina's house, hoping to find some degree of comfort and reassurance from Trina. The one thing

Trina always did when Shelly came over with the boys was to have prayer with her. Shelly always felt better after they prayed together.

Tony, coming home drunk, and finding the doors locked, had to fumble for his keys, then fumble to find the keyhole. Sometimes it took him thirty minutes to unlock the front door. When he finally got inside, he immediately started cursing at Shelly, hitting and shoving her. Sometimes Shelly fought back. If Tony persisted in fighting her, she would grab the boys again, and run over to Trina's house, staying there till she figured Tony had finally gone to bed. This scenario became a ritual, almost every night now, and Shelly was quickly reaching her breaking point. When she wasn't praying with Trina at her house, she prayed silently day and night, alone, begging God to take away her fears, and Tony's drinking habit. She was near to total despair. It seemed her whole life was one never-ending battle, and she was tired of fighting.

Pondering her past, summing up her present, and losing hope for a future, she decided it was time to end it all. She concluded that she was the one common denominator in the sad and sorrowful equation that made up her life. She would remove herself from the equation, and then everything would be better for everyone. The one thing, more than any other, which she knew for certain was that she loved Tony, but now she wasn't so sure that Tony loved her. And if Tony didn't love her, then her life was worthless. She was tired of dealing with all the fear, and now, she couldn't bear the thought of being unloved by the one person she loved more than life itself. Looking at her two sons, she concluded that, somewhere out there, there was a lady more beautiful and loving than her – a woman who didn't have any fears and hang-ups, a woman who could be a good wife to Tony and a great mother to her children. She picked up the phone, calling Marcy first, telling her she loved her, and telling her goodbye. As soon as she hung up from talking to Marcy, Marcy jumped in her car and headed over to Shelly's house. While Marcy was on her way, Shelly called Beth, telling her she loved her, and telling her goodbye. Next she called her Dad, saying the same things she had said to her sisters. Hank nearly collapsed when Shelly told him she was going to end her life. He began begging her not to do it, and for the first time in his life, he apologized to her for all the things he had done to her, and for not doing all the things he should have done. He and Marcy arrived at Shelly's at the same time.

Each phone call Shelly had made to her family was a cry for help. Had Marcy and Hank ignored that cry, Shelly would have killed herself that night. She had the pills in the palm of her hand when Hank and Marcy arrived. She was about to put the pills in her mouth when Marcy pounded on the door, screaming – *"Don't do it Shelly, please don't do this, Dad is here now, and we love you Shelly."* With the pills clinched tightly in her fist, Shelly unlocked the door. Hank and Marcy embraced her between them, crying and hugging her, telling her how much they loved her. Both Hank and Marcy offered for Shelly and the boys to move in with them, assuring her they would do whatever it took to get her the professional help she needed. Even though Shelly knew she could never live in the same house with either of them, there was something in their sincerity that touched her deeply. Looking at her two little boys, and realizing how much she loved them, and how much they needed her, she put the pills back into the bottle. Even with all her imperfections, she was worth something to them, and she could never leave them.

Another of Shelly's many cousins, Carolyn, Phillip's sister, was looking for a job. Fortunately she had a car to drive around searching for employment. Not having any success at finding a job she liked, and for which she was qualified, she decided to take a break from job-hunting one day, and go visit her cousin Shelly, whom she hadn't seen in close to a year. Shelly was thrilled having Carolyn drive all that way just to visit her. As the two of them reminisced about old times, Carolyn told Shelly she was looking for work, wondering if there were any opportunities in her area. Shelly suggested the two of them become partners in their own house-cleaning business. Carolyn agreed it was a fantastic idea, and the partnership was sealed with a handshake. While the boys were in school, she and Carolyn, working together, cleaned three or four homes a day, five days a week. It felt so good having her own hard-earned money again, and not having to beg Tony for money.

After the births of her two boys, with all the complications she had experienced, Shelly presumed she would never have any more children. It came as quite a surprise learning she was pregnant again. In the fifth month of her pregnancy her doctor insisted that she either quit, or at least suspend her cleaning job. She was waking up in so much pain she couldn't get out of bed without Tony's help. Tony was the happiest man on earth, informing Shelly that this one was going to be a girl. He even picked out the name – Mary, after his Mom. Shelly grinned, nodding her agreement and approval. But the night before the baby was born she told Tony they needed to pick out a boy's name, just in case it was a boy. Tony refused – he just knew this one was a girl. And he was right. Tony was allowed in the delivery room the whole time during Shelly's C-Section this time. It turned out to be the easiest delivery Shelly had experienced. She was only mildly sedated, but awake the whole time. When the doctor announced it was a girl, Tony choked up. The doctor let him hold the baby first. Shelly could see the pure joy in his eyes as he gently held their little girl in his arms.

Tony gazed into the baby's face, speaking his first words to his little girl – *"Hi there little Mary, you sure are a beautiful little lady."*

Shelly hadn't been to church in many years now. She still prayed every night at bedtime, and kept a prayer in her heart every hour of the day. She wondered if God was hearing her prayers at all. She was a bit surprised when Trina invited her to go to church with her one Sunday. This was a large Baptist church, with a large congregation. Shelly was very impressed with the welcome she received from everyone, including the Pastor. She and Trina sat in on a young women's Sunday School class. Again, Shelly was very much impressed with the fellowship and the teaching. After the class ended, and everyone was seated in the sanctuary for the worship service, Shelly began to get really nervous. It got worse as the minutes passed. Finally the anxiety got so bad she asked Trina to take her home. Trina said nothing on the way home, just waiting for Shelly to break the silence. Shelly felt a bit ashamed, having to walk out of the church during the singing. She told herself she had failed again – she had failed God and she had failed her good friend.

Trina was very kind, and very discerning. She sensed that Shelly had some very real emotional issues. Arriving at Shelly's townhouse, she told Shelly she knew a well-respected psychologist who could help her if she would agree to talk to him, adding that she had been under his care herself. Shelly immediately accepted her recommendation, knowing she had to have professional help, and thanking Trina for caring so much. On her first visit to the psychologist, after only a few minutes listening to Shelly, he knew she was suffering from Panic Disorder. After less than an hour, he also correctly diagnosed her with Post Traumatic Stress Disorder. The dark horrors of her past, the hardships and trauma of her adolescence, along with all the stress she was presently enduring had left her deeply scarred psychologically. The doctor prescribed a single medication for Shelly. She was fearful of taking the medication, but wanting to get better, she followed his orders. To her great surprise, the results were much quicker than she anticipated. After only a few visits to Dr. Shaw, and taking her medication as prescribed, she began to feel much better. She found herself actually enjoying life, getting through several days without any anxiety at all. One night as she knelt to pray by the bedside of the two boys, she found herself talking to God more intimately than she ever had before. Among the many things for which she was thankful, she thanked Him for Dr. Shaw, and for her good friend Trina.

The next time Trina invited her to church they skipped the Sunday School class, going straight into the morning worship service. Again she was welcomed by nearly every person there. This time there was something special in the singing. Even though she didn't know the words to the hymns, she caught herself humming along to the melody. The size of the crowd, which would have overwhelmed her before, now seemed to offer her comfort and safety. She had never been to a Baptist Church before this one, but now that she was here, she loved what she saw, what she heard, and what she felt in her heart. Folks she had never met came to her, hugging her neck, smiling, and treating her like she was family. The preacher was different also, quite the opposite of Rev. Stuart. When Pastor Ben got up to preach, a hush fell upon the congregation. When he opened his mouth, the words came from his mouth, but the message came from Heaven. The Holy Spirit took control of his mouth and his mind. What he said ministered grace to those who heard him. It was evident that he was in touch with God. God was speaking through him.

Pastor Ben possessed great wisdom, and with that wisdom he had a heart that reached out to everyone, with a genuine concern for their spiritual well-being. He often reminded the congregation that the messages he delivered were for everyone in general, but for someone in particular. He never knew exactly who that particular person was, but he knew the Holy Spirit was speaking to someone's heart. Today that someone was Shelly. Pastor Ben stepped slowly behind the pulpit, reached into his coat pocket, and pulled out a poem he had found, a poem entitled simply – The Prodigal. As he began to read, many eyes filled with tears, as Pastor Ben seemed to be reading their own histories from the page:

The Prodigal
Have you, like the Prodigal, wandered afar, to a land so strange and unknown;

Are you, like the Prodigal, reaping the harvest, of the bitter seeds you have sown;

Have you, like the Prodigal, wasted it all, and found that you have not a friend;

Have you, like the Prodigal, spent all you have, and facing a road with no end;

Are you, like the Prodigal, wallowing now, in the muck and mire with the swine;

Do you, like the Prodigal now recall, your Father's table so fine;

Do you, like the Prodigal, now realize how much your Father loves you,

Will you, like the Prodigal, make up your mind, as to what you're going to do;

Will you, like the Prodigal, rise up and come back home to your Father so dear;

Do you not see Him running toward you, is that not His voice you hear;

Yes, dear Prodigal, it is He, who welcomes you home again;

He cares not what you may have done, but He sees, and He feels your pain;

Come now my child, and let us dress you in garments fit for a king,

Let all my servants dance with gladness, and let all the maidens sing;

For this my child was lost and undone, but now he is safe and whole,

Rejoice, Rejoice, and praise ye the Lord, Bless the Lord, Oh my soul!

Tears were streaming from Pastor Ben's eyes as he slowly read the poem. His heart throbbed with compassion and gratefulness as one by one folks rose from their pews, coming forward to the altar, with Shelly at the head of the line. That Sunday marked a major turning point in her life. Kneeling there at the altar with scores of others, she poured out her heart to God, asking His forgiveness for all the bad things she had done, and for all the good things she had left undone. Then and there, she made a firm commitment, re-dedicating her life to God and His service. This time, she meant it with all her heart. There would be no turning back.

Shelly and Tony had now lived in the townhouse for five years. Tony had built a good reputation with his work ethic and skill, especially in cleaning and polishing floors. It seemed no one could make a floor look as good as Tony could. As a result of his hard work and dedication he began to get requests from several individuals to clean and polish their floors also. And now it had turned into a small business. Tony had to hire a small crew in order to keep up with the demand. After doing everything at the church where he worked, he stopped by all the other places on his way home, inspecting the work his crew had done, making sure their work met his standards. Soon he and Shelly had saved up a sizeable bank account – enough, in fact, to purchase a new three-bedroom ranch home in one of the finer neighborhoods.   For the first time in a long time, Shelly now believed she understood what real happiness meant. Yes, God did hear, and answer her prayers. Seeing Shelly so happy made Tony happy, and seeing Tony and Shelly so happy had a positive effect on the children. It was such a joy to watch them running and playing, laughing with pure delight – something Shelly had never known as a child.

Not long after they got settled into the new home, several neighbors came over, bringing little housewarming gifts, introducing themselves and their children, and welcoming Shelly and Tony to the neighborhood. Shelly couldn't help but notice that most of the neighbors attended the same church where she and Trina were going. It all seemed almost too good to be true. She and Tony had the nicest house they'd ever had, in the nicest neighborhood they'd ever lived in, and no bill collectors had to call for any reason. She and Tony began taking the children for walks in the evenings, stopping and chatting with a neighbor or two, and letting their children meet all the other children. Shelly prayed another silent prayer as they strolled hand in hand along the new, clean sidewalks.

Tony was still drinking, but not as heavily as he had before – or so Shelly wanted to believe. Tony didn't come home drunk every night like he used to, but did most of his drinking on the weekend. But the drinking he did on the weekends made up for the nights he didn't drink. Sometimes he'd still come home staggering drunk, yelling at Shelly, and provoking her into shoving matches. When these arguments escalated, Shelly began to panic again, losing control of her faculties. She was at her wits end with Tony's drinking, not knowing what to do, or where to turn. Again, it was Trina's sense of discernment that came to Shelly's rescue. Shelly didn't want Trina, or anyone else, for that matter, to know about Tony's drinking problem and the fights they were having because of it. But without Shelly saying anything, Trina somehow knew there was something wrong at home. In her calm and loving way, she told Shelly about a support group she should attend – a group of women who, like herself, had husbands who drank heavily, and provoked fights with their wives.

At first Shelly didn't want to admit that Tony's drinking problem was as bad as it was, not even to herself. She reasoned that since Tony only drank on weekends, he really wasn't an alcoholic. In fact, there were times when, with a bit of begging on her part, Tony had gone for a whole month without drinking. What she didn't know, however, was that Tony was actually drinking every weekend, but was keeping it well hidden from her. After a few more episodes of his coming home drunk, she decided it couldn't hurt to attend one of the meetings. At the first meeting, she discovered some of the ladies whose husbands had the same problem Tony had were some of her neighbors. They were there for the same reason she was there – to try to find answers. She also learned at that first meeting how alcohol had affected whole families, and not just the one who abused it. Some of the ladies began to share with her some things which they had had to do in order to protect themselves and their children from a drunken husband. Before leaving the meeting, all the ladies joined hands and prayed with, and for, one another, for their husbands, and for their families.

Shelly had gone back to cleaning houses with her cousin Carolyn, which, in itself, took her mind off all the negative things for a while. She kept going to church every Sunday, and every Sunday brought new strength, new knowledge, and a deeper understanding of her purpose in life. Slowly she began to understand that her life was not about herself, but about God and those around her. It was there, in church, worshiping Christ with other believers, and feeding upon God's Word, and feeling the very presence and power of God Himself that somehow shut out everything else. There, in the presence of the Holy Spirit, nothing else mattered. In those precious moments, her heart and mind were at peace with God and man. She was learning what it really meant to love, and to be loved. All her children were now in Sunday School every Sunday, and all attended Vacation Bible School during summer vacation from school. Somewhere deep in her heart, she believed God was going to make her family whole again. Shelly prayed about everything now – every decision she made was preceded by prayer. But the one person for whom she prayed more than anyone else was Tony. She didn't know how or when God was going to answer her prayer, but no matter how long it took, she would keep on praying, and she would keep on believing. But one of the many lessons Shelly was about to learn was that God does not always answer our prayers when we expect Him to, and more often than not, He answers our prayers in a manner we neither expect nor prefer, simply because His ways are not our ways, and His thoughts are not our thoughts. But He will always answer in a manner which glorifies His Son, and which is best for us. His timing is always perfect, and His way is always best.

Tony, like so many other men who are addicted to alcohol, refused to admit he was addicted. Also like many others, the next day after a night of drinking found him very sick in the morning, vomiting and promising he would never do it again, and unable to remember all the fun he'd had the night before. Then, after a few days of recuperating from the sickness, he would go right back to it again. One of the many things Shelly had learned at the meetings was to get the children as far away from a drunken man as possible, not only for their physical protection, but also to hopefully prevent them from hearing the cursing and yelling . Each time Shelly heard Tony pounding loudly on the front door, not being able to find the lock, she immediately put the children in the back bedroom, locking the door. She had made up her mind that the next time Tony came home drunk and raging, she was going to confront him with an ultimatum. And with that ultimatum, she was going to put her faith to the test, and leave the consequences up to God. That test came in the wee hours of Saturday morning. Tony went out drinking with his friends Friday night after work. All the *"good 'ol boys"* agreed they were going to *"tie one on."* When Tony hadn't called or come home by midnight, Shelly knew it was going to be one of those nights. She put the children to bed around 9:30 p.m., kissed them good night, and knelt by their beds, praying with them, and for them, reminding them to say an extra special prayer for Daddy.

She was still praying when Tony pounded on the door, yelling at her to *"hurry up and open the damn door."*   She met him at the door, begging him to stop yelling, telling him the kids were asleep. Tony shoved her backward, totally ignoring her pleading. He had to get to the bathroom, and quickly. Shelly heard him retching in the bathroom. He stayed in the bathroom almost an hour, vomiting and rinsing his mouth with water and mouthwash. Shelly waited patiently, praying for God to give her proper words to say to Tony. When he finally came out of the bathroom, Shelly asked him to sit down on the sofa. There was something in Shelly's tone he had never heard before. She was very calm, not raising her voice at all like she used to do when he came home drunk. There was a certain seriousness in her voice he couldn't ignore. Shelly looked him straight in the eye, holding his hand, speaking in a sweet and even tone:

"Tony, you know I love you. There's nothing I wouldn't do for you if I thought it would make you happy. Well now I'm going to do just that. It has become quite clear to me that you are not happy with me, and I realize it's all my fault. I'm not the kind of woman you deserve. I have so many fears and emotional problems to deal with, and it's not fair to you for me to keep putting you through all the trauma. I'm leaving Tony, so you can find a good and decent woman who can make you a lot happier than I can, a woman who doesn't have all the hang ups I have. I'm packing my things tomorrow Tony, and I'm taking the kids with me."

This was one time in their marriage when Shelly's words had a sobering effect – literally. Reality hit Tony where it hurt the most – in his heart. Seeing the sincerity in Shelly's eyes, and hearing it in her voice suddenly awakened all his dull senses, drugged by the alcohol. She was going to leave him! Glancing toward the children's bedrooms, then back into Shelly's face, he knew he couldn't live without her, or without his children. Hanging his head in shame for several moments, he finally found the courage to look into Shelly's eyes. The deep hurt he saw there was more than he could bear. Now it was his turn to speak. Struggling to hold back his tears, he began:

"Shelly, I'm so sorry for being so stupid for so long. It's not your fault baby, it's mine. I've been using the deaths of my Mom and Dad as an excuse to get drunk, lying to myself, and neglecting you and the kids. And I know I've hurt you deeply. I need help Shelly, and I want help. I can't bear the thought of losing you and the kids. I know I'm an alcoholic, and I promise I'll get help." Shelly reached into her purse, taking out a small piece of paper with the phone number of a rehab center for alcoholics.

Tony wasted no time in getting into a recovery program. The church where he worked agreed to stand behind him for the duration of his treatment, holding his job for him until he completed the program. To Tony's amazement, his insurance was willing to pay the full cost of his recovery, with the stipulation that he had to remain in the program until the doctors and counselors agreed he was sufficiently recovered to return to work, and he was to follow up with going to the Alcoholics Anonymous meetings for further counseling. He found it very touching that everyone who attended the church where he worked was so supportive and encouraging. No one condemned him. Many of the staff and congregation came to visit him at the rehab center, offering him their prayers and support, telling him he was a good man, and how they understood the sorrow he had endured in the loss of his parents.

Shelly kept working with her cousin Carolyn, cleaning homes and offices. While Tony was in rehab, the church where he worked offered her and Carolyn the job of cleaning the church, paying Shelly Tony's full salary. Shelly never mentioned Tony's addiction and recovery effort to her church. Everyone had been so good to her since she had started attending there, she just couldn't bring herself to burden them with another one of her problems. But the whole time Tony was in recovery, she went to the altar every Sunday, praying for him. Each time she went to the altar, all her friends came with her, kneeling beside her, praying with her. She never left the altar without thanking God for answered prayer.

The initial program into which Tony was placed lasted thirty days. He missed Thanksgiving with his family, but got to go home before Christmas. Tony came home a different man. Never had he been so thankful and happy to see his wife and family, and never had his family been so thankful and happy to see him. After a long round of hugs and kisses from everyone, he saw the big chocolate cake, (his favorite,) sitting on the dining room table. It was a time of family celebration like nothing either of them had known growing up. The glow on Tony's face as he looked around the table at his wife and children said more than mere words could ever say. From this day forward, his family was all that mattered to him. Tony attended the AA meetings faithfully, determined he would beat his addiction. Never again would the smell of alcohol be found in his home.

Shelly's Aunt Elizabeth had been such a blessing to everyone in Shelly's family. Whenever anyone needed a babysitter, or someone to clean their house, or to run an errand, Elizabeth was always there to help any way she could. She had been a godsend to Marcy when Marcy was in the workhouse for six months. But while Elizabeth was busy taking care of everyone else, she was neglecting herself, especially her own health. Not wanting to burden anyone else with her troubles, she never told anyone about going to the clinic, where she was diagnosed with polyps in her colon. She was told the polyps needed to be surgically removed immediately, because they could be malignant. She ignored the doctor's advice. She had no income, no health insurance, and no one who could afford to pay for any kind of surgery, and she was too proud to ask anyone for help. She continued to help everyone else for as long as she was physically able. But, like the doctors had predicted, the polyps were malignant. She got weaker and weaker, losing her appetite, and losing weight rapidly. When she could no longer function, she had no choice but to go to the hospital. She had waited too late. The cancer had now spread throughout her body. The doctor told her he could perform surgery on her colon, and perhaps prolong her life for six months at best. She agreed to the surgery, but insisted he allow her to tie up some loose ends first.

Shelly had often called her aunt, inviting her to go to church with her, but Elizabeth had always found an excuse not to go.

She had been to church perhaps three or four times in her life. Now she was afraid – afraid of death, and more afraid of what might await her after death. With Shelly's next call, she quickly agreed to go to church with her. There was one loose end she dared not leave untied – the destiny of her immortal soul. She had seen a definite change in Shelly's life, a change that stood out in sharp contrast to what Shelly used to be. There was a radiance in Shelly's face, and a sweet peacefulness that could not be explained in any common terms.   Shelly had undergone some kind of transformation, something which no earthly doctor or medicine could induce. Whatever Shelly had, Elizabeth wanted it.

The doors of Crestview Baptist Church were seldom closed. There was some kind of activity going on nearly every day of the week. But no matter what the agenda was on any given day, there was always prayer and singing beforehand.   Elizabeth's surgery was scheduled for Wednesday morning. She went to church with Shelly on Tuesday evening. Stepping out of the car in the parking lot, Elizabeth looked around slowly. It was the largest parking lot and church building she had seen. But there was something else which impressed her even more than the size of the place – standing there just looking around, there was a certain sacred aura which seemed to hover about the whole place. Suddenly she recalled a sermon she had heard as a little girl, something about Moses removing his shoes when God told him he was standing on holy ground. That's how she felt now – she was standing on holy ground. Shelly, seeing the strange look on her aunt's face, understood exactly what she was feeling, for she had felt it too, the first time she had come to the church with Trina. She smiled, taking her aunt's hand, as the two of them walked slowly together toward the door of the sanctuary. When Elizabeth stepped inside the church, her heart began to beat faster. Before anyone said a single word to her, she already knew why she had come. Jesus had been waiting for her for a long time.

She and Shelly sat down near the back of the church. As the song leader stood up, he announced – *"Let's all stand and sing the old Baptist anthem, Amazing Grace!"* The sweet harmony of everyone singing in unison brought back precious memories from long ago. How she wished she had gone to church more! The first two lines of the old hymn brought tears to her eyes – *"Amazing grace, how sweet the sound, that saved a wretch like me. I once was lost, but now am found, was blind, but now I see."* Shelly saw the tears streaming down her aunt's cheeks. Putting her arm around her, she asked, *"Aunt Beth, do you want to go to the altar and give your life to Jesus?"* Elizabeth nodded her head. As the hymn continued, she and Shelly stepped into the aisle to walk down to the altar. Everyone in the pew behind them stepped out to follow. As they passed each row of pews, everyone in that row followed them to the altar, kneeling to pray with Elizabeth. Pastor Ben was already there. No one had to say anything to Elizabeth – they all sensed her reason for coming. After only a few moments at the altar, she raised her head, asking Pastor Ben to baptize her. Pastor Ben smiled, asking her – *"Have you accepted the Lord Jesus Christ as your personal Savior?"* With a big beaming smile, and tears of joy now streaming down her face, she replied – *"Yes Pastor, Jesus has saved my soul, and I want to be baptized tonight if it's possible."* Hearing her aunt say that she was saved were the sweetest words Shelly had heard in a long time. Her heart rejoiced, knowing that one more member of her family was now saved, and God was answering her prayers. Pastor Ben had one of the ladies find a baptismal robe for Elizabeth. The whole congregation remained to witness her baptism. Shelly left the church that night happier than she had been in a long time, praying with each step for each member of her family. A few days after her surgery, Elizabeth was dismissed. Pastor Ben came to visit every day, sitting beside her in her bedroom, praying with her. Six weeks after the surgery, Elizabeth went home to be with the Lord.

The Darby family, George, Cheryl, and their two children, a boy and a girl, lived in the big house directly behind Shelly and Tony. Shelly and Cheryl had become close friends not long after she and Tony moved in. Shelly had often remarked to Cheryl how beautiful her house was, and how she would love to have a house like that someday, but knew they could never afford it. Cheryl smiled, thanking Shelly for the compliment, but adding – *"Well, you never know Shelly, someday soon you may just be able to move into a house just like this one."* Shelly grinned, appreciating the encouragement, but certain that she would never be able to afford a house like this. Cheryl continued – *"As a matter of fact, George and I are looking at another house way out in the country. The only problem is, we have to sell this house as soon as possible in order to buy the one we want. Let me talk to George tonight when he gets home, and see if we can come up with a plan to sell this house to you and Tony."*

Again Shelly thanked her for her offer, but in her heart she knew it was next to impossible for her and Tony to buy the house. As she got up to leave, she told Cheryl – *"I'll be praying for you and George to get that house in the country."* A few days later, George (who was an attorney,) and Cheryl came over to talk to Tony and Shelly. He said he had a little business proposition for them. Shelly and Tony couldn't imagine what kind of business proposition the Darbys could possibly have with them. George asked Tony if he would be interested in buying the Darby's house. Tony, like Shelly, was a bit shocked, knowing he couldn't afford a house like that.

With as much grace as he could muster, Tony replied – *"George, I'd love to have your house, but there's no way I could afford to pay you what it's worth."*

George insisted – *"Well, just hear me out before you say no. What if I can make you a deal you can afford? Would you be interested?"* Tony assured him he would definitely be interested. George continued – *"Here's what I'll do. You put your house up for sale, and whatever you get for your house, that's the price I'll ask for my house. As you know, I'm an attorney, and I will take care of all the paper work, no charge. I'll make it as easy on you as I possibly can."*

It was a deal too good to pass up. Both Tony and Shelly were in awe, not knowing quite how to respond. Tony thought there must be a catch somewhere. George assured him there would be no fine print, and no legal fees. All he needed was Tony's hand shake to seal the deal. Less than two months later, Shelly and Tony moved into their dream home. They didn't know it at the time, but this would be their home for the rest of their lives. Every night found Shelly on her knees, thanking God for all His blessings. She was now thirty-two years old, Tony was thirty-one, Tony Jr. was twelve, James was nine, and Mary was five. Looking around at her family gathered around the supper table, her mind drifted back to how things used to be, and the many old and ramshackle houses in which she had lived as a child. It made her heart swell with gratitude.

Shelly had now regained her driver's license. Now she was able to take the children to church and Sunday School herself. She also stopped and picked up as many other children as she could get in the car. By the time she got to church, she usually had seven or eight children with her. She kept asking Tony to go to church with her, but to no avail. He insisted he was Catholic, and had no desire, and no intentions of becoming anything else. Shelly finally stopped asking him. Pastor Ben couldn't help but notice how the children seemed to be drawn to Shelly like a magnet. Several of the Sunday School teachers noticed it also. Mrs. Wiser, one of the elderly teachers, informed Pastor Ben that she was no longer able to teach the children because of her health and her fading vision. She recommended Shelly for the position. Shelly loved all the children, but wasn't sure she was qualified to be a teacher. Mrs. Wiser assured her she was qualified.

Up to this point, Shelly had been faithful in her attendance, in her giving, and in inviting and bringing as many folks with her as she could persuade to come. But she had never actually joined the church yet. Pastor Ben told her he would love to have her teach the children, but she would have to become a member of the church first. Shelly joined the church the following Sunday. The following Sunday she was teaching the children's class. Looking back at her own childhood, and all the dark horrors she had endured, it was a bit difficult for her to grasp how God was using her in His service. Looking around her Sunday School room, seeing all the smiles and sweet innocence of the children, it was humbling to be entrusted with the duty of teaching them about Jesus and His love. She loved watching the children's excitement as they hunted the eggs she hid on Easter. But more than anything else, she loved the response she got from them while she taught them. Whenever it came time for Vacation Bible School, Shelly was one of the first teachers to volunteer for service in any area where she might be needed.

The excitement of what God was doing in her life was more than Shelly could contain. She had to share her joy with others. She began by witnessing to her own family - her Dad, her sisters, her cousins, aunts and uncles, inviting them to church every time they got together for any family event. But her family was living totally different lives. They wanted no part of church and religion. Each time Shelly invited them to church, some of them would make fun of her, especially Hank, calling her by the name of the wife of a certain well-known "televangelist." And to further insult her, they would go on with their cursing and fighting. Shelly was happy when the family event was over. But she kept praying for all of them. Her prayers did not go unanswered. The one person she least expected to show up at church was Hank. He was the first one to show up.

With all that Shelly had experienced up to this point in her life, all the shame she had known as a child, all the abuse, the neglect, the dangers she had faced, and the many fears she had dealt with, she doubted that anything that might happen from this point on could really make much difference, one way or the other. But her life was about to be shattered yet again. It must be said, however, that many other folks of lesser character, faith and strength would probably have been broken spiritually, had they been subjected to the trials through which she was about to go. Her faith was about to be put to yet another test, and in a way she would never have suspected. Here is a single life, a real life, a life which, in the face of all adversity, serves as a shining exemplary standard through which God's amazing grace and faithfulness can be clearly seen.

Shelly's sister Beth and her two children, Stephanie and Josh, moved out to Bedford close to where Shelly lived. It was so nice to have family close by again. Beth had accepted a job working for the school system and suggested that Shelly apply for a job also. Not long after applying, Shelly landed the job as a cook at the school where her children attended. It was a dream job for her, because she could work, and still be at home with the children in the afternoon. Her years of experience at the fast food restaurant, and the recommendation she received from her former boss paid off. The pay was decent, and there were some good benefits that came with the job, health insurance being one of the most important.

It didn't take long for Shelly to establish herself as a hard worker, and like she had always done at every job, she went the extra mile, pitching in and doing things she was not required to do, just to help out. When she wasn't cooking, she was cleaning up, or doing dishes. And it didn't take her long to win the hearts of her co-workers. Her outgoing personality brought a bit of humor to an otherwise dull atmosphere. She brightened up the place.

The work was by no means easy, having hundreds of meals to prepare every day, but a positive attitude, hard work, and a bit of laughter seemed to make the time go just a bit faster. And then there was a paycheck every week, which helped pay the bills. After about a year, Tony got a job at the school, doing what he loved – maintenance, and cleaning and polishing the floors, especially the big gymnasium.   Working at the school also gave Shelly the opportunity to get acquainted with a lot of other children – all the friends her three children had gotten to know. Whenever Shelly walked out onto the school grounds, a circle of children soon gathered around her. There was something about Shelly that drew children to her. She showed a genuine love for all of them, and patiently listened to what they had to say. Not long after she began working at the school, she was bringing several of the children to Sunday School and church.

Both of her sons, Little Tony and James were in the Youth Group at church now. They were also into different sports – soccer, baseball and basketball. Between going to their games, working, being a wife and mother, and teaching Sunday School, she had very little free time, but was thoroughly enjoying every minute of all of it. Tony attended a few games, but he was never really interested in sports. But it made Shelly and the boys happy when he did show up. Mary and her cousin Stephanie, who was about the same age as Mary, were in the Girl Scouts. Since they had first met, they soon became inseparable, just like Shelly, Beth and Marcy had been when they were younger. The Troop Leader, who had been with the girls for many years had to quit because of her health. Reba, Shelly's step sister, Barb's daughter, was appointed as the new Troop Leader, with Shelly as her assistant. It was another dream come true for Shelly, getting to spend a lot more quality time with Mary, something she had never known with her Mom. She sadly reflected upon the many hours and days she had missed doing fun things with her kids because of all her anxieties.

It happened rather suddenly. Shelly began noticing when she got up in the morning, she would suddenly lose her vision in her right eye for just a second or two. Then it would come back just as suddenly. The ophthalmologist she had seen nearly a year ago had given her a good report, telling her she didn't have any problems with her vision at all. When she began to have these momentary black outs, she diagnosed herself with poor circulation. But the temporary loss of vision became more frequent, and more prolonged. A friend of Shelly's, who saw the same family doctor as Shelly, needed a ride to her appointment. While there Shelly mentioned these episodes of vision loss to her doctor. He immediately recommended she see an ophthalmologist as soon as possible. This quick recommendation scared her just a bit, but she promised she would make and keep an appointment. Returning to the same ophthalmologist she had seen a year before, she and Tony waited in the waiting room. When the doctor came out and saw Shelly sitting there, he scowled at Shelly, being downright rude to her, asking her why she had come back after he had told her last year that her vision was fine. Both Tony and Shelly were very much offended by his attitude. Shelly got the impression he was trying to make her look stupid. Shelly told him about her episodes of vision loss, and that her family doctor had referred her back to him.

While examining Shelly's eyes this time, his whole demeanor changed quickly. He had discovered an inflamed optical nerve in her right eye. He immediately called the hospital, ordering an MRI and complete blood work for Shelly, and giving her another appointment so see him after getting the results of those tests. The very thought of being inside a machine in such a confined space frightened Shelly. She had never had an MRI, but had heard other folks talking about the experience. Tony assured her he would be there with her every moment. The day of the scan Shelly told the nurses she had panic attacks, and was claustrophobic. They allowed Tony to stand beside her, and rub her legs during the procedure. The nurse told her that if they found anything serious they would have to inject contrast into her IV and take more pictures. This, of course, frightened her even more, but she knew she had to have it done, and just wanted to get it over with as soon as possible.

As she lay there inside the machine, she prayed for everyone she could think of, being grateful that she was able to talk to God. When the lady told her they were going to have to inject the contrast, she nearly went into panic, knowing they had found something really bad. After the MRI and blood tests were all completed, and the results verified, she and Tony returned to the ophthalmologist.   After reading the results, he told Shelly he had good news and bad news. Shelly wanted the good news first. The doctor now appeared to be very sad, as he told her – *"The good news is - you don't have a brain tumor. The bad news is*

- you do have a tumor on your optical nerve, and I've never seen anything like it before." The surgeon, and director of the practice where Shelly's ophthalmologist worked, was in surgery while Shelly was there. Her ophthalmologist called him out of surgery to take a look at Shelly's results. He immediately gave her an appointment to come back and see him. On the way home Shelly remained silent. The word *"tumor"*, to her, meant *"cancer"*. She jumped to the conclusion that she was going to die as a result of this tumor. And even though she was not afraid to die, she wept, thinking she was going to die and leave Tony and her children. How could she break the news to her children? That night, as she had evening devotions with the boys and Mary, she told them what the doctors had found. All three of the children joined hands with her, praying for her. James was so devastated, thinking his Mom was going to die of cancer, he ran upstairs to his bedroom, not wanting the family to see his tears.

Through several sources, including co-workers, Tony heard of another doctor – Doctor Moser, who specialized in eye surgery. Doctor Moser was a Christian doctor, who had prayer with every one of his patients before any surgical procedure. After reading all of the results from Shelly's other tests, and examining her himself, he was 90% certain the tumor was not cancerous, although he admitted he had never seen anything like it in his career. Since Shelly still had good vision in that eye, Dr. Moser recommended that no surgery be done unless the tumor grew, and for now, it hadn't grown any. But Dr. Moser also recommended that she get several other opinions from other doctors. One of those doctors was Dr. Grant, a brain specialist, who also performed several different tests, including more MRI's, keeping a close watch on the tumor in particular.

Shelly continued to work at the school while all her tests were being done. Several specialists continued to monitor the tumor and her vision. With only a minimal loss of vision detected over a seven year period, all the doctors agreed the loss was due to age, and not from the tumor, so there was no need for surgery yet. Then it happened.   Working beside her friend Jan in the kitchen, Shelly was chopping up vegetables on the long butcher block. Suddenly Jan jumped backward, screaming – *"Shelly, you almost cut my finger off!"*   Shelly didn't even see Jan's finger. She knew she was losing her vision in her right eye.   She knew she needed to go see doctor Moser again. Dr. Moser recommended she get an appointment with a prominent brain surgeon he knew – Dr. Jordan.   While Shelly was making the appointment, all her records were being sent to Dr. Jordan. When she got to his office, he ordered one more MRI. While waiting on the results, he and Dr. Moser collaborated on Shelly's condition. Looking at the results of the last MRI, they both agreed she needed surgery as soon as possible. The tumor was spreading horizontally, toward her left eye. If it was not removed soon, it would blind her in both eyes. It wasn't easy breaking the news to Shelly and Tony, but Dr. Jordan knew it couldn't be avoided. Shelly had a ton of questions, and Dr. Jordan tried to answer all of them as honestly as possible, yet trying to give her as much hope as his professional knowledge would allow. Shelly left his office with tears in her eyes that day. Both she and Tony were really scared.

Shelly's whole family was afraid for her to have the surgery, but especially Hank. He begged her not to have the surgery. But Shelly asked all of them to have faith, and to pray that God would get her through this. Of course everyone in her church was praying, along with all her other friends. As the day approached for her to have the surgery, Shelly began to panic. She tried to be strong, but as she pondered what Dr. Moser had told her, her fear grew worse. The surgery would last about nine hours, and there was a possibility she would wake up totally blind in her right eye. Now she was praying for courage to make it through another day without a panic attack.   It happened that one of her little nieces, Kimmy, who was four years old, came to stay with Shelly and her family while her parents were away on vacation. She slept in the half bed opposite Shelly's bed. Each night Shelly would kneel beside Kimmy's bed as they prayed together.   A few nights before Shelly's surgery, after she and Kimmy had their devotions, Shelly fell asleep. Little Kimmy came over to her bed, waking her up.

Shelly, thinking the little girl was scared, or needed to go to the bathroom, asked her what she wanted. Kimmy smiled, petting Shelly on her shoulder, saying – *"Aunt Shelly, you have got to have this surgery. Jesus knows you have been through a lot in your life, and He brought you through it all, and He will bring you through this surgery too."* Shelly was speechless. Kimmy was only four years old, and didn't know anything about her life and all the things she had been through.   Maybe God was using this little girl to give her a little more comfort and courage for what she was about to endure. She gave Kimmy a big hug, telling he how much she loved her. She slept much better that night. But as the day of the surgery drew closer, she began to get really nervous again. Dr. Moser had prescribed some medications to keep her calm, but she had not been taking them.   She stopped eating much of anything, and was losing weight. Mary, noticing Shelly's weight loss and frantic activity, begged her to take her medication.   When Mary took her to see her family doctor, Dr. Stanz, he scolded Shelly for not taking her medication, and for not eating properly, reminding her she needed to be as physically strong as possible when she had the surgery.   Shelly took his advice. After getting on the medications, and eating properly, she began to feel a lot better, physically and mentally. A few days before the surgery, she began receiving flowers, gifts, cards and letters from all her friends at church, encouraging her, and assuring her they were all praying for her daily. But the best gift of all was from Tony Jr. and his wife Sarah – a little grandson – Harrison Anthony Davidson.

The night before her surgery, Shelly prayed for a beautiful day full of sunshine. The first thing she noticed when she woke up that morning was the sunlight coming through her window. She smiled, thanking God for another answered prayer. Arriving at the hospital, the waiting room was packed with folks from Crestview Baptist Church, including Hank, in his wheelchair. Shelly, knowing her Mom was not emotionally stable enough to be there for her surgery, had called and asked Sheila to pray for her at home. Sheila was relieved, because she also knew she couldn't handle being there. Tony and the children, along with every family member there, all kissed her before they took her downstairs. Hank rolled forward in his wheelchair, holding her hand, bowing his head, praying out loud for her safety and recovery. That prayer meant more to Shelly than all the gifts, flowers, cards and letters she had received.   All her fear vanished. She was at perfect peace, no matter what the outcome might be.

Ten hours later Shelly woke up in her hospital room. Someone was standing over her, crying. It was her daughter Mary. When Shelly asked her what was wrong, Mary quickly recovered from her shock. She hadn't expected her Mom to be so swollen and discolored from the surgery.   Not wanting to frighten Shelly, she told her everything had gone great. Tony came over to her bedside, taking her hand, assuring her everything went well. When Dr. Moser came in, Shelly was fully alert, waiting for his report. Shelly asked him not to mince words, but to just give it to her straight. Dr. Moser was amazed at how alert and coherent she was so soon after the ten-hour ordeal. He told her Dr. Jordan had removed all of the tumor, but both he and Dr. Jordan were pretty sure she would not be able to see again with her right eye. They were right. Shelly was totally blind in her right eye.

The doctors expected a long recovery period for Shelly, telling her she would probably have to stay in the hospital from one to two weeks. To their surprise, she was ready to go home after only four days. Tony and Mary stayed with her the whole four days. Tony missed four days of work, and Mary missed four days of school. Marcy came with Tony and Mary, but stayed outside in the waiting room. Hearing Tony and Mary describe Shelly's appearance, she couldn't bear seeing her sister in that condition. As thrilled as she was to get home, Shelly was still too weak to take care of herself. Tony and Mary tended to her every need. She kept telling herself today would be the day she would have the courage to look in the mirror. But each day brought new fear. Finally she decided it was time to face her fear. Her first glance at herself in the mirror was horrifying. She gasped, thinking – "*I look like a monster!*" Now she understood why Tony and the children hadn't said anything about her appearance. But the longer she stood in front of the mirror, the more she thanked God for bringing her through the surgery, and for sparing her the loss of both eyes. When she went for her first checkup with Dr. Moser, he was well pleased with her appearance, telling her she had healed a lot faster than he had expected. Before she left his office that day, Dr. Moser had prayer with her. His parting words to her were – "*Shelly, I believe God has great things in store for you.*"

The following Sunday was Easter, and Shelly desperately wanted to go to church even though her appearance was noticeably altered from how she used to look. But this was a very special day – the day of the resurrection of her Lord and Savior. She wanted to honor Him by being in His house with all her friends on this special day, regardless of her personal appearance. Mary drove her to church. As Mary held her Mom's arm, guiding her into the church, several folks got up from their pews, offering Shelly and Mary their seat close to the aisle. Shelly sat through the singing, but was too weak to stay for the whole service. She was grateful God had given her the strength to be there.

Shelly had lost count of all the visitors who came to see her during her recovery. Nearly every person from her church had been there within two weeks after she got home. Every person who came offered their services to both her and Tony, and each person took the time to have prayer with her before leaving. All her cousins, including Phillip and Carolyn, drove more than twenty miles to visit her.   She kept wondering why Marcy had not come to visit her. After all, they had been so close all their lives. Marcy's son, Buck Jr., now had a daughter of his own. When she was born, she looked so much like Marcy Buck Jr. decided to name her after his Mom. She would grow up being called – Little Marcy.   When Marcy finally got the courage to come and see Shelly, she brought Little Marcy with her. Seeing Shelly's closed eye for the first time was a bit of a shock for Marcy, but she was so happy to finally see Shelly, they embraced in a long sister's hug, crying tears of joy.

Shelly kept trying to hide the right side of her face from Little Marcy, thinking it would frighten her. Each time Marcy would bring her over, Shelly would deliberately sit on Little Marcy's right side so that she could only see the left side of her face. After Shelly had recovered sufficiently, Marcy started letting her babysit Little Marcy once in a while. And like every other child who ever came within arm's reach of Shelly, Little Marcy fell in love with her great aunt immediately. She sat and watched Shelly brushing her long beautiful hair. And as young as she was, she couldn't help but notice Shelly always keeping the right side of her face turned away from her while she brushed her hair. One day while Shelly was sitting on the opposite end of the big sofa, Little Marcy picked up the hair brush in one hand, holding a beautiful butterfly hair clip in the other.   Shelly watched her coming toward her, smiling. Little Marcy came over to Shelly's right side first, laying the butterfly clip on the end table, sitting down on Shelly's right side, in full view of her right eye. Slowly she began brushing Shelly's hair, ever so gently. When she felt she had brushed her hair enough, she picked up the butterfly hair clip, fastening it into Shelly's hair. Stepping back a few steps, she looked Shelly over, commenting – *"There now Aunt Shelly, you are so beautiful."* Shelly's eyes filled with tears as she held Little Marcy in her arms, hugging and kissing her. A little girl, more mature than Shelly had given her credit for being, had just given her a gift she would never forget.

Shelly wasn't so sure the school would allow her to return to work in the kitchen with her being totally blind in one eye, especially after she had almost cut off Jan's finger. To her pleasant surprise, however, everyone welcomed her back. It took her a few days to get re-adjusted to things. She found herself bumping into things and people. But everyone was so glad to have her back, they all made some adjustments themselves, giving Shelly just a bit more room when working in close quarters with her. After two weeks, Shelly was right back in the swing of things, doing her job as efficiently as she had before the surgery.

Shelly had been writing short poems ever since she was thirteen. Whatever came to mind, she wrote it down, never dreaming any of her poems would have any meaning to anyone else.

At work, she couldn't help but notice the sadness in her friend Jan's face. She didn't know it, but Jan was going through one of the roughest times of her life. Jan tried not to let her feelings show, but Shelly could tell she was not the same happy, fun-loving Jan she had known before her surgery. Shelly was never one to pry into her friends' affairs, so she did what she did best – she prayed for Jan every day and night, asking God to give her a kind word of encouragement for her friend. She began writing little poems for Jan every day, leaving them in Jan's locker. Each poem contained a message of hope and encouragement. Sometimes she would catch Jan standing in front of her locker, reading one of the poems, smiling as she read.   After reading several of Shelly's poems, Jan approached Shelly, telling her how much she enjoyed the poems, and how each one had encouraged her, adding that Shelly should consider having all her poems published in book form.

The idea of having her poetry in a book had never occurred to Shelly. She laughed, saying to Jan – " *I'm just a school cook Jan, I don't have a clue as to how to go about putting a book together, and besides, it would cost a lot of money – money that I don't have."* But Jan was very serious, insisting – *"Shelly, you just don't know how beautiful your poems are, and how they would affect other people. If you don't have them published, I will."* Seeing how sincere Jan was, Shelly began searching for someone who might help her get her poems published. As it turned out, her church had a book full of the names, addresses and phone numbers of local Christian businesses who advertised in the book. It was there she found Sandy, a lady who published books for Christian writers.   Mary drove her to talk to Sandy about getting a small booklet published.   Shelly was very nervous about the whole thing, still not confident that her poetry was worthy of being in a book. But Sandy guided her through the whole process, answering all her questions. Mary also offered some suggestions about the design and colors of the cover. Shelly decided to begin with a small booklet instead of a large book. Her first published work, containing about forty short poems, was entitled – Hope In The Storms. As far as Shelly was concerned, it would probably be the only book she would ever have published, but as she was about to discover, God had other plans.

When Crestview Baptist Church had a dinner, it was never a small affair - it was a feast fit for a king.   In order to get Shelly off his back, Hank decided he'd attend one of the dinners, thinking he would not have to listen to any preaching at a church social. But he didn't know Pastor Ben. And he didn't know how the Holy Spirit arranges men's circumstances without their knowledge. At some point, either before or after the dinner, Pastor Ben made sure there was a time of prayer and singing. After the singing, he would deliver a short message. The thing Hank and so many others don't understand is that, no one can hear the   Gospel and remain totally unaffected by it. Whenever the Gospel is preached in the power of the Holy Spirit, it has an effect, because it *must* have an effect. The effect of the Gospel of Jesus Christ will produce one of two effects, depending upon the relationship of the one who hears it. As the old preachers used to say – *"The Gospel will either bless you, or it will burn you."*

After being cordially welcomed by everyone, Hank sat in the back row. He wanted a clear and quick path out of the church in case someone tried to compel him to go to the altar. What he didn't know was that no one at Crestview ever did that to anyone. They allowed folks to make their own decisions, with no coercion from anyone. Hank let Shelly know he didn't want to go to any altar, and he didn't want to be asked to go. Shelly assured him no one would try to persuade him to do anything he didn't want to do on his own. To Shelly's surprise, Hank came back a few more times, always sitting in the back row.

Every time he heard the Gospel, his heart pounded in his chest, as he felt the Holy Spirit drawing him like a magnet draws a piece of steel. But he wouldn't move.   But another thing Hank didn't understand was the power of prayer, and now a whole congregation was praying for him every day and night.

Hank's first diagnosis was diabetes. Next he was told he had congestive heart failure, among other things. He was in and out of the hospital every few weeks. Shelly was becoming more and more concerned. But Hank was like a cat with nine lives – each time he was dismissed from the hospital he went right back to driving his cab. Shelly tried to enlist Beth and Marcy into her prayer group, but it seemed they knew very little about prayer. Hank's wife, Barb, stayed by his side every time he was admitted to the hospital. Then Shelly got a phone call from the hospital. Her Dad was really sick, and the doctor didn't think he was going to make it this time. Shelly bowed her head, praying God would let Hank live till she could get there. When she, Tony and Mary arrived at the hospital, the whole family was there, gathered around Hank's bed.

Shelly didn't know if he was alive or dead. Stepping closer to his bed, she saw he was awake. Leaning over, she kissed his cheek, whispering – *"I love you Daddy, I'm praying for you, and so is the church."* Hank's response shocked her more than any words she had ever heard come from his mouth. With anger in his voice, he looked up at Shelly, nearly shouting – *"It's your prayers that's got me in this shape in the first place, your prayers are my problem, I don't need your prayers, and I don't want your prayers."*   Everyone in the room could see the hurt in Shelly's eyes. No one spoke as Shelly bowed her head in sorrow, crying, leaving the room without saying goodbye to anyone.   Marcy called Shelly every day that week, telling her Hank was getting worse.

Shelly's best friend, Emily, and her daughter, Jenny, who was Mary's best friend, came to visit Shelly Friday evening. As the conversation shifted to Hank and his condition, Mary interjected – *"Mom, we have to do something, Papaw has to get saved."* Shelly asked Emily to please pray for her Dad. Before they could bow their heads in prayer, Lori, Emily's neighbor knocked on the door.   Emily asked her to join them in prayer for Shelly's Dad. The five of them joined hands in a circle, praying for Hank's health, and for his salvation.

When the phone rang Saturday morning, Shelly, seeing the number on the caller ID, was afraid to answer, fearing her Dad may have died during the night.   When she finally picked up the phone, it was Hank himself, sobbing uncontrollably, while trying to talk at the same time. Shelly was afraid he was going to give her bad news. Quietly she asked – *"What's wrong Dad?"* The words she was about to hear were the sweetest words she'd ever heard. Between sobs, Hank managed to make her understand – *"Oh, Shelly, I'm so sorry for all the mean things I said to you.   I want you to be the first to know, God came into my room last night, and He came into my heart. I've never felt anything like this, I'm so happy Shelly, I can't stop crying."* Hearing Hank sobbing and talking, the nurses came into his room, wanting to know what was wrong. Hank immediately replied – *"Nothing's wrong now, everything's right. The Lord has forgiven me of all my sins, and I'm telling my daughter about it."* The nurses left with a strange look on their faces, as Hank continued talking to Shelly – *"When I get out of here, I'm coming to church, and I'm going to the altar, and I promise you, I'll never turn my back on God again."*

Shelly and her friends had been praying for Hank for eight years. Tony was thirty-nine, Shelly was forty, Tony Jr. was now twenty, James was seventeen, and Mary was thirteen. Hank kept his word to Shelly.

He went to the altar, was baptized, and attended church faithfully, sitting up near the front of the church with Barb, every Sunday. The diabetes had gotten worse – so bad, in fact, Hank had to have his left leg amputated. After he had sufficiently recovered from the surgery, he continued to go to church in a wheel chair, and he still rolled up to the front, where he could hear the singing and the preaching. Fortunately, with his medical insurance, he had a prosthesis made, which enabled him to still drive his cab.

The change in Hank Smith's life was radical, to say the least. He had always been able to make friends easily, but now it seemed the whole world loved him, and he loved everyone. He had a whole new outlook on life, and a much better attitude. He and Shelly now had long conversations, with no yelling, no cursing, and no judgment. Hank could now look his daughter in the face, and tell her he loved her, and really mean it, which was something he had never done when she was little.

Hank's conversion was a lot like Shelly's conversion – he had a testimony he couldn't keep inside. He had to share his newfound faith with everyone he met, and he met a lot of people. Hank's reputation as a cab driver had gained him some recognition and respect, even among the more well-to-do citizens, officials, and a few dignitaries in the greater Columbus area. Whenever a high-ranking official needed a cab from the airport, they called Hank first, knowing he would be there on time, his cab was always immaculately clean, and he was easy to talk to. Hank had even become friends with a Senator. The local newspaper wanted to do a big story on Hank and his cab, but Hank refused. From the day he received the Lord Jesus as his Savior, he never failed to share his testimony with every passenger he picked up.

Many men and women got out of Hank's cab with tears in their eyes, having heard his story of how Jesus had saved his soul, and changed his life. Hank's life was so radically different from what it had been, most folks who knew him before could hardly believe the change they saw in him. He had a spring in his step, a smile on his face, and a song in his heart. Whereas before he would engage in off-color conversations and dirty jokes with his friends, now he would not condone foul language in his home or in his cab. Soon after meeting him, wherever that might be, he would steer the conversation toward God, church, and the Bible.

But while Hank was growing stronger in his faith, his body was growing weaker. All the drinking, consuming too much sugar, and rough living he had done, had all taken their toll. And driving his cab twelve to fourteen hours a day, six days a week, which cut off blood circulation to his legs, and not getting enough exercise, all contributed to his failing health. He already knew he had congestive heart failure, and now his kidneys were failing. He could no longer sleep in his bed. He had to sleep in a reclining chair in order to breathe a little better. But none of these things stopped him from going to church. No matter how bad he felt, he never complained, trying to convince everyone he was just fine. But Shelly and her sisters knew better. They could see the steady decline in his appearance. His doctor insisted that he go on dialysis treatment, but Hank refused. Seeing Hank's stubbornness, the doctor begged him to at least have a port installed, so that when he got worse, which was a certainty, they could begin the dialysis immediately. Reluctantly, Hank finally agreed to have the port installed. When he came home from the hospital, it was all Barb could do to keep him from going back to driving his cab. She knew he was in no condition to be driving.

Two weeks before Christmas, Beth came to visit her Dad. Leaning back in his big recliner, Hank still pretended he was fine, trying to keep the conversation as light-hearted as he could, but Beth could tell he was much worse than he had been the last time she saw him in the hospital. As she held his hand, looking into his eyes, Hank knew he wasn't fooling her at all. It was time to be totally honest with his youngest daughter. His voice trembled slightly as he managed a weak smile, but he wanted her to know the truth, and perhaps prepare her for what he knew was going to happen soon. Each sentence was a struggle for him now, as he had to hesitate between every few words to catch his breath:

*"Beth, sweetheart, I love you so much. I know I haven't told you that as much as I should have, and I know I haven't shown it like I should have, but...*Beth stopped him, seeing he was struggling for breath, replying – *"It's ok Dad, you don't have to say anything. All of us know you love us, and you always have. All of us love you too. You just need to rest and do what the doctors tell you, so we can all enjoy Christmas together."* As Hank gripped her hand softly, the expression on his face saddened. She knew he wanted to say something else, and she was terribly afraid of what he might say. Hank drew in a few deep breaths, gripping her hand a bit tighter. He wanted to get it all said before she left: *"Daddy won't be here for Christmas this year honey. And I want you to promise me that all of you will celebrate Christmas just like you always have. But I'll be in Heaven, celebrating Christmas with Christ Himself."* Beth didn't know quite how to respond, but she was trying desperately not to cry. Even though her heart was breaking, she smiled, nodding, letting him know she understood. Just before she closed the door behind her, she turned, taking a long look at her Dad. The frail person in that recliner was a poor representation of the strong, stalwart man she used to know.

The following week, Shelly called her Dad every day. Knowing he couldn't talk very long, she tried to keep her conversations short, but Hank kept her on the phone as long as possible. On the phone he seemed so happy and full of life, he almost had her convinced he was getting better. Shelly even had him laughing, telling him about some of the mischief she, Beth and Marcy used to get into when he was at work.   Each time she hung up the phone, she prayed, thanking God for giving him another day, and praying that God would spare him any pain and suffering.

On December 20th, late in the evening, Barb called Shelly. Hank had had a heart attack. She had called the life squad, and they were there, trying to revive him, but not giving her much hope. Hank was not responding. His pulse was barely discernable. They were going to have to get him to the hospital as quickly as possible. One of the paramedics quickly put an oxygen mask over his nose and mouth, turning the oxygen pressure up to ten. Barb told Shelly they were loading him into the ambulance. Shelly had a bad habit of throwing things when got extremely upset, and this was one of those times. She threw the phone against the wall, venting her frustration. Tony took her in his arms, holding her tightly, trying to calm her, reminding her they needed to rush to the hospital.

When Shelly and Tony arrived the doctors had already put Hank on life support. As Shelly approached his bed, he appeared as if he was just lying there asleep. Shelly began rubbing his hair, speaking softly – *"Daddy, if you can hear me, I want you to know, if you want to go on and be with Jesus, we'll be ok, we don't want you to suffer."* Shelly knew how much her Dad loved singing, and although she never fancied herself a singer, she began singing one of Hank's favorite gospel songs, entitled – Because He Lives. After singing to him, she prayed for him, hugged him, and kissed him goodbye. Shelly dried her tears as she left the hospital, knowing she would never see her Dad alive again. The doctors told Barb they were fairly certain Hank was brain-dead, and that she needed to make the decision to unplug him from the life support.

On the morning of December 22nd, Shelly's step sisters began calling Hank's friends, family, and folks from the church, asking them to come to the hospital, so they could be there when Hank was taken off the life support. The doctors told them Hank wouldn't last more than a few minutes when the machine was unplugged. Shelly, Marcy and Beth refused to go, not wanting to see their Dad take his last breath. But to everyone's surprise, including the doctors and nurses, when the machine was unplugged, Hank started breathing on his own. He lived until the afternoon of December 23rd, two days before Christmas. His funeral was to be on Friday, two days after Christmas, at Crestview Baptist Church.

There may have been a bigger fan of the Ohio State Buckeyes than Hank Smith, but seeing him at one of their games, or hearing him cheering for them while watching them on TV, you wouldn't have thought so. As Shelly used to say, Hank loved, lived and breathed OSU. At his funeral, all his grandsons wore their OSU T-shirts under their dress shirts. After the funeral, they all removed their dress shirts, carrying Hank's casket out of the church wearing their OSU T-shirts.   It was their last gift to him.   Barb said it would have made Hank proud. Shelly and her sisters nodded in agreement.   As the procession left the church to go to the cemetery, a long line of taxi cabs followed behind the family. Shelly sobbed uncontrollably, knowing she would never get to be in church with her Dad again, but yet thankful that she had been instrumental in getting him to come to church, and knowing he was with Jesus now, and she would see him again someday.

When Shelly got her first order of books from Sandy, she prayed, asking God to let the books be a blessing to whoever read them. She made sure her friend Jan, who had encouraged her to get it published, got the first copy. As word began to get around about the booklet, everyone who read it gave Shelly positive reviews, telling her how much they enjoyed reading her poems. Several others sent her letters, telling her how one or more of her poems had helped them through some rough situations. She was especially touched by a letter she received from the school secretary, who told her how much her poems had meant to her while she was going through her radiation treatments. Shelly responded to that letter, telling her it was God who had given her the gift of writing the words, and He deserved all the glory. Shelly brought one of her books to the school kitchen, laying it on a table where anyone who saw it could pick it up and read it. She noticed some of the teachers coming into the kitchen, picking up her book, and reading it with tears streaming down their faces.

Shelly, thinking her poems had caused tears of sadness, began to apologize to them. The teachers assured her their tears were not tears of sadness, but tears of happiness. Shelly could hardly believe how God was using such a small thing as her book of poetry to bless so many others. Then a local card store agreed to take some of her books on consignment. The widespread distribution of her book was more than Shelly could absorb. It had gone so far beyond her expectations, it was hard for her to accept. Then she remembered how she had asked God to make it a blessing to everyone who read it. It was simple – God was answering her prayer. That night, as she lay in bed she began to talk to God, telling Him how unworthy she was of His blessings: *"Dear Lord, surely You have chosen the wrong person for this task. There has to be someone else out there who can do a much better job than I can. I'm just a school cook with a lot of anxieties. I have*

panic attacks, I am afraid to travel, I have only one eye, and I just don't fit the mold You have made for me."

The next morning after praying, Shelly was reading from her book of daily devotions. The words she read seemed to leap off the page at her – *"Broken shells can touch a life in a way no perfect shell ever can."* Tears filled her eyes as she looked up toward Heaven. She was God's broken shell, cracked and broken in so many places, and yet a vessel that He could use to His glory. Then and there she made God a promise that she would do whatever He wanted her to do, and this time, her promise would not become pie crust. After that Shelly could hardly believe the doors that started opening. First the local newspapers did a story on her. Then the biggest newspaper in town did an even bigger story, telling how this little booklet by a local author was touching so many lives. Now Shelly could hardly keep up with the demand for her book. Total strangers were coming up to her asking for the book. She now had to keep some books with her wherever she went. Tony noticed folks coming to Shelly in the grocery store, either asking for a book, or telling her how much they enjoyed reading it. She had now lost count of how many books she had given away for free.

Not long before Mother's Day, Shelly got a call from a local television station, asking her to be on their program on Mother's Day. They told her they wanted to interview her, and promote her book. Shelly's heart leaped into her throat. She was so afraid she would panic, and mess up the whole program. The caller assured her they would take care of any mistakes she might make. When she told Tony, he became more excited than Shelly, telling her how proud he was of her accomplishments. He drove her to the TV Station, staying with her while she waited to be called back for the taping of the show. Shelly paced up and down nervously, praying for strength to get through this without embarrassing herself on public television.   And again, her fears were totally unnecessary. The program went like clockwork. Now Shelly's phone number was out there for everyone to see. As soon as she got home from taping the program, her phone was ringing. As orders for her book kept pouring in, Shelly began sending them out before receiving payment for them. She simply trusted everyone to do the right thing. Many of the checks she received had a nice note with them, telling her how much they appreciated her book. Every day when she checked her mail she looked for a note before looking for a check. She kept and cherished every note she received.

While reading an article in a local paper about a cancer support group, Shelly noticed the group was in a nearby church. Her first thought was to give some of her books to the group. Since the book had turned out to be such a blessing to so many others, perhaps it might be of some value to these ladies. On her way to work Shelly stopped by the church. Melody, the spokesperson for the group, greeted Shelly. Recognizing Shelly from her pictures in the paper, and seeing Shelly's books in her arms, Melody asked Shelly what she was doing Thursday evening. Without thinking about it, Shelly told her she didn't know of anything she had to do Thursday, but that she had just stopped by to see if any of the group might want to read her book, and if so, she wanted to donate as many as were needed. Melody accepted Shelly's donation immediately. As Shelly turned to leave, Melody added – *"Since you don't have anything scheduled for Thursday, you can come and speak to our group."* Shelly froze in her tracks, stammering nervously – *"What? You want me to speak to a group? I've never done anything like that, and I would be too nervous, but thank you for asking."* But Melody was persistent. Calling another lady out into the lobby, she asked Shelly to join hands with them in prayer. Shelly wasn't sure what they were going to pray for, but bowed her head with them. Melody asked God to give Shelly the courage and strength to come and speak to all the cancer patients in the group. Hearing the sincerity in Melody's voice, Shelly stood there totally silent. When Melody raised her head, she smiled at Shelly, shaking her hand, saying – *"We'll see you Thursday at 7:00 p.m."* Shelly nodded in agreement, handing all the books to Melody. As she left, she thanked God for folks like Melody, a lady who voluntarily gave of herself in order to help others in need.

Arriving at the church at 6:50 p.m. Thursday evening, Shelly almost held her breath as she sneaked quietly into the group, keeping her head down as if she didn't want to be seen. She had no idea what she was going to say to this group. As the time drew closer for her to speak her heart raced wildly. Her mouth was dry as cotton. She kept her head bowed, praying for guidance. When Melody stood up to open the meeting, she announced – *"Ladies, tonight we are blessed to have a very special, well-known personality with us...*Shelly looked all around the room, wondering who this special person could be. Maybe she could get their autograph before leaving! Melody's next sentence announced – *"We have Mrs. Shelly Davidson, the author of this book of poetry, entitled "Hope in the Storms", and she is going to be our keynote speaker this evening."* Shelly's mouth fell open. Her face turned beet red. Never in her life had anyone referred to her as being *"very special"*. When Melody motioned for Shelly to come forward, all the ladies applauded as Shelly turned to face them. Before Melody sat down Shelly blurted out – *"Ladies, I'm just a school cook and dishwasher, and I'm not anyone special at all."* Melody interrupted – *"Don't let her kid you ladies, her writings are awesome, and she really is a very special person."* With the tension broken, Shelly began by telling the ladies how God had taken control of her broken life. As she continued to speak, the words now came easily. She silently thanked God for calming her nerves, and for giving her this opportunity to offer encouragement to others who were suffering. Her speech was short, but powerful. As she opened her book of poetry and began reading, she looked out over the crowd. Nearly every lady in the room had tears in her eyes.

When Shelly ended her reading, every lady in the room came forward, hugging her, and thanking her for coming. After that first visit, Melody called Shelly to come back and speak to the group several more times. Everyone in the group became her friend. With Shelly's permission, Melody sent Shelly's phone number to several other churches throughout the greater Columbus area. Not long afterward, she was called to speak to several other ladies groups, making more friends wherever she went. It was still difficult for her to grasp how God could use someone like her.

Any time Shelly's phone rang before 7:00 or 8:00 a.m., she was afraid to answer it, fearful that something terrible had happened to someone. This morning she was startled awake at 5:00 a.m. She jumped up trembling as she picked up the phone. It was Tony's younger sister Marie, and she was crying. Shelly knew something was terribly wrong. It was even worse than Shelly expected.

Marie's best friend, Julie Singleton, and her husband Robert, whom Shelly and Marie had known for about seventeen years, early in their marriage, had almost given up on having children when finally they had been blessed with a son, Jenson, now sixteen. Marie's voice trembled as she broke the news to Shelly. Jenson had died in an auto accident that night. Shelly thought her heart was going to stop beating. She couldn't imagine the horror Julie and Robert were enduring. She began praying for the family immediately. Julie, who had read Shelly's book of poems, called Shelly later that same day, asking her if she would write the obituary for Jenson's funeral.   Shelly assured her she would do her best to honor her son. It was the least she could do for a friend. A few days after the funeral, as Shelly continued praying for her friends throughout the day, as she prayed, the words – *"Letter From Heaven"* kept popping into her mind. She wondered if this was God's way of telling her to write something else. As she continued to think about the broken-hearted family, those words – *"Letter From Heaven"*, kept ringing in her conscience.   By now Shelly had come to a place in her spiritual life wherein God's still small voice was unmistakable. He wanted her to write a poem in memory of Jenson. But like she had done so many times before, she began to doubt her ability to write anything that would be worthy of Jenson's memory.   She was afraid she would horribly disappoint the family. She began trying to think of some way to get out of writing the poem. Then she would become ashamed of herself, reminding herself of how many times she had worried needlessly, and God had never let her down.   Back and forth, all day long, she halted between two decisions. Then that still small voice whispered again - *"Do it now."* Sitting down at her desk, Shelly had the poem written in about ten minutes.

As Shelly read the poem silently, tears filled her eyes. She knew she couldn't have written something this beautiful and comforting by herself. She had gotten into the habit of always giving God the credit when ending her poems, adding – *"Written by Shelly Davidson, inspired by God."*   Finding the prettiest embossed paper she could find, and a nice picture frame, she re-typed the poem, putting it inside the frame. She was still just a bit nervous about taking the poem to Julie and Robert, not knowing how they might react.   But again, her anxiety proved needless.   Julie read the poem out loud as Robert stood beside her, reading it silently. Before they got to the end, they were both crying. Julie grabbed Shelly in a tight embrace, thanking her for honoring their son with such a beautiful poem. To this day, the poem sits on a special table by itself in their family room. That meant so much to Shelly she drove straight home, falling on her knees, apologizing to God for trying to get out of writing the poem. She had no idea how many more lives that single poem was going to touch.

Letter From Heaven

If I could write a letter and send it down to you,
There's so much I would tell you, there's so much here to do.
There are angels on every corner, the beauty is so grand,
When I first arrived here, God Himself He took my hand.
I've met all of my family, they're so loving and so kind,
I gave them all an update on everyone they've left behind.
Their smiles are never-ending, they tell me their happiness never ends,
For here in heaven, there is no heartache, for it's not been touched by sin.
My first thought was for my family and my loved ones I hold so dear,
There were so many things I would have said knowing my homecoming was so near.
I would have told you how much I loved you, and thanked you for all that you've done for me,
All of you are the very best, God gave me such a loving family.
I know this is very hard on you and your tears seem never ending,
That's why I asked God to please allow me to send this letter I'm sending.
Heaven is so very beautiful, I've walked on streets of gold,
There is no sickness here or pain, and no one ever grows old.
All the fields here are filled with flowers, there is greenery everywhere,

There's so much love, laughter and fun, and our Father who really cares.

I talked to God about you and poured my love out to Him,

He put His arms around me, and reassured me we'd be together again.

For now He sends His strength and love, and He'll carry you if need be,

I want you to know He's such a loving God, I know someday you will see.

I want you all to please be strong and carry me close to your heart,

You have the rest of your lives to live, my prayer is that you will start.

The joy you gave me through the years, I want that joy for you,

Take time to live, to love, to laugh, and through you, let me shine through.

And when you think of me, don't think of me with tears, think of me with laughter,

For God has given me a home where I'll live happily ever after.

Written by Shelly Davidson,
Inspired by God

Every day of Shelly's life was now filled with ongoing activity of one kind or another. From the time she awoke till the time she laid down at night, she was busy. However, between babysitting for friends and family, working three hours at the school, writing, keeping all her speaking engagements, being interviewed by different folks from newspapers and magazines, responding to fan mail, being a wife and mother, and attending her son's sporting events, the term *"busy"* falls extremely short of defining her life. But of all the people who came to love Shelly's writing, her Mom, Sheila, was her biggest fan. No one could be around Sheila for very long without hearing her boast about how gifted and famous her daughter Shelly had become. This, of course, embarrassed Shelly to no end. She didn't accept praise very well, not even when it came from Mom. Shelly still considered herself as being somewhat beneath everyone else on the social scale, not wanting to exalt herself above measure, and not wanting anyone else to exalt her. Whatever might become of her life, she wanted God to have all the glory at all times.

Shelly's sister, Beth, had long since divorced her first husband, and married her new husband, Shawn Matheson. Shelia had also divorced her husband, Mick. Beth and Shawn had bought a small house with an acre of land close to the one in which they lived, cleaned it up, and moved her Mom into the smaller house. Now Shelly had her sister and her Mom living closer to her. She could walk to Beth's house in ten minutes, or drive to her Mom's house in less than fifteen minutes. Together, she and Beth kept a close eye on Sheila and her activities, but especially her finances. With Beth owning the house, there was no chance of Sheila being evicted for not paying her rent. Sheila's mental health was failing again. She was extremely paranoid, and simply ignored paying her bills. She had taken in several stray cats and two dogs. Cleaning up after her pets occupied a great deal of her time. Beth insisted that cleaning up after her cats and dogs was a condition she had to meet in order to remain in the house. Shawn kept the grass mowed and the house maintained.

Shelly and Beth understood their Mom was on a fixed income, and couldn't afford a lot of extra things, but had she managed her finances properly, there would have been sufficient money to pay all her bills, and have money left. Sadly, however, that was not the case. She was constantly having repairs done on her old car which had been her Aunt's, and still insisted on going to every yard sale and garage sale she could find, spending money on stuff she didn't need, and would never use. She smoked a special brand of cigarettes that cost more than most other brand names, and she smoked a lot – sometimes more than a pack each day. And now, to make matters worse, she had begun sending money to several television preachers, who convinced her that sending her money to them would somehow guarantee God's blessing upon her own finances. At the end of every month, she ran short. Beth and Shelly were having to help her pay her bills, and buy her cigarettes. Finally, Shelly and Beth had to step in and take control of their Mom's financial affairs. Beth took Sheila's checkbook and her bills, making sure each check was made out in the correct amount, and sent to the right place. Sheila was not happy with the arrangement, but soon discovered it was for her own good. She knew she had to trust someone, and she trusted her girls more than anyone else in the world.

Marcy still lived in the neighborhood where she and her sisters were raised. The area had been in steady decline for years now. The streets were full of potholes, the sidewalks cracked and sunken, and the houses dilapidated, with several being condemned. The house in which Sheila had lived was one of the condemned ones, which was another reason Beth had bought the other house close to Bedford City, to give her Mom a place to live. Marcy missed her Mom terribly. It broke her heart when Sheila was forced to move out. With Shelly and Beth living so far away, Marcy had been Sheila's only friend after Mick moved out. Now she seldom got to see her Mom, not only because of the distance between them, but also because of having to take care of her own family.

Shelly and Beth now shared the responsibilities of seeing that their Mom kept her doctor's appointments, and had the things she needed. Shelly drove her to the doctor, Beth took her to the grocery store, and Shawn took her everywhere else she wanted to go – mostly to yard sales and smaller stores all over town.   Every time one of them went to see her, she seemed somewhat more paranoid than the last time they were there. She was convinced there was an invisible person in her house, watching her every moment. Shelly tried to explain to her that there was no such thing as an invisible man. Sheila insisted that the government had secretly developed a spray that made people invisible.   Nearly every day she misplaced something in the house, and when she couldn't find it, she immediately accused someone of stealing it. When either Beth or Shelly came over and found the article that had supposedly been stolen, Sheila insisted the invisible person who stole it must have gotten a guilty conscience, and secretly returned the item.   She also insisted the government had tapped her phone, and was listening in on all her conversations. When the girls tried to assure her none of those things were true, she would become very angry with them, scolding them for trying to correct her. An hour later, she would call them, having no recollection of their last visit, or anything they had said. They both loved their Mom dearly, but, as Beth commented to Shelly – "*We have our hands full.*"

Shelly's reputation as a published writer preceded her wherever she went.   Her reputation as a hard worker did the same. Other schools began to call her, inviting her to come and apply for a job. She was reluctant to accept another job, but one school offered her an additional hour of work – four hours instead of three. It wasn't all that much, but it was closer to home, and her friend Jan had now gone to work there. These two factors were enough incentive for her to accept the job.   Her nervous energy soon manifested itself, as she kept busy doing her job, plus helping out in other areas, cleaning and washing dishes, doing little things she was not required to do, simply because she wanted to help. While other cooks took breaks for whatever reason, Shelly kept working, stopping only long enough to give Tony a quick call once in a while.

But, like everyone else, at one time or another in their careers, Shelly had a really bad day once in a while - one of those days when Murphy's Law prevails, when everything that could possibly go wrong, does go wrong. Add to that the fact that both her mind and body were near exhaustion, and you can understand how she might sink into deep depression.   But Shelly had determined that she was not going to let her emotions get the best of her this time – she would sing, whistle, work, or do whatever it took to bring herself out of her gloom. And since she wasn't such a great singer, she decided that keeping busy would take her mind off things better than anything else. She just wanted to get through this day, and put it all behind her.

The school custodian had put down new mats on the concrete floor for all the cooks to stand on. The mats were supposed to serve a twofold purpose – first, to prevent falls on the concrete floor, which sometimes got quite slippery from spilled water or food that had been dropped onto the floor. The second purpose, and the one for which the ladies were the most thankful, was that the mats were supposed to serve as cushioning for the ladies' feet. The new mats were almost twice as thick as the older ones. Approaching her work station, Shelly, not noticing the thicker mats, tripped on the corner of the mat. Before she could regain her balance, her right knee hit the concrete floor hard. The pain was excruciating. After sitting on the floor for a few minutes, recovering from the shock, two of the other ladies helped her to her feet. She was barely able to stand. Limping to the bathroom, she examined her knee. It was badly bruised. Not wanting to appear as a weakling in front of the other ladies, Shelly finished her shift that day, putting most of her weight on her left leg. When she got home, the knee was swollen and red. Tony advised her to go to the hospital, but Shelly refused, thinking, and praying, it would heal overnight.

For two more weeks Shelly limped into work, doing her job while almost screaming in pain. She knew she couldn't go on like this. It was time to swallow her pride, and go to the hospital. The first MRI revealed a torn meniscus. She would have to have surgery. She tried desperately to talk the doctor out of doing the surgery, but he insisted it had to be done if she wanted to get back to work, and it would probably be a long time before she could return to work. During the surgery, the doctor found more damage which the MRI hadn't picked up. The surgery would take longer than anticipated, and so would her recovery time. The damage was so extensive, it was impossible for her to endure physical therapy after the surgery. Against her doctor's wishes, she still wanted to return to work. After four months of MRI's and X-rays, Shelly returned to work. Her supervisor assigned her to the cash register, where she would have to stand in one spot for four hours. Shelly pleaded with the supervisor to put her back on the line with the other cooks, where she could move about, flexing the knee, and giving it more blood circulation. The supervisor refused her request. Shelly was forced to retire from the work force on disability. She took it all in stride, believing this was God's way of giving her more time to do what she loved, namely, writing. And that's exactly the way it turned out.

It had been nearly two years now since she had sent her book to a Christian magazine, hoping they might do a story about her life. Having received no response from them, Shelly decided to give them a call. After reminding the secretary that she had sent her book two years ago, the secretary told her the magazine didn't publish biographical stories, but would love to advertise her book in the magazine.   Shelly explained that she wanted her life story to be in print, as a testimony to others girls who may have experienced the same hardships, abuse and molestation she had experienced. Perhaps if they could understand how that, no matter what the situation might have been into which they were born, and no matter how many bad decisions they had made, there is yet hope and deliverance in Jesus Christ.   Shelly had reached another plateau in her life, perfectly understanding her God-given purpose for being born. She was created to glorify her Creator and Redeemer, and He had given her the means through which she could fulfill that purpose.

The secretary listened patiently as Shelly gave her a brief summary of the more traumatic scenes of her life, adding that as a result of some of those horrors she had endured, she was left with a lot of physical   and emotional scars, including her panic attacks, from which she would never be totally free. The secretary was so touched by Shelly's story she asked Shelly if it would be alright for them to have prayer together. Shelly welcomed the prayer of someone she had never met, hundreds of miles away, who took the time to listen, and cared enough to pray for her. After they had prayed together, the secretary asked for Shelly's e-mail address and phone number. Two days later she received an e-mail from the editor of the magazine. He wanted to do a story on Shelly's life. Shelly's jaw dropped in shock.   Then the phone rang. It was the editor, wanting Shelly to fill in some details about her story, promising her he would send her a copy of the magazine, complete with her story and her picture. It was clear that God was still working in her life, using her as an instrument through which to bless others. The very thought of being chosen by the Lord to be used as a vessel of honor was so humbling. When she received the magazine, the story they had done brought tears to her eyes. Again she realized how unworthy and undeserving she was of any of His blessings.

Surfing the internet, Shelly found a Christian website where she could share her poems with new and old friends, and also read poems written by other folks from all over the world. The site also provided a comment section where poets and authors could leave comments about the poems. It was very encouraging to have other poets comment on, and critique each other's work. One dear lady, after losing a loved one, found comfort in reading Shelly's poem – Letter From Heaven. But the poem also caught the attention of Steve Politte from Missouri, who had developed a website of his own, called Open My Eyes Lord, where, when he found a poem that really touched his heart, contacted the poet, asking for permission to put the poem to music, making it into a video. Shelly's poem, Letter From Heaven was one that got his attention. Not long afterward Steve made it into a video, which has since been seen around the world, bringing hope and comfort to countless numbers of folks who have lost a loved one. Seeing the video for the first time, Shelly was amazed at how Steve had enhanced her poem with pictures and music. It was quite humbling to realize how God can take such a small thing, from the hand and heart of one so unworthy and undeserving, and turn it into a blessing to so many others.

As Shelly's poems and her book continued to gain wider circulation, many who had read her first book began to encourage her to write another. Having gained some invaluable experience from the publication of her first book, and having plenty of time to write now, Shelly soon had two more small books published – Showers of Blessings and Everyday Grace, both of which have touched countless lives. Shelly sometimes pondered – *"I wonder if the folks who have read my books would think of me differently if they knew my past, and where I came from?"* Maybe someday God would arrange the circumstances for her to do just that – write a book that would reveal her whole life, so that folks could get to know the real person behind the poems, and maybe get to know the God who inspired them. After all, she concluded – *"Our lives are not about us, who we are, what we do, or even what we give; it's all about the Giver of all life, the One who...gives us all things richly to enjoy."*

Shelly's life was changing rapidly. Through her writing she had acquired more friends than she had ever dreamed of having. That, in itself, can sometimes help us deal with many of the strains and stresses of life. Sometimes we just need a friend who is willing to listen, a strong shoulder on which to lean, or cry. Shelly's Christian counselor was such a man – a man of unimpeachable integrity and boundless compassion, who never judged, criticized or condemned, but rather sympathized, and offered sound advice, based upon God-given wisdom. But he also prayed with Shelly before bringing any counseling session to a close.

But there are some things which no amount of counseling, however well-intended and executed, can ever completely wipe away. There were fears and nightmares, stemming from Shelly's past, from which she would never be entirely free. At night, when the rest of the family slept peacefully, Shelly was still haunted by painful, horrible dreams of her childhood. In those dreadful nightmares she was back in that house where she had seen the ghastly face of an evil spirit staring at her. One day while talking to Marcy on the phone Shelly told her about her dreams. A long silence followed. Finally Marcy responded, telling Shelly that she had also had the same nightmares about that old house, and her childhood there. They both agreed that old house was haunted by evil spirits. They wondered if their younger sister Beth had ever had nightmares related to the house. When Shelly called Beth, telling her about her own nightmares, Beth assured her she had never had any bad dreams about her childhood in that house.

Marcy, who still lived in that same neighborhood, suggested to Shelly that the two of them should go back to the old house, and walk through it. Her reasoning was that if they could face the thing that had caused them so much pain and fear (the house) and walk through every room without being harmed or haunted, this would prove the house was never haunted, and all their fears had been groundless, and they would finally be free of those fears. But while Marcy's theory made some sense, Shelly immediately rejected the idea, replying – *"Not for a million dollars; I will never set foot in that house again, not even on the porch."* Her memories were just too painful to go back there, and risk having those feelings stirred up again.   Her reasoning was that she would rather endure the nightmares she already had than go back there and perhaps create new ones.

Sheila, Shelly's Mom, was now nearly seventy-four years old. And considering all she had endured, both physically and mentally, she was blessed with relatively good physical health. She had never been hospitalized, and had never undergone surgery. And until moving out to Bedford City, she avoided doctors as much as possible. That was about to change.   When Shelly and Beth had agreed to share the responsibilities of taking care of their Mom, the responsibility of watching after Sheila's health had fallen to Shelly. Accepting that responsibility, and taking it seriously, Shelly made sure her Mom kept regular doctor appointments, and that she submitted to all the tests the doctors ordered. So far Sheila had received only good reports. In one regard, Sheila was a lot like Shelly, always giving God the credit, the glory and the thanks for every good thing in her life, including her health. But nature and other forces were at work in Sheila's body, and not for the better. Several factors contributed to her decline. She had smoked cigarettes since she was seventeen; she seldom maintained a healthy diet, and she didn't get enough exercise, to name only a few. Shelly and Beth had talked to their Mom on the phone so often that both of them could detect the slightest variation in her tone when speaking to her. This day, Shelly could tell Sheila wasn't feeling well by the weakness of her voice. But when Shelly asked if she was ok, Sheila insisted everything was alright – she was just having some strange symptoms she hadn't experienced before. After describing those symptoms to Shelly, Shelly insisted upon taking her to the doctor. Sheila refused at first, but Shelly persisted, finally convincing her it was best to find out what was causing her symptoms.

After listening to her symptoms, and having some blood work done, the doctor ordered a colonoscopy to be done immediately if possible. But due to a scheduling conflict, the test was postponed until the next morning. The results were not good. Sheila was diagnosed with colon cancer.   But thankfully, her cancer was not the aggressive, fast-spreading type, and the doctors agreed they had caught it in time to remove it before it could cause any serious damage.   Sheila, Shelly and Beth all agreed to the surgery. Marcy vehemently objected, fearing for her Mom's life, afraid she was going to die the same way her Aunt Elizabeth had died of cancer. But although Sheila dreaded the surgery, she convinced Marcy it was for the best. Sheila's doctor referred her to the best cancer surgeon he knew. The surgery was a total success. The cancer had not spread, and the surgeon was able to remove all of it.

On Sheila's first night home from the hospital, Marcy stayed all night with her Mom. It would prove to be a night she would never forget. Sheila had seven well-fed, spoiled cats. Seeing the fat cats, Marcy understood why her Mom had lost so much weight. She had been feeding her own food to the cats, while going hungry herself. And she slept with six of the cats!   One of the cats was wilder than the other six, and for reasons known only to God and the cat himself, after eating downstairs with the other cats, he would run upstairs, and hide from Sheila. Tonight, he was hiding under the bed on which Marcy was going to sleep. Marcy woke up to the rank odor of cat urine. Raising up, she discovered she had been sprayed by the big tom cat. Her sheet and underwear were soaked. To say that she was not happy would be putting it mildly.

Shelia healed from the surgery, and was doing exceptionally well. Then, after two years, the girls began noticing a radical shift in her behavior. She was becoming confused easily, sometimes forgetting the names of her grandchildren, and calling Shelly and Beth as many as twenty times a day. Sometimes she even got her girls confused, calling them by the wrong name.   When Beth took her to the grocery store she would buy the same food she already had at home. Beth tried desperately to talk her out of it, and sometimes she would listen, but more often than not, she would insist she needed everything she was buying. The girls were under the impression that she was cooking and eating properly until they noticed she was losing weight again. On her next visit to her doctor, he prescribed medication for the treatment of dementia. Shelly made certain that Mom took the medication exactly as prescribed.   It was breaking her heart seeing her Mom like this.

The girls finally agreed it was not safe for Sheila to be alone. Marcy's son, Buck Junior, and his girlfriend LeAnn, moved in with Sheila. Living with Sheila was no easy arrangement, not so much because of Sheila herself, but because of the seven cats and two dogs. From all appearances, the cats had more control over the house than Sheila. Sheila protected the cats as if they were her children, always afraid someone was going to hurt one of them. In order to pacify Sheila's fear, Buck Jr. would occasionally pet one of the cats, assuring her he loved the cats also, and would never hurt them.

Shelly and Beth went to see their Mom every day, with Shelly giving Sheila her medicines, and Beth making sure she had everything she needed, including her *"cat treats"*. With Buck Jr. and LeAnn living with Sheila, Shelly and her sisters felt just a bit better about her safety, knowing Buck and LeAnn would look after her. Sometimes Shelly would call before coming to give Sheila her medicines. When LeAnn answered the phone, she sounded reluctant to talk to Shelly. Shelly knew something was wrong. One of the cats had run out the front door, and Sheila had gone running after it. Before LeAnn could catch her she had fallen. Before LeAnn could say anything else, Shelly hung up and hurried to her Mom's house. Sheila appeared to be fine, but Shelly insisted on taking her to Urgent Care just to make sure. The doctor said she was fine, but at her age she needed to be more careful, because her bones were far more likely to be broken from a fall than when she was younger. Shelly thanked God for watching over her Mom. Most of the women on Sheila's side of the family had lived to be quite old, and all of them were still in their right mind when they died. Shelly wished the same for her Mom.

Sheila's birthday, December 17th, was quickly approaching. She would be seventy-seven. The girls were getting more worried with each passing day. Sheila was not eating much of anything, and it seemed she had lost interest in just about everything. As the days went by Shelly noticed her Mom walking much slower than usual, and it seemed she was deliberately distancing herself from everyone and everything. Shelly knew how much her Mom loved celebrating her birthday with the girls and grandchildren, and she was determined to make this one the best birthday party her Mom had ever had. The whole family planned on surprising Sheila by bringing the party to her house. When the big day arrived, everyone came with their gifts and food for the party. Sheila sat quietly through most of the evening, not saying much to anyone, seemingly unaware they were there to celebrate her birthday. All the girls noticed she wasn't enjoying herself at all. The next day, when Shelly called, Sheila asked – "*Shelly, am I dying?*"

Trying not to reveal the shock in her voice, Shelly quickly answered – "*Why, no Mom, you're not dying. Why would you even ask such a question?*"   Sheila asked – "*Then why was everyone here last night?*"   Shelly explained that the whole family had been there last night celebrating her birthday.   With that, Sheila seemed to snap out of her gloom immediately, laughing and joking as if she had enjoyed every minute of the party. And although Shelly's heart was breaking, knowing her Mom had dementia, it was good to hear her laugh again.

With Sheila's family, Christmas had always been the biggest holiday of the year – the one they celebrated with more pomp and circumstance than any other. It was a time when the whole family – Sheila, Hank, the three girls – Marcy, Beth and Shelly, along with their husbands and children, had always gathered at Hank and Sheila's for a big dinner, singing, and exchanging gifts. Since Hank had moved out and married Barb, the rest of the family still celebrated Christmas at Sheila's house whenever possible. There was something about Christmas that seemed to cause everyone to put all their differences, and all their troubles on hold for a while. No one complained about their personal problems, their financial woes, or even their bad health. The joy of having all the children, grandchildren, and in-laws together at the same time, in the same house, laughing, singing, and having a good time, seemed to make all their troubles disappear for just a little while.

But this Christmas would be different. As much as Sheila wanted to join in the festivities with her family, her excruciating pain would not allow her to even smile. Everyone could see the pain in her eyes. She could barely hold her head up. Shelly wanted to take her to the Emergency Room that night, but Sheila refused, not wanting to spoil Christmas for everyone else. The day after Christmas, Shelly came over to Sheila's house, insisting her Mom let her take her to the hospital. This time Sheila was in so much pain she didn't argue. She had to have some relief from the pain. The first thing the doctor ordered was X-rays of her back. There was a hairline fracture in one of the lower vertebrae. After asking Sheila and Shelly a few questions, the doctor agreed that her back had most likely been fractured when she fell, chasing the cat. He gave her a prescription for pain pills, and recommended therapy for her spine. Shelia's pain increased to the point that she now had to wear adult diapers because there were times she just couldn't make it to the bathroom.

Shelly invited her Mom to come to her house for a big New Year's Eve dinner, but Sheila had already promised Beth she would come to her house on New Year's Eve. After wishing each other a happy New Year, there was a short silence. Sheila and Shelly never hung up the phone or left one another's house without saying - "I love you". They had become so close that either one could detect the slightest difference in the voice of the other, whether on the phone, or in person. When Shelly said – "I love you Mom", that momentary hesitation, and the slight quiver in Sheila's voice when she responded – "*I love you too Shelly,*" broke Shelly's heart. She heard more than – "*I love you too Shelly,*" she knew she was hearing her Mom's "*goodbye*".

Two days after New Year's Day, LeAnn called Shelly, asking if she had a TV tray she could use to put Sheila's food on. When Shelly asked why she needed a tray, LeAnn told her Sheila hadn't been out of bed for two days. She hadn't gone to Beth's house for New Year's Eve.   Shelly was very upset that no one had called her.   Rushing over to her Mom's house, she discovered Sheila hadn't eaten anything in about three days. Both LeAnn and Buck Jr. had begged her to eat something, but Sheila refused everything they offered her. Shelly tried to get her to eat, but to no avail. She said she was hurting too much to eat anything. Shelly called Beth and Marcy first, then the Emergency Squad. Beth and Shelly arrived at the hospital the same time as the ambulance. After an initial examination, the doctor told the girls he was going to admit Sheila to the hospital. He was almost certain she was going into renal failure. Her kidneys were shutting down. The girls sat in shock as the hours dragged by, waiting for any news about their Mom's condition. When the doctor finally came into the waiting room, his countenance spoke almost as loudly as his words. Not only were Sheila's kidneys shutting down, but now they had discovered she had all the symptoms of a rare form of cancer. They were going to do one more test that would either confirm or deny their suspicions. The doctor warned the girls in advance that if they did find that Sheila had the cancer, it would most likely be spread throughout her body, and if so, there wasn't much hope of her surviving more than a few weeks at best. Still in shock and denial, Shelly and Beth decided they'd better call Marcy and tell her what the doctors had said. Hearing the bad news, Marcy tried to be brave, and not show her emotions. But when she hung up the phone, she was sobbing.

Sheila was transferred to a nursing home not far from the girls. Beth, refusing to give up on her Mom, was still insisting they give her Mom the physical therapy her other doctor had ordered, hoping that maybe it would help her. The doctors didn't want to take away the thread of hope the girls had for their Mom, but neither did they want to give them a false hope. There was no easy way to tell the girls their Mom was dying. But in order to give them any shred of hope they possibly could, they gave Sheila the therapy, knowing it would not help her condition. Shelly and Beth came to the nursing home every day. It was torturous for both of them, watching their Mom grow weaker and weaker, day by day. Sheila was now bedfast. The girls had now accepted the sad truth – their Mom wasn't going to live much longer. Marcy started coming at night to relieve Shelly and Beth.

Knowing she was going to lose her Mom, Shelly turned to the one, and the strongest source of consolation she knew – prayer. She knew her Mom loved the Lord Jesus, and was ready to go in peace, and no matter how much pain she was suffering, Sheila still lifted her hands toward Heaven, saying -   *"Thank you Jesus."*   Each time Shelly came to see her Mom she prayed with her, kissed her, and told her she loved her. The doctors at the nursing home finally told the girls they had done all they could do for Sheila. She would have to be transferred to the Hospice section of the nursing home. After only one day in the Hospice facility, none of the three girls was happy with the care and treatment their Mom was getting. Beth told them she was taking her Mom to her house, and would take care of her herself.

Beth, her husband Shawn, and their two children, Stephanie and Josh, lived right around the corner from Shelly. Stephanie and Josh came over every day, doing whatever they could do to help out.

Sheila had now stopped talking altogether. She wouldn't even take anything to drink now. The only movement the girls noticed was when she would open her eyes for a few moments. Each time Shelly had to leave, the pain was almost unbearable, not knowing if her Mom would be alive when she came back. Sheila hadn't spoken a word in about ten days. Sitting beside Sheila's bed one afternoon, rubbing her hands and talking to her, Shelly detected the slightest motion in her Mom's lips. Suddenly Sheila began humming. Shelly didn't recognize the tune, but to her, it was the sweetest sound she had ever heard. She listened spellbound as Sheila continued to hum.   As Sheila's eyes barely opened, Shelly smiled. She was certain her Mom was looking into Heaven.

Two days later, at 5:00 a.m., Shelly's phone rang. It was Beth, sobbing – *"Shelly, Mommy's gone, please come over here now."* Shelly ran to Tony, telling him her Mom had passed away. They were at Beth's house five minutes later. Shelia looked so peaceful. Shelly couldn't stop rubbing her hands and face and kissing her while they waited for the funeral home to pick her up. Marcy, hearing of Sheila's death, was so distraught she couldn't come to Beth's house that night. The next day Shelly and Beth went to the funeral home to make the arrangements for Sheila's funeral.   Sheila had refused to allow anyone to purchase a life insurance policy on her, insisting she didn't need any, because she was going up in the Rapture.   Beth and Shelly paid for their Mom's funeral with their charge cards. Shawn, Beth's husband, bought her the most beautiful gown and robe. And if it can be said that there is such a thing as a beautiful funeral, then Sheila's was beautiful.

Shelly could hardly bear saying goodbye to her Mom. She kept standing at the head of the casket, talking to her Mom, and rubbing her hands, weeping. Finally, Mary came and gently walked her away from the casket. It was the first time in a long time Shelly had seen tears streaming down Tony's face. It wouldn't be very long till Shelly realized just how much she missed her Mom. They had been through so much together, both in her childhood, and as an adult. But one thing Shelly would always remember was the promise she had made to her Mom before her death – the promise that she would always love Jesus, and never fail to share His love with everyone she possibly could.

Somewhere in her childhood, she couldn't recall exactly when and where, she had read a poem with the words... *"a promise made is a debt unpaid."* Shelly's promise to her Mom was a promise she found no difficulty in keeping. From the moment she made that promise, everything she would write thereafter would be written as if her Mom was standing behind her, looking over her shoulder, smiling, and encouraging her to keep up the good work. With all the lives she had already touched through her poetry, she clearly understood that her writing was not a talent she had developed over time, but a gift from God, to be used for His glory, and to bless others in some way. In seeing and hearing the thousands of testimonies from folks all over the world, her own heart was touched, even overwhelmed at times by the reality of how God can take a broken, shattered vessel like her, put it back together, and make it a blessing to someone else.

Shelly took her own personal testimony to God's grace seriously, she guarded that testimony vigilantly, and shared it eagerly. She also took all of her friendships seriously. The thousands of friends she had met on social media were more than names and faces on a computer screen. One of the many things that kept her humble and grateful was that so many of her friends had become more than friends – they had become *"followers"*, which, on social media, meant they followed everything she posted. Whenever a friend on social media sent her a prayer request, no matter how many, and no matter how grave or minor the situation, Shelly prayed for each need as if it was her own.   The thought often crossed her mind – *"If only the world would follow what God has posted in His Word, what a difference it would make!"*

Shelly had learned a blessed secret that seems to escape so many Christians. She had learned to listen to the voice of the Holy Spirit, and to follow His leading. She understood her life was not her own, but His, to use as He pleased. Through the study of His Word, and the guidance of His Spirit, she understood her life was being steered by an unseen hand. Every decision she made was preceded by prayer, and waiting for Him to answer. It didn't matter if she was happy, sad, healthy or hurting, she was determined to honor Him in all of it. And in honoring Him, she was honored.

Shelly found another magazine online called Life's Journey, with articles, stories and pictures which featured many of the most well-known   authors, sports figures, ministers and celebrities in the world. Her immediate reaction was the same as it had been so many times before – she felt unworthy of being mentioned in the same breath with any of these people. At the same time, she prayed for God's guidance.   After prayer she wrote a short simple note to the editor of the magazine, asking – *"Do you do stories on nobodies?"* She sent the note, but never in her wildest dreams did she expect an answer from the magazine. And even if she did get a response, it would probably be a graciously written rejection. She soon forgot all about sending the note, and kept writing poetry. Almost two years later she received an e-mail from the editor of the magazine. They not only wanted to publish her story, they sent her instructions on how to submit it!

It would be difficult to describe Shelly's emotions upon reading the e-mail. She was extremely excited and grateful they had read her note, and had responded to it, but now that they had, she was doubtful they would actually accept and publish her story. Then it hit her like a bolt of lightning – *"Oh me of little faith! If it was God's will for her story to be told, He would arrange the circumstances for it to be done. It was her duty to simply obey Him.* She sent the story, along with two of her poems. Within less than an hour, when she checked her e-mail, there was a response from the magazine. They wanted to publish her story, along with one of her poems, and a picture of her in the March issue. In addition to publishing her story, they asked for her permission to publish one of her poems every month, giving her her own page in the magazine.

Shelly's heart pounded with gratitude, thanking God for His amazing grace. When she received the March issue of the magazine, it was still so hard to believe what was happening in her life. Many times she lifted her eyes toward Heaven, telling Jesus – *"Lord, You never cease to amaze me!"* But God was not done with her yet. Shelly had no idea how far her influence had already gone, and no idea how far it was yet to go. Shelly's heart's desire was to reach out to others who were hurting, many of whose lives were quite similar to her own. She realized there are thousands, if not millions of young girls around the world who may have suffered many, if not all, of the same things she had been through, but were too afraid, and too ashamed for their stories to be publicized. To this day, Shelly Davidson prays every day that perhaps God can take the story of her own life, and bring a ray of hope and deliverance to someone else, just as He did for her. And God made a way for that to happen. Presently, along with all her writing, including another book of poetry, Shelly now hosts a radio program once a month. Her voice can be heard online, and on three continents, including

North America, South America, and The United Kingdom, on radio station KCWG The Truth, based in California. On her first program Shelly shared her own story of how God delivered her from a life plagued with poverty, perversity, and punishment, into a life blessed with grace, mercy and peace. With tears in her eyes, she thanked God for His mercy, while wishing her Mom could see what God was doing in her life. She thought – *"Maybe Jesus is telling Mom all about it right now."* Now Shelly finds and invites other people from all walks of life who loves God, to come on her program, to share their stories with the world.

Another blessed secret Shelly discovered in her journey with Jesus, and another which so many others seem to miss, is that God loves to talk to His children, and He loves for His children to talk to Him – not once a year, not once a month, not once a week, nor once a day, but in an ongoing, moment-by-moment communion between Father and child. Shelly has learned that every breath and every heartbeat are gifts from God. We cannot live a single moment without Him, therefore every moment belongs to Him. Reflecting upon her life, Shelly realized how far God had brought her from what she used to be. And no matter what she had done, or how many times she had done it, He had loved her in the midst of it all. And His love is everlasting. He promised He would never leave her nor forsake her. God had somehow taken even the worst things in her life, and had used them as tools to mold her into a more loving, compassionate and forgiving person.

Today Jesus Christ is the light and love of Shelly's life, still blessing her, and still using her as an instrument of His grace. Shelly smiled as she signed off from the radio program, thinking – *"I've always been a child of God, even when I was lost. I was His by creation then, and now I am His by redemption."*

POEM

From Trash To Treasures

I couldn't stop the memories from coming again,
I felt like a piece of trash how could I mean anything to Him.
The one who was perfect in every way,
I needed God to love me and I asked Him everyday.
Looking around I knew that I had nothing to give,
There was so many bad things that happened in this life I lived.
From the time I was young there was so many things,
I felt so unworthy of His love and all the blessings it brings.
Down on my knees I heard Him as He whispered so softly,
My child gather all of your trash and bring it to me.
You keep trying to run from all the trash in your life,
With me you can take time to heal I'll make everything all right.
Like a pile of compost made from so many things,
Over time turns into something with so much beauty it brings.
I can use all of your trash, and the things you've been through,
To touch so many lives there's so much you can do.
My love for you is endless and could never be measured,
You are a child of the King who will turn your trash to
treasures.

Written By Eva Dimel
Inspired By God ©

ABOUT THE AUTHOR

Eva Dimel, from Grove City, Ohio, has suffered much heartache in her life, along with panic disorder and brain surgery to remove a tumor that left her blind in the right eye. She is happily married to Tom Dimel, and are proud parents of three grown children and five grandsons, who are the joy of their lives. God gave Eva the gift of writing poetry to praise Him and help others who are hurting. He is leading her in paths she never imagined for herself.

Eva has published four books of poetry, the newest one called Eva's Inspirations, Inspired by God; she posts a new poem every day on her face book page; is a public speaker, sharing what God has done for her; she has a line of gift items featuring her poems, and is host of her radio show on kcwgthetruth.com originating from California and broadcast worldwide.   Her joy in life is her Savior, Jesus Christ, her family, and hearing from people all over the world who have been blessed by something she has written.

One of the many passages of scripture that means a lot in her life is Proverbs 3:6-7, Trust in the Lord with all your heart, lean not to your own understanding; acknowledge Him in all your ways and He will direct your path

"I know God is directing my path, and I love Him with all my heart."

Eva Dimel.